PRAISE FOR

WHAT'S GOD SAYING HERE?

I commend Eric Bargerhuff and Matthew Kim for reminding preachers, and the rest of us, not to skip over the Bible's hard passages. Literary critic George Steiner once suggested that perplexities in literature may reflect perplexities in life. Understanding what God is saying often requires effort. A preference for ease and simplicity subverts the need for serious work in biblical interpretation. I came away from Bargerhuff's and Kim's struggles with these hard texts with a better understanding of how to do this serious work.

Kevin J. Vanhoozer, research professor of systematic theology, Trinity Evangelical Divinity School

I am a big believer in the importance of wrestling with the passages of Scripture that do not come easily to us, and *What's God Saying Here?* delivers on what it promises. Eric Bargerhuff and Matthew Kim expertly guide readers through a selection of some of the most challenging passages of Scripture to unpack their complexity without losing sight of the coherence of Scripture's teachings as a whole. This is a very helpful book for preaching pastors as well as for readers of the Bible seeking to go deeper in understanding. The interpretive approach modeled here will be meaningful to any church ministry that values a fuller, authentic witness in the proclamation of Jesus Christ.

Jennifer Powell McNutt, Franklin S. Dyrness Professor of ..., Litfin Divinity School, ... author, *The Mary We Forgot*

CW01497424

Eric Bargerhuff and Matthew Kim have provided the church and her pastors with an invaluable resource—a theologically rich, homiletically sound guide to challenging passages from across the Scriptures. These are passages we've all struggled to understand and preach, wondered what they say about God's nature, and tended to avoid. With this book, the church and her pastors are better equipped to engage the full counsel of God and see the fullness of God's purposes in the world.

Joel Lawrence, president, Center for Pastor Theologians

What's God Saying Here? is the kind of book every thoughtful Christian needs on their shelf—especially those with a pulpit ministry. With pastoral care and scholarly insight, Drs. Bargerhuff and Kim tackle some of the most morally difficult passages in Scripture—not to explain them away, but to help us read them rightly. This book will strengthen your trust in God's Word and deepen your confidence that even the hard texts are good news when we read them in context and in light of Christ.

Amy Gannett, Bible teacher, author, church planter, and founder of Tiny Theologians and the Bible Study Schoolhouse

What is true of Paul's letters is no less true of the Christian Scriptures: "There are some things in them that are hard to understand" (2 Peter 3:16 ESV). Instead of simply ignoring "awkward, troubling, and bizarre" texts, Eric Bargerhuff and Matthew Kim pose and respond to thirty perplexing questions arising from careful, thoughtful biblical reading. Moreover, they show us how we might do likewise. This book is of considerable value in no small measure because it can rescue us from a hermeneutic of convenience and preference on the one hand and from creating a "canon within a canon" on the other.

Todd D. Still, Charles J. and Eleanor McLerran DeLancey Dean and William M. Hinson Professor of Christian Scriptures, Truett Seminary, Baylor University

Eric Bargerhuff and Matthew Kim tackle head-on the most theologically challenging, obscure, and uncomfortable passages in the Bible. This is a resource not just for preachers, but for every believer. As a ministry leader and teacher for more than thirty years, I found my mind and heart challenged in new ways. Kudos to Bargerhuff and Kim for boldly going where few others dare to trod.

Angie Ward, PhD, director of the Doctor of Ministry program and associate professor of leadership and ministry, Denver Seminary

Awkward, uncomfortable, confusing, disturbing—these are understandable responses to challenging parts of the Bible that have troubled many of its readers. Regrettably, some have turned away from Scripture when difficult passages aren't sufficiently resolved. But can they be? Eric Bargerhuff and Matthew Kim provide an invaluable resource. Not only are some of the stickiest passages tackled; more importantly, the authors employ a hermeneutical and applicational method that provides guidance on how to approach any passage of God's Word. The proof of these pages is that God and his Word can endure the most probing scrutiny.

Rick Holland, PhD, senior pastor, Mission Road Bible Church, Kansas City, Kansas

As a shepherd for several decades, I've never had someone walk away from the flock over questions regarding the deity of Christ or the application of the Nicene Creed. But I've witnessed a trainload of sheep being discouraged and diverted by questions they couldn't answer. *What's God Saying Here?* answers these questions. I eagerly give this outstanding resource to every new member of The Shepherd's Church. For the sake of the flock, I recommend you do the same.

Stephen Davey, pastor/teacher, The Shepherd's Church; president, Shepherds Theological Seminary; principal Bible teacher, Wisdom International

What's God Saying Here? is a one-stop sermon resource that equips preachers and teachers to navigate the Bible's sticky wickets with clarity, simplicity, and creativity. Drs. Bargerhuff and Kim courageously address the pertinent passages that every biblical communicator wants addressed. I highly recommend it.

Keith Krell, PhD, senior pastor, Crossroads Bible Church, Bellevue, Washington

What's GOD Saying Here?

What's GOD Saying Here?

How to Navigate **Awkward**, **Troubling**, and **Bizarre** Passages We Would Rather Skip

Eric J. Bargerhuff and Matthew D. Kim

ZONDERVAN REFLECTIVE

ZONDERVAN REFLECTIVE

What's God Saying Here?
Copyright © 2025 by Eric J. Bargerhuff and Matthew D. Kim

Published by Zondervan, 3950 Sparks Drive SE, Suite 101, Grand Rapids, MI 49546, USA. Zondervan is a registered trademark of The Zondervan Corporation, L.L.C., a wholly owned subsidiary of HarperCollins Christian Publishing, Inc.

Requests for information should be addressed to customercare@harpercollins.com.

Zondervan titles may be purchased in bulk for educational, business, fundraising, or sales promotional use. For information, please email SpecialMarkets@Zondervan.com.

ISBN 978-0-310-15913-1 (audio)

Library of Congress Cataloging-in-Publication Data

Names: Bargerhuff, Eric J. (Eric James) author | Kim, Matthew D., 1977- author
Title: What's God saying here? : how to navigate awkward, troubling, and bizarre passages we would rather skip / Eric J. Bargerhuff and Matthew D. Kim.
Description: Grand Rapids, Michigan : Zondervan Reflective, [2025]
Identifiers: LCCN 2025020931 (print) | LCCN 2025020932 (ebook) | ISBN 9780310159117 paperback | ISBN 9780310159124 ebook
Subjects: LCSH: Bible—Homiletical use
Classification: LCC BS534.5 .B35 2025 (print) | LCC BS534.5 (ebook) | DDC 251—dc23/eng/20250701
LC record available at https://lccn.loc.gov/2025020931
LC ebook record available at https://lccn.loc.gov/2025020932

HarperCollins Publishers, Macken House, 39/40 Mayor Street Upper, Dublin 1, D01 C9W8, Ireland (https://www.harpercollins.com)

Cover design: Darren Welch
Cover images: © Conoby / Getty Images
Interior design: Denise Froehlich

Printed in the United States of America

25 26 27 28 29 LBC 5 4 3 2 1

To Dr. Michael F. Gleason—
one of my longtime mentors of the faith,
whose initial impact on my life and
encouragement along the path
have helped shape my love for Scripture and the glory of God.
Thank you, brother, you are a testimony to faithfulness.

ERIC J. BARGERHUFF

To Peter and Grace Kim—
dear friends and former church members,
whose constant encouragement enriched my
teaching and preaching ministries
while serving as your pastor.
I thank God every time I remember you in prayer.

MATTHEW D. KIM

CONTENTS

INTRODUCTION

MATTHEW D. KIM

Imagine a movie studio deciding to take on a massive new project—turning the entire Bible into a feature film. Once the insurmountable task of scripting, casting, and filming this epic movie is complete—not to mention the extensive practical work and visual effects this film would require—it would need an official movie rating. What rating do you think *Bible: The Movie* would receive? Would it be considered G or PG? Probably not. Scripture can be troubling—even downright disturbing—at times. Many scenes in Scripture would undoubtedly get an R rating. And others, even if they don't contain episodes of explicit violence or sexuality, are extremely difficult to understand, explain, and digest. These scenes would be considered unfilmable.

Similarly, I've often treated these passages as unteachable. Over the years, I have placed asterisks next to numerous portions of the Bible. My guess is that you have too. While reading the Bible—either devotionally or while preparing for teaching—have the hairs on the back of your neck ever stood up as you tried to figure out why you're seeing a certain passage there, what it means, and what you're supposed to do with it as Jesus' disciple today? Perhaps you've wondered why God would include *that* phrase, *that* verse, *that* paragraph, *that* story, or even *that* book or letter in his Holy Word.

Pastors have great latitude when it comes to text selection. The temptation for all preachers is to skip over the verses or passages that cause interpretive or applicational troubles. Sometimes the biblical author writes a complex paragraph that juxtaposes seemingly contradictory points. Since we don't know how to reconcile that inconsistency, we choose to skip the passage. I remember while preaching a sermon series through the gospel of Mark titled "Who Is Jesus?" I came across a rather shocking narrative concerning the naked man in Mark 14:51–52. Giving myself an escape path, I conveniently skipped over the account of Jesus' arrest that included these two verses. I thought, *This doesn't have anything to do with who Jesus is, so let's move on.* Thankfully, Eric took up the challenge in this book to guide us through this peculiar detail and who this man is. It's only natural to want to gloss or pass over the uncomfortable or bizarre.

Part of our reason for writing this book is to explain some of the seemingly bizarre things God says, does, and requires of his people in both Testaments. Sometimes the strangeness of Scripture emerges in what God permits according to his divine sovereignty. By no means are we attempting to speak on behalf of God or apologize for him. To help mitigate some curiosities or fears we have regarding God's Word, in Isaiah 55:8–9, God explains our infinite smallness in relation to his incomparable greatness: "'For my thoughts are not your thoughts, neither are your ways my ways,' declares the LORD. 'As the heavens are higher than the earth, so are my ways higher than your ways and my thoughts than your thoughts.'"

Even if we appreciate this gap between our understanding and God's and trust that his ways are higher than our ways, our task of teaching these many peculiar and troubling texts in the canon isn't made any easier. However, just because we question or wonder about what's included in Scripture doesn't mean we should avoid preaching and teaching on difficult, perplexing passages. Just the opposite, in fact. We wrote this book to embolden you not to shy away from the weirdness or wonder of Scripture.

We are staunch believers in teaching and preaching all of

Scripture. In 2 Timothy 3:16–17, Paul instructs, "All Scripture is God-breathed and is useful for teaching, rebuking, correcting and training in righteousness, so that the servant of God may be thoroughly equipped for every good work." Every iota of God's Word is significant to the lives of Christians today. The Bible is God's perfect instruction manual for the Christian life, free from error in the original manuscripts and written for believers to pursue Christlikeness, holiness, and righteousness.

In other words, preachers are expected to preach "the whole counsel of God" (Acts 20:27 ESV). Yet we tend to quickly bypass troubling texts and verses. We cherry-pick from passages and Bible books we like and understand but conveniently stray from texts, verses, or books that are bizarre, obscure, or confrontational. Many preachers ask, "How do I teach *that*? Let's just move on to the next verse, next passage, or next book."

In *What's God Saying Here?* we provide counsel on how to handle thirty of the most confusing verses, passages, sayings, and stories in the Bible. With our advice, encouragement, and reliance on the Holy Spirit's illumination, we trust you'll be less apprehensive about teaching and preaching on such confounding passages. We engage in this challenging work of explaining Scripture because we love God, his Word, his people, and his church.

So what's the best way to read this book? The chapters are grouped into five thematic headings, with appropriate passages falling under each umbrella topic. You'll first find an introduction that has a quick word of advice on how to handle these kinds of passages. While some may choose to read the book straight through, others may first pick out texts or topics most intriguing to them or select a chapter based on the passage or theme of future teaching or preaching projects. Whatever works best for you is great. In each chapter, you'll find a good dose of exegetical, biblical, and theological explanation of the given text and some guidance into how to communicate it to your people. At the conclusion of each chapter, you'll find a set of summary statements—Principles for Reflection—that highlight what the text means in its original historical and cultural context, what it means for us today, and what to do as a response.

After reading each chapter, we hope your confidence will be built up and that your first instinct will not be to skip to the next verse or page anymore. While no interpreter is flawless, we strive to be wise guides in your study and preparation. Though we've made our share of mistakes in the past, our faith and love for God and his Word have been fortified through the writing of this book. It's emboldened us to be more intentional about scrupulously teaching biblical passages for sermons, Bible studies, and even in our classrooms. We will have succeeded in our goal if you commit yourself to greater study and service in providing others with the whole counsel of God while relying on the Holy Spirit through prayer, engaging in biblical exegesis, and communicating the message of God's Word—the straightforward parts, the strange parts, and everything else found in the Bible.

PART I:
AWKWARD

How to Teach Things That
Make Us Uncomfortable

Sometimes it's hard not to be embarrassed when we read God's Word. The passages in this section give a glimpse into some of the most uncomfortable texts that make us squirm in our seats. We often don't know how to deal with awkward subject matters like nudity, graphic violence, suicide, or politics, to name a few. Much like in general conversation, there are a few principles to keep in mind when approaching uncomfortable matters in the Bible.

Perhaps a good way to broach the topic is to give your listeners a trigger warning. For instance, "I'm going to be talking today about an awkward story or subject matter from Scripture, and it's _____." Giving your listeners a heads-up before diving into the passage enables them to mentally check in and prepare their hearts for what's coming.

Certain awkward texts can be best introduced with some degree of levity. While we won't make a mockery of Scripture or make fun of God, it can help to acknowledge the elephant in the room with measured humor. "Isn't it strange that this is in the Bible? It's actually a bit funny. We can laugh about it together."

Uncomfortable passages are often invitations into a larger conversation. We're not going to solve in one sermon or Bible study lesson centuries-long disputes about politics or women's roles in ministry. However, we can engage in dialogue about views we share or disagree about.

Awkward Scripture texts force us to respond in either positive or negative ways. Make your best effort to read the room. Ask the Holy Spirit to help you as you teach your people what God's Word has to say to them—even when it comes to uncomfortable things.

CHAPTER 1

WHY IS THERE A HORROR STORY IN THE BIBLE?

Judges 4:1–24

MATTHEW D. KIM

Until a monarchy was set up in 1050 BC, human judges oversaw a grueling three-hundred-year period of Israel's history.[1] Among all the judges of Israel, I can safely say I'd be most afraid of meeting Jael on an unlit street corner. At least, if we knew what we know now about her, any reasonable person would avoid her. Mimicking a gory scene from a horror film, Jael's story is as strangely disturbing as it is arresting. But what does God want us to learn from Jael's narrative? As we know from the spiritual climate toward the end of Joshua and later in Judges, the book of Judges showcases the steep moral decay of Israel and its surrounding nations.

God assigns two judges, Deborah and Barak, to "confront the enemy Jabin, king of Canaan, who reigned in Hazor."[2] Beginning

---

1. See David L. Palmer, *Casket Empty: God's Plan of Redemption Through History* (Casket Empty Media, 2016), 93.
2. Jason S. DeRouchie, *How to Understand and Apply the Old Testament: Twelve Steps from*

with Judge Deborah (a prophet and the wife of Lappidoth), a common pattern emerges: "Again the Israelites did evil in the eyes of the LORD" (4:1). The backdrop is one of war. Deborah makes the following bold prediction: "Because of the course you [Barak, the military commander] are taking, the honor will not be yours, for the LORD will deliver Sisera into the hands of a woman" (v. 9).

Here's the sequence of events in verses 7–9: God commands Barak, son of Abinoam, to take ten thousand soldiers to Mount Tabor to overtake Sisera, Jabin's army commander, with God's help. Not trusting fully in the Lord, Barak issues an invitation to Deborah: "If you'll go with me, I'll go; but if not, I won't go." She then takes the opportunity to humiliate Barak: "I'll definitely go with you. However, the path you're taking won't bring honor to you, because the LORD will hand over Sisera to a woman" (CEB).

While clearly the hero of the story is the Lord, it is Deborah who holds Barak accountable and keeps him focused on God. The story continues with verse 14: "Deborah said to Barak, 'Go! This is the day the LORD has given Sisera into your hands. Has not the LORD gone ahead of you?'" As God fights the battle, Sisera escapes temporarily and goes to Jael's tent—a seemingly safe place, since "there was an alliance between Jabin king of Hazor and the family of Heber the Kenite [Jael's husband]" (v. 17). Jael proceeds to dupe Sisera and convinces him of her protection. Yet in the middle of Sisera's sleep, Jael takes out a tent peg and drives it into his temple with a hammer. Jael kills Sisera in her tent.

In her actions toward Sisera, Jael breaks several conventional Jewish customs:

(1) In offering hospitality to Sisera she usurps her husband's exclusive right as a male to offer hospitality to a male. (2) In killing Sisera she violates the covenant between Heber and Sisera's superior. (3)

_____

Exegesis to Theology (P&R, 2017), 29.

In killing Sisera, who had sought hospitality and protection in her house, she violates the fundamental right of guests. As in the Middle East today, in the ancient Near East hospitality toward strangers represented one of the highest social values—even superseding a man's responsibility for the well-being of his children (19:22–26).[3]

Scholars make loose comparisons between Jael's story and the crucifixion of Jesus. An eerily similar moment takes place as Sisera asks Jael for a drink before his bones are crushed, just as Jesus asks the Roman centurion for a drink before being nailed to the cross. Significantly, the narrator notes that Sisera asks for water and yet Jael gives him milk, knowing that milk's properties (hypnagogic effect) could speed up and perhaps deepen Sisera's sleep process.

Nicknamed "the slayer of Sisera," Jael warrants a brief character study. What do we know about her? The name Jael means "ibex," or "mountain goat." She is a Kenite and not an Israelite (1:16).[4] Her marital status is clear from the text. She is married to Heber the Kenite (4:17). It's important to note that the narrator wants us to know that an alliance has been formed between Jabin (the king of Hazor) and Heber (the Kenite) in verse 17 as well.

In verse 18, Jael enters the scene. With social grace, she leaves the tent to invite Sisera. Jael establishes relational rapport with her prey, then methodically woos him into the tent (4:18). Sisera shows no sign of hesitation in accepting Jael's invitation.

It's fascinating that no physical harm comes to Sisera when his army of nine hundred chariots surrounded him. Eventually they all die by the sword, except for Sisera. He goes to the only "safe place" he knows, which is in the tent of his supposed Kenite ally, Jael, but ends up losing his life to Jael's tent peg.

What could we emphasize in teaching Jael's story? Let's begin

---

3. John H. Walton and Craig S. Keener, eds., *NIV Cultural Backgrounds Study Bible* (Zondervan, 2016), note on Judges 4:18–21, p. 416.

4. D. A. Carson, ed., *NIV Zondervan Study Bible* (Zondervan, 2015), note on Judges 4:17, p. 440.

by discussing what the story of Jael does not mean. I do not believe the story of Jael is a rah-rah feminist manifesto championing women to "own the moment."[5] This is a misreading of the text. Not every circumstance warrants women to seize their moment and, in this case, murder another person. Using this text as a call to empower women is dangerous. While this was God's unique call on Jael's life, women are not mandated to murder as a gospel, kingdom-expanding order. This was a one-off moment in Israel's history in which God commanded murder of the one (Sisera) for the greater good of a nation (Israel).

Nor is this text an apology for committing sin and getting away with it. Notice that this text seems to approve of two sins in particular: *deception* ("Don't be afraid" [v. 18]; "She opened a skin of milk" instead of giving him water [v. 19]) and *murder* ("She drove the peg through his temple into the ground, and he died" [v. 21]). Some may make the case that God is pleased in someone's death. Not at all!

What then is the point of this account in Judges 4? First, the narrator wants us to know that God is faithful to fulfill his promises. Deborah knows that something significant is about to happen to Sisera. She even names it. She prophesies that Jael will complete the mission of conquering Jabin's army through this act (5:24–26). How did Jael know this was her God-ordained moment to kill the enemy? Was she thinking this even before Sisera entered the tent? Did God speak to her in a dream or audibly give her this command? While we can't answer these questions, it's clear that Jael knows this is what needs to be done for her people to be free.

Second, this is a story of role reversal. God uses a Kenite, not an Israelite, to save God's people from their enemies. Similarly, in Jesus' parable of the good Samaritan, the hero is not a Jew but rather a Samaritan. The emphasis of the Judges 4 narrative seems to be centered on those God chooses to do his work. Here, "Jael has in effect

---

5. For example, Yolanda Stith's interpretation misses the mark (*Jael's Tent: A Clarion Call to Women to Own the Moment* [self-published, 2022]).

conquered both Sisera (by depriving him of his life) and Barak (by depriving him of the honor)."[6] It would have been culturally and socially embarrassing for Barak to witness a dead man lying on the ground brought about by the hands of a woman. It was *his* enemy to defeat and conquer, not Jael's.

Third, Deborah praises Jael in Judges 5:24, calling her "most blessed of women." Jael's action must be seen positively, or as blessed, in some light. The primary storyline is fulfilled in the last two verses of Judges 4: "On that day God subdued Jabin king of Canaan before the Israelites. And the hand of the Israelites pressed harder and harder against Jabin king of Canaan until they destroyed him." For God's mission to be fulfilled among the Israelites, Jabin and his army need to be defeated. Jael does the will of God in an unlikely scenario of being called on by God to kill the Israelites' enemy.

Let me end this chapter with a couple of preaching or teaching aids. In *The Art of Preaching Old Testament Narrative*, Steven Mathewson provides helpful literary/genre clues for how a teacher/preacher might explain this text. He observes three types of irony in narrative passages: "(1) verbal—the character says one thing and means something else, (2) dramatic—the character says something but does not understand its full implications, and (3) situational—the situation is the opposite of what is expected or appropriate."[7]

For our purposes, it's dramatic irony, according to Mathewson, that Sisera instructed Jael to tell any visitor that nobody was there with her in the tent. And yet "Sisera did not realize the truth behind the answer he instructed Jael to give. There would not be anyone present because he would be dead with a tent peg driven through his temple!"[8]

What is the application for the congregant or student? This clearly is not a prescriptive text that points us to full obedience. We are not,

6. *NIV Zondervan Study Bible*, note on Judges 4:22, p. 440.
7. Steven D. Mathewson, *The Art of Preaching Old Testament Narrative*, 2nd ed. (Baker Academic, 2021), 58.
8. Mathewson, *Art of Preaching*, 58.

as Jesus says, to "go and do likewise." One takeaway is that God can choose to use anyone who is willing. Circling back to our previous discussion, we are not privy to what was taking place in Jael's mind. Did she know this was her divine assignment? Probably not. What she did know was that the only way to defeat the enemy was through convincing Sisera that she could offer safety and protection. It's also ironic that Jael is not one of the judges of Israel. She is a foreigner and a minor character.

The primary judge in this chapter is Deborah. Barak is too fearful and timid to take on a leadership role. Barak says to Deborah, "If you go with me, I will go; but if you don't go with me, I won't go" (4:8). Barak is again humiliated at the end of the chapter. "Barak came by in pursuit of Sisera, and Jael went out to meet him. 'Come,' she said, 'I will show you the man you're looking for [the one you were supposed to kill]'" (v. 22).

Another teaching element pertinent to today's context is courage. Will we be courageous to fight for the Lord—to speak, to act, to carry out what he requires of us? The teaching or preaching has nothing to commend regarding violence; rather, it's an invitation to be agents of obedience to fulfill God's commands. Because of Jael's obedience, Deborah sings her praises: "Most blessed of women be Jael, the wife of Heber the Kenite, most blessed of tent-dwelling women" (5:24).

Principles for Reflection

1. In an act of irony, God uses Jael, an unlikely heroine, to advance his mission by saving his people from corrupt rulers. God uses those who are able and willing to do his work. This story is a fulfillment of prophecy that Jael, a Kenite woman, would be the one who successfully eliminates Sisera.

2. We may see this as a story of missed opportunities and moments of courage. Barak is too fearful to take charge. Whatever his issue was, he did not become a confident and obedient leader. Not everyone needs to take a leadership role, but we must consider how God can use those who are willing to stand up and fight for the Lord.

3. Many Christians today lack courage and a backbone. We must not shy away from fighting the Evil One. What might God be asking us to do to fight evil and injustice in this world?

CHAPTER 2

IS SUICIDE THE UNFORGIVABLE SIN?

Matthew 27:3–9; Acts 1:18–19

ERIC J. BARGERHUFF

Every year in the United States, approximately 1.6 million people attempt suicide, and 50,000 people die from it. It is the eleventh leading cause of death in this country, and men are nearly four times more likely than women to die from it.[1] Nearly everyone knows of someone or has a relative who has attempted suicide or died from it. If you are one of the few who haven't been touched by this tragedy, consider yourself fortunate.

It is by far one of the saddest and most heartbreaking realities we face in this fallen world, and it underscores the crisis of mental health and spiritual emptiness that grips our society. Though it is not the unforgivable sin, as many wrongly suppose, it nevertheless must be

---

1. "Suicide Statistics," American Foundation for Suicide Prevention, accessed February 17, 2025, https://afsp.org/suicide-statistics/.

seen as a sin—as an act of self-murder. We are all created in the image of God, and therefore our lives matter and have inherent value.

Anyone who teaches the Bible should not avoid this subject just because it's uncomfortable to think or talk about. Many people we encounter walk in silent pain, wishing they could talk with someone about their thoughts, feelings, and struggles. One of the worst things we can do is avoid addressing suicidal thoughts, because God wants us to be delivered from the temptation to think it is an escape, the only way to solve life's difficulties or hardships. God's grace and power far exceed our understanding, and his transforming love can rescue anyone even in their darkest and most hopeless moments.

The Bible records six instances of suicide. Not surprisingly, the first one is in the book of Judges, which covers a dark period in Israel's history. Abimelech, the son of Gideon and a judge of Israel, commands his armor-bearer to take his life after Abimelech's skull was fractured by a large millstone dropped on his head from a tall tower by a woman. Because he was more concerned about his reputation than anything else ("Draw your sword and kill me, or they'll say about me, 'A woman killed him'" [Judges 9:54 CSB]), he chose to end his own life via proxy.

One of the more famous suicides is that of King Saul, Israel's disgraced first king, who was wounded by archers in battle with the Philistines. He, too, commanded his armor-bearer to strike him down rather than let him die at the hands of the Philistines. The armor-bearer was too afraid to lift his hand against God's chosen king of Israel, so Saul fell on his own sword, followed shortly after by the armor-bearer himself, who took his own life as well (1 Samuel 31:4–6).

Next is the story of Ahithophel, former adviser to King David, who betrayed him in the conspiracy with Absalom, David's son, to usurp the throne. When Ahithophel's advice to Absalom in the skirmish with David was not heeded, he considered himself useless, both to the king's son and to the king he had betrayed, and he hanged himself (2 Samuel 17:23).

Another Israelite king, Zimri, who had killed Elah, the previous king of Israel, along with all his family and friends, also took his own life after just seven days of serving as king, the shortest reign in Israel's history. When the army loyal to King Elah heard of Zimri's murder and treachery, they named their own commander, Omri, as a rival king and went after Zimri. When the city Zimri lived in was captured, he set fire to his own royal palace and died in it (1 Kings 16:18).

Before we turn to the suicide of Judas Iscariot, note that some commentators think that Samson was guilty of suicide in Judges 16, but the Bible never portrays his death as such. Rather, he is seen as sacrificing his own life in the war against the Philistines for the sake of the people of Israel. Praying to the Lord for strength, which was granted to him, he pushed against the two middle pillars of the temple, where his enemies were gloating over him. The temple collapsed and killed them all, which led to his own death as well. Scripture states that "those he killed at his death were more than those he had killed in his life" (Judges 16:30 CSB).

Interestingly, the Bible lists Samson as one of the heroes of the faith in Hebrews 11:32. Despite his shortcomings and obvious sins, Samson was regarded as a warrior who fought for the cause of the Lord and the Israelites in the Old Testament. His status as a hero of the faith wouldn't have merit had he committed suicide. Rather, his death was seen as a self-sacrifice.

By far, the most controversial and well-known suicide in the Bible is that of Judas, one of the twelve disciples Jesus lived with and trained for ministry. Judas is infamously known as the betrayer (Matthew 27:3), the coward who sold out Jesus for thirty pieces of silver to the chief priests and elders who were plotting to kill Jesus.

Judas was not a true believer. Jesus pronounced him spiritually unclean at the Lord's Supper (John 13:10–11). Earlier in John, Jesus said, figuratively speaking, that Judas was "a devil" (6:70).[2] Satan

---

2. For more on the difference between Jesus saying to Peter, "Get behind me, Satan!" (Matthew 16:23) and Jesus calling Judas a devil in John 6, see my book *The Most Misused Stories in the Bible: Surprising Ways God's Word Is Misunderstood* (Baker, 2017), 111–12.

himself was said to have entered Judas (13:27), a true sign that he was an unbeliever who could be possessed and used by Satan. Later, Jesus would refer to Judas in his prayer for his disciples as the lost one, the "son of destruction," whose role as the betrayer was a part of God's sovereign plan "so that the Scripture may be fulfilled" (17:12 CSB).

Judas's impending judgment for his treachery was so bleak that Jesus pronounced a woe on him and said, "It would be better for him if he had not been born" (Matthew 26:24). John called him "a thief" (John 12:6), with his lust for money on display in his betrayal of Jesus (Matthew 26:14–15). Peter's attitude was that this betrayer of Jesus "left to go where he belongs" (Acts 1:25 CSB), a likely reference to hell.

The betrayal itself was especially heinous. A prearranged sign was agreed on between Judas and those who came to arrest Jesus—a kiss, a Middle Eastern custom used as a sign of affection between those who were quite familiar with each other, perhaps even friends. Michael Card captured the horrific nature of this betrayal: "Why did it have to be a friend who chose to betray the Lord? Why did he use a kiss to show them? That's not what a kiss is for."[3]

The Bible says that Judas later regretted and felt guilty about his decision to betray Jesus, saying he had sinned by betraying innocent blood (Matthew 27:4). Once he saw Jesus condemned by the Jewish and Roman authorities, he tried to give back the money the chief priests and elders had bought him off with, but to no avail. They didn't care about the money; they were interested in only one thing—Jesus.

Judas ended up tossing the money back into the temple courts, and the chief priests refused to use it for temple purposes because it was "blood money" (Matthew 27:6). Instead, they bought an open field as a place where strangers (people known by no one) who died in Jerusalem would be buried. The field was known as the "potter's field," apparently because its dirt had a claylike texture used for the making of pottery. The field was then renamed "Field of Blood," since

---

3. Michael Card, "Why?," track 6 on *Known by the Scars* (Sparrow Records, 1984).

it was bought with the blood money (27:8). Luke tells us that since the field was bought with Judas's money ("unrighteous wages"), it was as though Judas had bought the field himself (Acts 1:18 CSB).

After tossing the money back, Judas went out and hanged himself (Matthew 27:5). The graphic detail of his suicide is described by Luke: "He fell headfirst, his body burst open and his intestines spilled out" (Acts 1:18 CSB). Commentator Darrell Bock suggests that "this kind of gruesome detail matches the description of the death of Herod Agrippa I in Acts 12:23, making a similar point about God's judgment."[4]

Many have tried to reconcile the idea that Judas hanged himself with that of him falling headfirst, since hanging by the neck wouldn't necessarily give the idea of the head falling before the body fell. But taking the Matthew and Acts passages together doesn't seem to present a problem if Judas hanged himself and then after the hanging fell in a way that caused his head to fall first and his body to rupture.[5] Bock remarks, "The image is vivid and graphic, intended not only to describe but also to leave an emotive impression on readers to prevent their following Judas's negative example of unfaithfulness and betrayal."[6]

The preacher/teacher who teaches on this passage should recognize several things. First, as we've said, Judas was never a true believer. John teaches that those who may have once professed to be followers of Christ may eventually demonstrate through defection and apostasy that they never were believers to begin with: "They went out from us, but they did not belong to us; for if they had

---

4. Darrell L. Bock, *Acts*, Baker Exegetical Commentary on the New Testament (Baker Academic, 2007), 84.
5. In *The Acts of the Apostles* (Pillar New Testament Commentary [Eerdmans, 2009], 124–25), David Peterson makes another suggestion: "There is also the possibility that the Greek expression *prenes genomenos* in v. 18 means 'swelling up' instead of 'falling headlong', in which case we can imagine the corpse becoming bloated in the heat and bursting open while still hanging. Whatever the precise meaning, the sense of the passage is that this was a form of divine retribution for his evil betrayal of Jesus (cf. 12:23 note)."
6. Bock, *Acts*, 85.

belonged to us, they would have remained with us. However, they went out so that it might be made clear that none of them belongs to us" (1 John 2:19 CSB).

Many people have walked away from Jesus (John 6:66) in spite of having full knowledge of who he was, even after seeing or experiencing evidence of his divine power. And the writer of the letter to the Hebrews seems to suggest that those who do walk away will never circle back and genuinely repent (6:4–6). It is the ultimate rejection, despite all the evidence. Judas clearly rejected Jesus.

Second, the difference between worldly sorrow and godly sorrow is clearly evidenced in this text. Judas may have felt guilty for his sin of betrayal, but it did not lead him to truly repent. Paul tells us, "Godly grief produces a repentance that leads to salvation without regret, but worldly grief produces death" (2 Corinthians 7:10 CSB).

In Judas's story, we do not see him embrace the kind of repentance that leads to "times of refreshing" (Acts 3:19), the kind that erases sin and brings about salvation. Rather, Judas continued in his rebellion by murdering himself. This is not to suggest that anyone who takes their own life sins in such a way that they are destined for hell. Surely believers can fall prey to this temptation in moments of weakness. It is not, as we suggested earlier, the unpardonable sin. God's grace covers all our sins—past, present, and future—if one is truly saved.

Remember, the Bible makes it clear that Judas never believed in Jesus, and that his greed, betrayal, and subsequent suicide reveal a heart rooted in rebellion—one that stayed rebellious all the way to death. He intentionally rejected and turned away from the grace of God made available to him in Christ.

Third, and finally, this passage will always be challenging when there are people in your audience who have been impacted by, thought about, or attempted suicide. A gentle and compassionate manner of communicating when teaching this text is essential. You must be prepared to give people hope by proclaiming the availability of the grace that covers all sin.

Principles for Reflection

1. Be prepared to speak on the value of human beings who are created in the image of God and valued to the extent that God would send his Son to earth to pay the penalty for our sins and shortcomings, all so that we can find healing in and reconciliation with him. And be ready to share the gospel. There is victory over sin, death, shame, and guilt—for our Savior took on all of that for us—and was raised victorious so that we, too, may be "more than conquerors" (Romans 8:37).

2. You would do well to have resources to recommend to people who may need counseling or materials to help them (or someone they know who may be in a crisis moment). The Bible has much to say about how God helps us in our moments of weakness (Romans 8:26; 2 Corinthians 12:8–10) and how fellow Christians should come alongside brothers and sisters in need (Romans 12:13; Galatians 6:1–2; 1 Timothy 5:3; James 2:15–17; 1 John 3:17).

3. We should never avoid teaching on painful and difficult topics like this one. You may save someone's life if you engage this issue. But be prayerful and prepared. Hurting people abound both inside and outside the church and we have the Christ they desperately need.

CHAPTER 3

HOW DID A NUDE RUNNER MAKE IT INTO SCRIPTURE?

Mark 14:51–52

ERIC J. BARGERHUFF

The first instance of nakedness in the Bible goes back to the Garden of Eden, where our first parents, Adam and Eve, realized they were naked after they had sinned and disobeyed the Lord's commands (Genesis 3:7). In that context, sin brought forth shame. Prior to that, their natural state was nothing to be ashamed about (2:25). They had a clean conscience because they knew no sin. But everything changed when both of them ate the forbidden fruit of the tree of the knowledge of good and evil.

It was then that they hid, and when the Lord appeared and called out to them, Adam confessed to hiding from God due to his nakedness. Their solution was to sew fig leaves together to cover themselves, but the Lord decided to show them the real impact of their sin and covered them with animal skins, thereby giving us the first instance of physical death in the Bible. Something else died in their place—perhaps previewing the idea of substitutionary death—namely, animals.

From this point on, the Bible mostly portrays *public* nakedness or nudity in a negative light. Except for the concept of sharing intimacy in marriage, undergoing examination or surgery in medical contexts, or perhaps the innocence of a child who lacks self-consciousness about their body, the idea of being naked and exposed in front of others is frowned on and shameful. Sin has twisted that which was originally good, and the lusts of the flesh have taken over.

To be sure, the human body is an amazing work of art, a design unmatched in all creation from a loving and all-wise Creator. Only humanity is said to be created in God's image, and this includes our whole being—body and soul. But the adult naked body, because of humanity's fall into sin, is designed to be kept private and only seen publicly in the aforementioned contexts.

In the Bible, public nakedness is for the most part connected to promiscuity, humiliation, guilt, and shame.[1] For those who regularly indulge in the sin nature, or the flesh, that which should be shameful is proudly flaunted with no shame at all. The illicit sexual nature of our culture today has seared the conscience, and as a result, we have become increasingly desensitized to living in Babylon, so to speak.

So it comes as a bit of a surprise when we see an instance of public nudity among one of Jesus' followers. Now to be sure, this was inadvertent nudity, and therefore one must not be quick to condemn. The more shameful act was that of abandoning Jesus on the night of his arrest, an act that Jesus' disciples just hours before had said they would never do.

This account is found only in Mark 14:51–52. Already on this infamous night, Jesus had instituted the Lord's Supper at the Passover feast and spent extended time teaching and praying for his disciples

---

1. For more on nakedness in the Bible, including its metaphorical and theological contexts and implications, see "Naked, Nakedness," in *Dictionary of Biblical Imagery*, ed. Leland Ryken, James C. Wilhoit, and Tremper Longman III (IVP Academic, 1998), 581–82.

in their midst (Matthew 26; Mark 14; Luke 22; John 13–17), telling them of their abandonment that would take place in the heat of the moment: "All of you will fall away, because it is written: 'I will strike the shepherd, and the sheep will be scattered'" (Mark 14:27 CSB).

Peter, the brash, outspoken one, immediately denies that he will fall away. Jesus then prophesies that before the rooster crows twice, Peter will deny knowing Jesus three times. And we know that Peter ended up doing just that, though he said he never would: "If I have to die with you, I will never deny you" (Mark 14:31 CSB). And to a man, the rest of the disciples (except Judas, who had already departed to betray Jesus) lined up behind Peter's words and said they would never forsake him either. But they did.

Only hours later, when Judas arrives with the chief priests, elders, Romans soldiers, and temple police to arrest Jesus, each of the remaining eleven disciples flees, as Jesus predicted earlier that evening. And soon afterward, during Jesus' sham trial in the middle of the night, Peter will say three times that he doesn't know Jesus.

Mark gives us information we don't see in any other gospel account. As Jesus is taken away, a young man (not one of the twelve disciples) is apparently following him. He is soon discovered by the authorities, and a rather bizarre event takes place. Mark recounts the scene: "Now a certain young man, wearing nothing but a linen cloth, was following him. They caught hold of him, but he left the linen cloth behind and ran away naked" (Mark 14:51–52 CSB).

Who is this young naked runaway? We are not told, but many scholars believe it is none other than Mark himself, the writer of this gospel. After all, if all the disciples already fled, who would be left to give an account of this incident unless the author himself is the young man in question?

Though the exact location of the upper room where Jesus shared his final Passover feast with his disciples is not revealed in Scripture, it may have been at Mark's mother's house, which served as a sort of central headquarters in Jerusalem for the disciples. This may well have been the place where Jesus appeared to them after his resurrection and where they gathered and devoted themselves to prayer after Jesus' ascension (Acts 1:12–14). This was also the first place that Peter went to after his release from prison in Acts 12, that is, "the house of Mary, the mother of John who was called Mark, where many had assembled and were praying" (v. 12 CSB).

If this location was, in fact, where the Last Supper took place, surely Mark would have been aware of the evening's events, even if he hadn't been present in the room during the supper.[2] As the night went on and the disciples left to head to Gethsemane, Mark would very likely have gone to bed, only to be roused by a large detachment of soldiers with torches and clubs headed toward Gethsemane.[3]

This would easily explain why the "young man" (if it was Mark) who was following Jesus had nothing but a linen cloth (undergarments) on. He might have jumped out of bed to see what the commotion was all about. Lighting lamps to see to get fully dressed was not likely going to happen, for fear that he would miss out on the moment that was soon to pass him by.

Therefore the obvious question we might ask is this: Why did Mark include this brief encounter? Was it because, as some scholars have suggested, he wanted to put his own signature on this gospel account with his own hand? In other words, like an artist who signs their name on the bottom corner of a work of art, was Mark including a story about himself to put himself into the story?[4] Possibly. After all,

---

2. Remember, Mark was closely associated with the original Twelve, was a cousin to Barnabas (Colossians 4:10), was at one time a ministry companion to Paul (though they had a temporary falling out [Acts 15:37–40] only to be reconciled later [2 Timothy 4:11]), and later became like a son to Peter (1 Peter 5:13). It is these relationships that gave Mark the credibility to write this gospel in the first place, which was likely written on the basis of Peter's preaching ministry.

3. By the time Jesus concluded his prayer in Gethsemane, it was so late that Peter, James, and John had a hard time staying awake while Jesus was praying, as the narrative tells us (Mark 14:32–42).

4. David L. McKenna writes (*Mark*, Preacher's Commentary [Nelson, 1982], 289), "As an art lover who searches for the signature, initials, sign or number of the artist in the corner of a painting, I like the idea that John Mark put his imprimatur in the corner of his work."

it was a historically accurate story, and the gospel writers don't seem to have a problem including things that were potentially embarrassing to disciples. In fact, when they do so, it seems to argue even more for the gospel's authenticity.

Then why didn't Mark just come out and say it was him? Because it wasn't the practice of the gospel writers. If the writers are referred to at all, it is always in the third person, since they were simply telling the narrative and did not wish to bring attention to themselves. After all, this is the story of Jesus, and none of them wanted to rob him of that glory by using the first-person point of view. Even John, one of the three disciples of Jesus in his inner circle, refers to himself in his gospel account as "the disciple whom Jesus loved."

Further speculation as to why verses 51–52 are included in the story is not warranted, but we know, through the doctrine of the inspiration of Scripture (2 Timothy 3:16–17; 2 Peter 1:20), that the Holy Spirit wished to include this detail in the gospel account. But we can gain insights from it. It shows the fear of these disciples, the cowardice of the human heart in moments of weakness, and the difficult challenges facing those who want to follow Jesus.

This story gives the preacher/teacher an opportunity to show how the Bible often is authentic in its details in stories, especially those that do not flatter Christ followers. If someone wished to forge an ancient document or a story, they are not likely to include things that would undermine their own sense of greatness. This is just one reason we can trust the historicity of these accounts.

Further, the teacher or preacher can press on the conscience of the audience by asking, "What are we ashamed of when it comes to following Christ? Will we, like the disciples, run away when the heat is on? What price are we willing to pay to be associated with the Savior? In some cases, it may cost us our lives. Are we willing to count the cost?" Paul said it well: "I am not ashamed of the gospel, because it is the power of God for salvation to everyone who believes" (Romans 1:16 CSB).

The good news is this: Even though Jesus' disciples abandoned their Savior in a moment of weakness, God in his grace restored them. And not only that, but he used them to establish the foundational truths of the gospel message and ministry. Christ is building his church even today, using fallible human beings like us who fail all too often. He is a God of second chances, and his grace is greater than our sin.

Because of the cross and the empty tomb, those who believe will not stand naked and ashamed before God (spiritually speaking); rather, we are clothed with the righteousness of Christ given to us through faith. When the winds of persecution blow in our direction because we belong to Christ, may we stand firm in our faith, trusting in God's empowering grace to strengthen us so we will not run away in fear and shame.

Principles for Reflection

1. As eyewitnesses, the gospel writers did not call attention to themselves in the narratives they wrote; therefore, if they are mentioned, it is in the third person. Their motive was to keep the spotlight on Jesus. Those who preach and teach can take a cue from this. It is not inappropriate to use personal testimony when we are teaching biblical truths, but we must be careful that our teaching, preaching, and writing focus on "what does this passage teach me about God?" rather than letting our own stories steal the spotlight.

2. Certain stories included in the Bible that are potentially embarrassing for the heroes of the faith actually argue for the authenticity of an account. If the author was writing

something that likely wasn't true, presenting the characters in the best possible light would be the preferred approach.

3. Following Jesus isn't always safe. It comes at a cost. Oftentimes, we don't know what the cost is until we face a situation where we have to make a choice, sacrifice something, or risk public humiliation because of our commitment to Jesus and obedience to his will. Are we living in a distinctively Christlike way that could lead to persecution and awkward moments in the eyes of a skeptical world?

CHAPTER 4

MUST CHRISTIANS OBEY THE GOVERNMENT?

Romans 13:1–7

MATTHEW D. KIM

The subject of obeying the government is a hot topic for many Americans. During COVID-19, the government issued mandates for all its citizens. In certain state contexts, churches were ordered to close, sometimes for extended periods of time (even when it had become safe to reopen).[1] Some churches heeded the principle in Romans 7 to obey the government's directives, while others chose to disobey and reopen their worship gatherings despite restrictions. Does this mean the churches that reopened were disobeying the government and thereby disobeying God, even though God commands Christians to worship? Does this mean the churches that reopened before restrictions were lifted ought to be punished according to this

---

1. Melissa Quinn, "Houses of Worship and States Battle over Coronavirus Restrictions," ABC News, April 16, 2020, www.cbsnews.com/news/houses-of-worship-and-states-battle-over -coronavirus-restrictions/.

passage? What happens if, God forbid, another pandemic strikes our world? What does the church do then? I'll leave it to you to decide.

I haven't heard many sermons on this text in my lifetime—and perhaps for good reason. The subject of the government's influence in our lives is tricky and polarizing. It's interesting to note that Romans 13:1–7 is the "meat in the sandwich" between two pieces of bread: *love* (12:9–21) and *law* (13:8–10), where Paul speaks of love as our primary motivation as Christian and the fulfillment of the law.

Here Paul explains that God clearly has given government the authority to properly rule over its citizens. Let's first explore Paul's logic in the passage and the causal relationships he sets up. In other words, we do *this* because God does *that*.

First, it's expected that *everyone* submits to governing authorities because no authority exists apart from what God institutes. So is there truly a separation of church and state as we understand it today? Not according to Paul's teaching here. Second, in verse 2, anyone who disobeys what God has established (government) begets judgment. Third, do what is right and you will be acclaimed. Fourth, those who do wrong will incur "the sword." The government has God's authority to govern with an iron hand.

At first glance, the text seems to be rather straightforward to preach or teach. The late Haddon Robinson shared a sermon outline in a class session on Romans 13:1–7. Here's an example of how a preacher or teacher might expound on this passage.

I.   Christians must submit to governmental authority. Why?
    A. God has established government.
    B. If we rebel against government, we rebel against God.
    C. If we rebel against government, we will be punished.
II. Robinson's Conclusion
    A. God has established this authority.
    B. We are subject to God and submit to authority.
    C. Christians must submit to governmental authority.

D. God has established government.

E. If we rebel against government, we rebel against God.[2]

Yes, this is the basic structure of the text. We could preach or teach this text in this manner and then go straight home. Case closed. Just obey the government. Why? Because God said so, and not doing so is disobeying what God has created for us to obey.

Many incredulous students of the Word and hearers of the sermon, however, will want to ask questions. For instance, we'll begin with the big one: Does this mean we must obey the government even when officials tell us to disobey the Lord? If we take this text at face value, it seems that every person on the planet is mandated by God to follow the directives of the government in all circumstances. Failing to do so is rebelling against what God has instituted, and the consequence is judgment.

This sets up a clear problem because leaders in the government are fallen human beings who don't always do what's best for God and his people. Sin and corruption abound in governing systems. Many have witnessed the horrors of the judicial process and the way citizens are treated by those who create policies and laws. Timothy Terrell says, "Policy made with good intentions is not necessarily good policy. . . . The primary function of civil government is to promote justice—to punish those who do evil and commend those who do good (Rom. 13:4; 1 Peter 2:14)."[3] These ideals aren't always executed well.

Many Christians could do more to learn about our government and how it runs. Jonathan Walton notes, "The fact that America functions as a republic and not a democracy shouldn't come as a surprise to

---

2. Haddon Robinson, class notes from his introductory preaching course at Gordon-Conwell Theological Seminary.

3. Timothy D. Terrell, "The Need for Caution in Advocating for Climate Change Policies," in *Cultural Engagement: A Crash Course in Contemporary Issues*, ed. Joshua D. Chatraw and Karen Swallow Prior (Zondervan Academic, 2019), 196–97.

US citizens, but it does. . . . This lack of knowledge about the political process is not limited to the poor or those living in rural areas."[4]

When does a violation of the government occur? Scott Rae explains that this passage highlights the three areas that represent "the legitimate and God-ordained role of government': . . . protecting citizens, maintaining social order, and ensuring justice." Rae goes on to write, "Though submission to civil authority is not absolute, and though there is room for civil disobedience to unjust laws, the government is authorized to use force, if necessary, to fulfill its mandate."[5]

Sadly, my skeptical mind goes immediately to dystopian books or televisions shows depicting a government that takes absolute control to the extreme—erasing human rights and dignity one step and command at a time until all that's left of humanity is the numbing recitation of mantras that have brainwashed them over sound systems. Access to necessities like food, water, and shelter is nowhere to be found.

While God has authorized government for basic human order, protection, and justice, we recognize that God has also given humans cognitive and moral reasoning abilities, as well as the command to not commit idolatry. Thus, we obey the government to the extent that we do not commit idolatry or disobey the Word of God.

The blurring of earthly citizenship and heavenly citizenship deserves mention. We are temporary citizens of earth, but those who are in Christ are permanent citizens of heaven. In every election cycle, we face the momentous opportunity to be earthly citizens who have a future heavenly dwelling. We must not live as if earth is all there is, without an eternal destination. For many Christians, the election of governing officials (particularly a nation's president and vice president) has risen to the level of idolatry and political partisanship to

---

4. Jonathan Walton, *Twelve Lies That Hold America Captive and the Truth That Sets Us Free* (IVP, 2019), 78.
5. Scott B. Rae, *Moral Choices: An Introduction to Ethics*, 4th ed. (1995; repr., Zondervan, 2018), 410.

the abandonment of Christian wisdom. We've become so divided over politics that Christians no longer live in unity.

A brief word about the hermeneutics of politics. Anytime Scripture refers to government and rulers, such as kings and judges, we tend to take note and seek to massage scriptural instructions to fit our political leanings and systems. We must recognize the danger of misapplying the biblical teaching on government/politics. As Kaitlyn Schiess observes, "One difficulty with examining biblical arguments in American political life is the blurry line between direct reference and vague invocation of popular biblical language."[6] All too often, we cherry-pick verses or eisegete passages to support our agendas. Be careful!

This doesn't mean we don't take seriously biblical teachings on government or the fact that God intends for elected officials to serve in strategic, influential positions. In fact, commentator John Witmer points out that "a civil leader is God's servant, a concept often forgotten today."[7] Therefore, in response to texts such as Romans 13:1–7, our submission to the governing authorities comes in two forms that go beyond simple compliance to the law. The most natural way to support the government as Paul instructs is by paying our taxes. Jesus said this in the Gospels. "Give back to Caesar what is Caesar's, and to God what is God's" (Matthew 22:21; Mark 12:17; Luke 20:25). Paying taxes is a fundamental requirement of a citizen. Paying taxes is what allows the government to function by providing resources so they can focus on their deeds of service. They allocate monies based on the needs of the local community, region, state, nation, or province.

Another principle may seem more unnatural for human beings. Witmer continues, "So a Christian ought to give everyone what he

---

6. Kaitlyn Schiess, *The Ballot and the Bible: How Scripture Has Been Used and Abused in American Politics and Where We Go from Here* (Brazos, 2023), 176.
7. John A. Witmer, "Romans," in *The Bible Knowledge Commentary: An Exposition of the Scriptures*, vol. 2, ed. J. F. Walvoord and R. B. Zuck (Victor, 1985), 490.

owes him (lit., 'repay everyone his dues'), whether substance (taxes and revenue) or respect and honor."[8] Paying "respect and honor" to our governing officials can be easy to do if we align with that party but oh so challenging when we disagree. When we respect and show honor to our leaders, we pray for them and for their wisdom. We ask God to help them in their weakness and to draw them to put their hope and trust in him alone.

Only God can allow those in authority to govern judiciously. Immediately my mind goes to Israel's King Solomon, who asked the Lord for wisdom to govern rightly: "Give your servant a discerning heart to govern your people and to distinguish between right and wrong. For who is able to govern this great people of yours?" (1 Kings 3:9). I wonder how many government leaders pray for wisdom each day? If they are not seeking the Lord, we pray on their behalf that they will not rely on their own wisdom but on God's wisdom alone. And as part of the call to respect and honor our officials, we refrain from mocking or slandering them privately or publicly. Yes, easier said than done!

The challenge in explaining Romans 13:1–7 is that, in principle, it seems simple to tell others to obey the laws and submit to the government. Yet it's much more complicated when we're dealing with topics such as Christian nationalism or White supremacy, which are loosely related to government but also involve inequality, injustice, and privilege. We must recognize that because of their struggle with the sinful nature, governing officials at times create laws that benefit people who have similar views and who support them financially.

Let's pray for our government leaders—city, county, state, region, nation, and worldwide. How can submitting to and praying for the government become a more regular part of our daily rhythms? How can we declare Jesus as Lord of all—including in our politics and our votes on today's issues? How can we respect and honor the government

---

8. Witmer, "Romans," 490.

and stay in unity and fellowship with believers? The motive for our ethics and response to government is love for God and love for people. We submit to the government (within reason) as an act of love for God and neighbor.

Principles for Reflection

1. God expects all citizens to honor and follow governmental authority and obey the laws they create. We are called to pray for our leaders at all levels. Yet we must always obey God when the policies and procedures of the government contradict the teaching of Scripture.

2. We may not like who is in an elected office, but we are called to pray for governmental leaders and obey the laws of the land. We may think we are wiser than they are, but God permits people to hold certain offices, whether we like them or not.

3. Are we spending more time being critical of our leaders than praying for and honoring them? There may be people with whom we've unnecessarily had conflict over policies and practices. Who do we need to confess our sins to and ask for their forgiveness? Pray for our leaders' wisdom and character and that they would fear the Lord.

CHAPTER 5

ARE WIVES REALLY "WEAKER PARTNERS"?

1 Peter 3:7

ERIC J. BARGERHUFF

Because we live in a world of competing worldviews and concepts of reality, 1 Peter 3:7 is one of the most challenging verses to interpret and teach. We live in a culture where the devil has had his way with the world in his campaign to confuse society on the definitions and roles of men and women. Each week seems to bring about a new social construct in which subjective experience and imagination eclipse any claim to absolute truth—a place where clear definitions and boundaries exist.

Paul's description of God's judgment for exchanging his truth for lies seems fitting for the present day, as we see people given over to corrupt minds to pursue that which is unnatural, even becoming inventors of evil (Romans 1:28–30). In other words, God is letting sin run its course in all its destructiveness as a form of judgment for rejecting him and his truth. And with each new headline, the believer cries out, "Lord, have mercy."

Where, then, is the corrective to a society that has lost its way? Where do we find the truth when even objective scientific fact is rejected for the sake of sin's unbridled lusts? Jesus points to the source of truth in his prayer to the Father: "Your word is truth" (John 17:17). God's Word stands as the corrective to a culture in which desperately wicked hearts (Jeremiah 17:9) do that which is right in their own eyes (Judges 17:6).

The Bible makes it clear that humanity was created as male and female (Genesis 1:27; 5:2; Matthew 19:4; Mark 10:6). There are no other options, and this is identifiable even to the level of our physical chromosomes. Both sexes are equally created in God's image, and neither is inferior to the other in any way. They both possess rational and intellectual abilities, emotions, a will, and a capacity for spirituality. They are both created to reflect the glory of God and his image and tasked to rule over creation (Genesis 1:28). The Bible also clearly teaches that men and women were made to complement one another, each having their own strengths and weaknesses. These truths can be seen in the roles they are called to play in marriage, where God established an authority structure by which the relationship can function in a healthy manner.

Paul told the Ephesian church that wives are to be subject to their own husbands, and that husbands are to take leadership as the head of their wives (Ephesians 5:22–23). These instructions were to serve as a pattern for reversing the curse that came from sin (as recorded in Genesis 3). Unfortunately, humanity's sinful nature means that the harmony between a married couple is corrupted by selfishness—the wife will desire to usurp the role of her husband, and the husband will inappropriately dominate his wife (Genesis 3:16).[1] Paul aimed to

---

1. For an interesting discussion about the translation theory and interpretation of this verse, see Denny Burk's "Five Quick Points on the ESV's Rendering of Genesis 3:16," DennyBurk .com, September 14, 2016, www.dennyburk.com/four-quick-points-on-the-esvs-rendering -of-genesis-316/.

address this by setting forth a healthy pattern for the way a husband and wife can love each other within God's plan.

Yet reciting a passage like Ephesians 5:22–23 can cause deep angst in today's culture for fear of abuse, and in some cases, such fear is warranted. But the Bible must be properly understood in context if it is to be interpreted and applied in a way that glorifies God.[2]

The remedy is found only in being regenerated and born again through repentance and saving faith in Christ, experiencing the Holy Spirit's sanctifying power as God redeems us and transforms us and our relationships. Redemption's trajectory is to reverse the curse, and the apostles' instructions are meant to put things back into God's ordained proper order.

To this end, the Bible contains other passages in which the roles of men and women in the context of marriage are defined (for example, 1 Corinthians 7:3–5; Colossians 3:18–19; Titus 2:4).[3] As mentioned at the beginning of this chapter, the words of the apostle Peter in 1 Peter 3:1–7 have drawn a lot of attention. Peter's slightly different angle here is that he is talking about marriage roles in a unique context— mainly how to live in a mixed marriage where one person is a believer and the other is not: "Husbands, in the same way, live with your wives in an understanding way, as with a weaker partner, showing them honor as coheirs of the grace of life, so that your prayers will not be hindered" (1 Peter 3:7 CSB).

In Peter's first letter, he teaches the church how to live in the hostile world into which they have been dispersed because of persecution. The Christian witness is not to be tarnished by social action, militancy, defiance, or protest, but rather is to be defined by holiness (1:15), love (1:22), and submission to authority (2:13), to name a few virtues. The

---

2. In large measure, the problem begins when people place inherent value on particular roles, whereas any functional society must have a working authority structure to avoid chaos. This is true for governing authorities in society, as well as in society's essential building block—the family.

3. To limit the scope, I'll only address the roles of husband and wife in the marriage relationship rather than cover broader topics such as the role of men and women in society or the church.

theme of submission during suffering permeates this section, whether at the hands of the government, in the workplace, in the social environment (in their case, sometimes as slaves), or in the family.

Scripture tells us that Peter was married (Mark 1:30; Luke 4:38; 1 Corinthians 9:5). In his letter, he echoes some of the same instructions for husbands and wives that Paul presented.[4] But he specifically addresses wives who are married to non-Christian men:

> In the same way, wives, submit yourselves to your own husbands so that, even if some disobey the word, they may be won over without a word by the way their wives live when they observe your pure, reverent lives. Don't let your beauty consist of outward things like elaborate hairstyles and wearing gold jewelry or fine clothes, but rather what is inside the heart—the imperishable quality of a gentle and quiet spirit, which is of great worth in God's sight. For in the past, the holy women who put their hope in God also adorned themselves in this way, submitting to their own husbands, just as Sarah obeyed Abraham, calling him lord. You have become her children when you do what is good and do not fear any intimidation. (1 Peter 3:1–6 CSB)

Peter, like Paul, calls the wife to submit to her own husband (not to all men in general) and to let their beauty come more from within than without (as a matter of the heart more than fashion or style).[5] The idea of submission was not new, because it was to be the pattern for wives' relationships with their husbands whether or not they were

---

4. I contend that Paul had probably been married at some point, though not during his apostolic ministry. He may have been biblically divorced or widowed. He had been a Pharisee at one point in his life, and Pharisees in Jewish culture were typically married. So it would have been highly unlikely he would have been single. In the end, however, this is mere speculation, since the Bible doesn't address Paul's marital status prior to his apostolic calling.

5. Peter's example of a woman's beauty not coming from elaborate hairstyles, gold jewelry, or fine clothes is not an outright prohibition from possessing those things. Rather, his point is that a woman's ultimate beauty doesn't come from those things but rather is found in the internal character qualities of a "gentle and quiet spirit" (1 Peter 3:3–4).

believers, since in Ephesians 5:22–32, Paul said the same thing in the context of a Christian marriage. Furthermore, their lives were to serve as examples of godliness, even to the point that they might lead unbelieving husbands to Christ by the winsome nature of their character. This kind of result is ultimately what matters to God.

Drawing on a powerful effect that wives can have on their unbelieving husbands, Peter emphasizes the endearing and godly nature of a "gentle and quiet spirit" (1 Peter 3:4). Wayne Grudem makes this comment:

> Such a *gentle and quiet spirit* will be beautiful to other human beings, even unbelieving husbands (vv. 1–2), but even more importantly it is something which *in God's sight is very precious*. Why? No doubt because such a spirit is the result of quiet and continual trust in God to supply one's needs, and God delights in being trusted (cf. 1:5, 7, 8–9, 21; 2:6–7, 23; 3:12; 5:7).[6]

Peter then points to the fact that godly women in the past adorned themselves by embodying such beautiful character as they submitted to their husbands. He mentions Sarah as an example—how she submitted to Abraham's leadership, obeying him and even "calling him lord" (v. 6 CSB). On the surface, this sounds a little shocking. But as always, context is the key to proper interpretation. The Greek word *kyrios* can also be translated as "master," which only softens the effect ever so slightly to our modern-day ears.

In the Genesis context, for Sarah to call Abraham "lord" (Genesis 18:12) was a polite sign of respect, the same way "yes, sir" and "yes, ma'am" are used today. To be sure, you've heard of "lords and ladies" in British society, so we know there are other uses of *lord* in various societies based on title or position that show dignity and respect. Peter is

---

6. Wayne A. Grudem, *1 Peter*, Tyndale New Testament Commentaries (Eerdmans, 1988), 140, italics in original.

using an example of the winsome godliness of Sarah, demonstrated in her relationship with her husband, Abraham.

Of course, a wife should not submit when submission is inappropriate—including anything that violates the moral will of God as outlined in his Word (Acts 4:18–20; 5:28–29). And she should not fear or be intimidated by her unbelieving husband but rather entrust herself to God and to doing what pleases God. Our definition of *lord* is, of course, much different from our understanding of the divine nature of Jesus Christ, who, as we know, is the only true Lord of all in the highest sense.

Peter turns to Christian husbands in verse 7, addressing a situation in which Christian men are married to unbelieving women. The words "in the same way" indicate that the context remains. Peter has clear instructions for husbands. Notice that the word *submit* is absent, because nowhere does the Bible tell the husband to submit to the wife in terms of leadership, but there is a mutual submission (Ephesians 5:21) with respect to the proper duties and responsibilities outlined by God's Word. A husband is to live with his wife in an understanding way, submitting to his duty to love her as himself (v. 28), with a pure love (vv. 25–26), and with the goal of meeting her needs.

The "understanding way" mentioned in 1 Peter 3:7 (CSB) refers to a husband's sensitivity to a wife in every way—emotionally, relationally, physically, and spiritually (especially since she may not yet believe, and he wants nothing to hinder his prayers for her).

Peter calls the wife a "weaker partner," and with the entirety of Scripture in mind here, since we know she is equally made in the image of God, we know that Peter is primarily talking about physical weakness here. Those who preach and teach on this passage must make that point clear.

The woman is intellectually and emotionally—in every way— the man's equal in the sight of God. This is the clear implication of Genesis 1:27 and 5:1–2, where the Bible clearly establishes equality by stating that both male and female were made in the image of God, collectively calling them "man." The only difference is in the area of physical strength—a distinction that is by biological design and is empirically and scientifically verifiable.[7] Ironically, with the cultural confusion among the sexes today, the controversies about men who dominate in women's sports proves Peter's point. The husband's role is to protect, provide, and lead. His physical strength aids in those roles.

Peter once again reiterates the inherent equality of men and women as image bearers by calling women "coheirs of the grace of life" (1 Peter 3:7 CSB). Is it possible that eternal life is in view here? Not necessarily—if she's yet not a Christian. Yet the gift of life and marriage itself is enough of a reason to treat her in "an understanding way," with the intention of praying for and leading her toward her salvation. But if the wife does profess faith, Peter may be clearly reminding the husband what the New Testament so readily affirms— that men and women alike are both "one in Christ Jesus" and "heirs according to the promise" (Galatians 3:28–29). Either way, whether or not the wife is a believer, he is to show her honor.

Finally, it is a profound insight to point out that the way a husband treats his wife has a direct impact on the effectual nature of his prayers. His role, lived out correctly, will benefit the power of his prayers. If the wife is not yet a believer, the husband's treatment of her is directly linked to the effectiveness of both his prayers and his witness. The weight of this should weigh heavily on Christian men, for it is a great responsibility. If a husband loves a woman with a sincere, humble, selfless love, seeking ways to honor and please her while being sensitive to her feelings, emotions, opinions, and needs (as a

---

7. Thomas R. Schreiner writes, "In what sense are women 'weaker'? Nothing else in the New Testament suggests that women are intellectually inferior, nor is it clear that women are weaker emotionally, for in many ways the vulnerability of women in sharing their emotions and feelings demonstrates that they are more courageous and stronger than men emotionally. Nor did Peter suggest that women are weaker morally or spiritually than men. . . . The most obvious meaning, therefore, is that women are weaker than men in terms of sheer strength" (*1, 2 Peter, Jude*, New American Commentary [B&H, 2003], 160). Grudem suggests that the idea of weaker may also include "weaker in terms of authority within the marriage" (*1 Peter*, 144).

spiritual leader should be, with all that those needs entail—especially spiritually), there is a strong likelihood that a wife may submit with exceeding joy to his godly leadership.

Those who teach on this passage should prepare for some instances of pushback, which is an indictment of our cultural biases. But the Bible stands as a corrective. When we look at the life of Jesus, we see how much he loved us with a pure love, even while we were his enemies (Romans 5:8). He submitted to the Father's will throughout his entire life and ministry. He stands as both the model leader who initiates love and the willing and humble servant of the Lord who submitted out of love as well. Therefore, both men and women can find in Jesus the perfect example of the role they are called to play.

Principles for Reflection

1. Men and women are created equal in the sight of God, but there are differences in roles, physicality, and dispositions. Problems arise when we assign values of superiority or inferiority to these differences, which the Bible never does. We would do well to see these differences as God's gift to us.

2. It is a biological fact that men, on average, are stronger than women (with exceptions, of course), and this fact is what Peter is referring to when he says that a wife is the "weaker partner."

3. Understanding the doctrine of humanity as it is seen throughout the Bible helps us understand passages like this one by guiding us away from interpretations to avoid and toward those to accept.

CHAPTER 6

DID JESUS LITERALLY DESCEND INTO HELL?

1 Peter 3:18–20

MATTHEW D. KIM

Hell is not a comfortable conversation point for anyone, including Christians. In common Christian parlance, it is a literal and eternal place where the presence of God is absent and where Satan and evil rule. In *Erasing Hell*, Francis Chan confesses, "Until recently, whenever the idea of hell—and the idea of my loved ones possibly heading there—crossed my mind, I would brush it aside and divert my thinking to something more pleasant. While I've always believed in hell with my mind, I tried not to let the doctrine penetrate my heart."[1] Like most Christians, we want a ticket out of hell and into heaven.

Historically, the Universalist view (endorsed by the Universalist Church of America and others) is that all people on earth will end up in heaven. Heaven is the polar opposite of hell; it is the place

---

1. Francis Chan and Preston Sprinkle, *Erasing Hell: What God Said About Eternity, and the Things We've Made Up* (Cook, 2011), 14.

where God dwells for eternity. Origen (AD 185–254) supported the view that God will save all for heaven and eternal life.[2] According to Universalism, no one is outside the bounds of a heavenly future, regardless of one's religious commitments. If everyone ends up in heaven, a literal hell becomes unwarranted and a moot point. But since Scripture (including Jesus himself) names hell as a real place, we can't reasonably claim that hell fails to exist.

I first became conscious of the concept of hell as a child growing up in church. I found myself puzzled each week when reciting the Apostles' Creed about whether or not Jesus physically and literally went to the place of hell. If so, why was he there even temporarily and what did he do there? If not, why is this teaching a part of the Apostles' Creed?

Over the years, a debate has taken place over the line in the Apostles' Creed that reads, "He [Jesus Christ] descended into hell."[3] Between Jesus' death on the cross and his resurrection from the grave (the day we know as Holy Saturday), it is said that Jesus descended to hell. Some of the debate stems from the interpretation of 1 Peter 3:18–20 and other texts.[4]

Hell is a place of eternal suffering, and suffering is the dominant motif of 1 Peter. The apostle is writing to those who are undergoing various forms of persecution. In the section of chapter 3 leading up to verse 17, Peter has been telling the believers that those who are in Christ will suffer for his name and for the sake of righteousness. In connecting their suffering to holding on to righteous faith and behavior, Peter then names Christ's suffering: "Christ also suffered once for sins, the righteous for the unrighteous, to bring you to God. He was put to death in the body but made alive in the Spirit" (v. 18). Peter

---

2. Chan and Sprinkle, *Erasing Hell*, 23.
3. The phrase "descended into hell" is not found in any version of the creed prior to AD 390. Wayne Grudem discusses the phrase in great detail in his *Systematic Theology: An Introduction to Biblical Doctrine*, 2nd ed. (Zondervan, 2020), 725–36.
4. See related passages (including Acts 2:27; Romans 10:6–7; Ephesians 4:8–9; 1 Peter 4:6).

then writes, "After being made alive, he [Jesus] went and made proclamation to the imprisoned spirits—to those who were disobedient long ago when God waited patiently in the days of Noah while the ark was being built" (vv. 19–20).

These verses have generated discussion on whether Jesus went to hell to proclaim a message to "imprisoned spirits." What is peculiar in this text are the unnamed imprisoned spirits to whom Jesus went and proclaimed. Who is being referenced as the "disobedient long ago when God waited patiently in the days of Noah while the ark was being built"? Those who support the view that Jesus "descended into hell" believe that between his death and resurrection Jesus went to a place to preach to this specific group, who were in some type of hell or even a literal one.

There are three distinct interpretations of the phrase "he descended into hell."[5] First, Jesus, while hanging on the cross, endured the pains of hell. Second, Jesus, until the time of his resurrection, remained in a "state of death." Third, Jesus went to a physical place known as hell after the cross and prior to his bodily resurrection.

The remainder of our discussion will explore these chief concerns: Did Jesus literally go to hell, and if so (or if not), what difference does it make in our lives as twenty-first-century Christians? Greg Garrison writes, "The early church believed that after his death, Christ descended into hell to rescue the souls of the righteous, such as Adam and Eve. Jesus descends and breaks down the doors of hell, unbinds the prisoners and leads the just to heaven."[6] If this interpretation is correct, Jesus would have removed these individuals from hell (a permanent place). It would also mean Adam and Eve had been in hell.

Others hold opposing views. R. C. Sproul writes, "Peter doesn't tell us who the lost spirits in prison are or where the prison is. People

5. "Did Jesus Really Descend into Hell?," Zondervan Academic, April 14, 2017, https://zondervanacademic.com/blog/did-jesus-really-descend-into-hell.
6. Greg Garrison, "Did Jesus 'Descend into Hell' After His Death?," AL.com, updated September 29, 2024, www.al.com/life/2022/04/did-jesus-descend-into-hell-after-his-death.html.

are making a lot of assumptions when they consider that this is a reference to hell and that Jesus went there between his death and his resurrection."[7] Thomas Schreiner says, "First, Christ suffered for the unrighteous to bring believers to God (v. 18). Second, by the power of the Spirit he was raised from the dead and proclaimed victory over demonic spirits (vv. 18–19)."[8]

While it may seem like we're splitting hairs, the term *hell* needs to be defined in order to make a convincing case that Jesus went there. We must distinguish the Old Testament meaning of the place of the dead from the literal destination of hell in which God's presence is absent forever.

The following chart on ancient Israel's perspective on the afterlife gives us greater understanding:[9]

Hebrew Understanding of Death

THE PLACE OF THE DEAD	The Place of the Righteous Dead (Paradise, Abraham's Bosom)
	The Place of the Unrighteous Dead (*Hades, Gehenna, Sheol*)
	The Place for the Fallen Angels (*Tartarus*)

The place of the dead can be demarcated as three "places": the place of the righteous dead, the place of the unrighteous dead, and the place for the fallen angels.[10] The Old Testament word for the place of the dead is *Sheol*. The New Testament equivalent is *Hades*. The actual place of permanent separation from God and of eternal punishment

---

7. R. C. Sproul, "What Does the Apostles' Creed Mean When It Says That Jesus Descended into Hell?," Ligonier Ministries, accessed February 14, 2024, https://learn.ligonier.org/qas/what-does-apostles-creed-mean-when-it-says-jesus-d.

8. Thomas R. Schreiner, *1, 2 Peter, Jude*, New American Commentary (B&H, 2003), 180.

9. "The Fallen Angels in 'Tartarus,'" Emmaus Institute, March 22, 2024, https://emmausinstitute.net/the-fallen-angels-in-tartarus.

10. See Nick Hartman, "What Does the Apostles' Creed Mean by 'He Descended to the Dead?'," Youth Pastor Theologian, April 5, 2023, www.youthpastortheologian.com/blog/what-does-the-apostles-creed-mean-by-he-descended-to-the-dead.

is *hell*. Matthew Emerson further distinguishes terminology based on Latin roots: "The creedal Latin varies between *ad inferna* ('descended into hell') and *ad inferos* ('descended to the dead [ones]'), but these are synonyms until the Reformation."[11] It's crucial to know which perspective we'll adopt to help our listeners/students understand the doctrine.[12]

Taking a slight detour, what did Jesus say about this third category of "descended to the dead," or a literal hell as a permanent destination for the unrighteous? The imagery of hell is one of heat and fire (Matthew 5:22; 18:9; Mark 9:43; James 3:6). It's a place where body parts are figuratively thrown (Matthew 5:29–30; Mark 9:45, 47), where "soul and body" go to be destroyed (Matthew 10:28), where the unrighteous and unrepentant go to be sentenced (Matthew 23:33). It's a place to be feared (Luke 12:5) and a place of darkness (2 Peter 2:4). Jesus described it as a place "where there will be weeping and gnashing of teeth" (Matthew 8:12; 13:42, 50; 22:13; 24:51; 25:30; Luke 13:28).

Based on my reading, I find it more convincing that Jesus went to "the place of the righteous dead" and not to a literal permanent dwelling place called "hell." There is no biblical warrant to argue that Jesus died on the cross and traveled to a literal hell to pay the penalty for our sins and to be tormented by Satan on our behalf. And yet even if this happened to be true, what can we take away from what transpired on Holy Saturday?

---

11. Matthew Y. Emerson, *"He Descended to the Dead": An Evangelical Theology of Holy Saturday* (IVP Academic, 2019), 3–4.

12. Joe Rigney explains rather definitively here: "Following his death for sin, then, Jesus journeys to Hades, to the City of Death, and rips its gates off the hinges. He liberates Abraham, Isaac, Jacob, David, John the Baptist, and the rest of the Old Testament faithful, ransoming them from the power of Sheol (Psalm 49:15; 86:13; 89:48). They had waited there for so long, not having received what was promised, so that their spirits would be made perfect along with the saints of the new covenant (Hebrews 11:39–40; 12:23). After his resurrection, Jesus ascends to heaven and brings the ransomed dead with him, so that now paradise is no longer down near the place of torment, but is up in the third heaven, the highest heaven, where God dwells (2 Corinthians 12:2–4)." ("He Descended into Hell?," Desiring God, April 4, 2015, www .desiringgod.org/articles/he-descended-into-hell).

Like other mysteries in the Christian life, we don't know exactly what happened. Nor was it God's intention that we do. If it had been, God would have made it clear. What we can rejoice in is the fact that Jesus died and rose again. Where he might have gone in the time between the cross and the resurrection is unnecessary for our salvation. We take encouragement and find hope in the words written by Matthew Emerson:

> [Jesus] did not just experience dying only to rise again moments later, but he actually remained dead in the grave. He did not simply have his breath expire and then immediately rise to glory, but his body was buried and his soul departed to the place of the dead. And because he is God in the flesh, he defeated the place of the dead and the grave by descending into them and then rising again on the third day. In the Christian tradition, this hope is known as the doctrine of Christ's *descensus*—his descent to the dead.[13]

First Peter 3:18–20 is of great significance because it relates directly to the gospel message. The wrath of God was poured out on Jesus Christ, and not on us who deserved it. Because of what Jesus accomplished on behalf of professing believers, we don't have to experience hell. Whether Jesus physically went to the location of hell is known only by God. Yet the fact that we can live eternally with the triune God is astounding. This world minimizes hell or considers it a fallacy. This passage maximizes the weight of hell because the death and resurrection of Jesus is the crux of the gospel we proclaim. Hell is a real place and those who are in Christ won't have to experience it. As we face suffering in this life, Christians can stand firm on the fact that Jesus ascended to heaven, and he will descend once again from the clouds on the glorious day of his second coming.

---

13. Emerson, *"He Descended to the Dead,"* xi.

Principles for Reflection

1. According to God's Word, hell—a place marked by the absence of God—is a literal and permanent separation from the triune God. Jesus died on the cross on Good Friday and was bodily resurrected on the third day, which we know as Easter, or Resurrection Sunday. During the time and space between, we know that Jesus was separated from the Father. Whether he went to a literal place called hell is and always will be a mystery on this side of heaven.

2. The descent of Jesus to hell is an issue open to debate. But we can proclaim with confidence that Jesus died and rose again to defeat Satan and to execute the incomparable plan of God to redeem sinful humanity.

3. My goal going forward is to be more proactive in evangelism. I want to make Jesus' sacrifice on the cross and his miraculous resurrection a topic of conversation as often as I can. May we boldly share our faith and glorious gospel with every nonbeliever we meet. We may never know the eternal destination of the person we encounter, but we do know that Jesus has accomplished everything necessary for humanity to experience eternal life with him. In this light, we must renew our commitment to share and practice our faith.

PART II:
AMBIGUOUS

How to Teach Cryptic Passages

Ambiguity and uncertainty are particularly challenging for teachers and preachers. Even when we do our best to study a text, we find that at times we have no earthly answers to difficult passages. Here are some things to keep in mind when dealing with especially cryptic passages.

We will want to make it clear to everyone that life will always have its moments of uncertainty. We don't have all the answers because we're not God. While it may sound like a cop-out, it can be helpful to explain to others that because we are finite, we can't be certain; we've studied, prayed, and deliberated, and here's what we *think* a particular passage may mean, but it's really only our best guess. Of course, we wouldn't say this about every Bible text, since God's Word is clear on certain instructions and commandments. Yet in other instances, like the passages we're about to discuss, we can't necessarily offer definitive responses.

Cryptic passages invite ongoing opportunities for deeper study of Scripture. As you expound on the following texts, you may want to ask the church to study these texts in small group Bible studies. Is there anything more exciting for a ministry leader than to see church members engaged in studying God's Word together?

The struggle with ambiguous texts is that we hate to admit certain things are beyond our comprehension. Rather than dismissing the obvious, we have greater credibility when we confess that this ambiguity demonstrates strongly that we serve a God whose greatness transcends our human understanding. We don't know why God included this cryptic passage in the Bible, but it's there for a reason. Even in its ambiguity, it can give deeper insights into who God is and what his will is for us.

CHAPTER 7

DO ANCIENT FOOD LAWS MEAN ANYTHING TODAY?

Deuteronomy 14:21

MATTHEW D. KIM

While I'm not mageirocophobic (afflicted with a fear of cooking),[1] cooking is by no means my forte. Yet even for me, Moses' command to the Israelite community seems so odd that it doesn't require mentioning—of course no one would think to "cook a young goat in its mother's milk," right? What does that even mean?

Mentioned also in Exodus 23:19 and 34:26, this strange instruction's context is most fully described in Deuteronomy 14:21 where God commands the Israelites, "Do not eat anything you find already dead. You may give it to the foreigner residing in any of your towns, and they may eat it, or you may sell it to any other foreigner. But you are a people holy to the LORD your God. Do not cook a young goat in its mother's milk."

---

1. "Mageirocophobia (Fear of Cooking)," Cleveland Clinic, accessed February 14, 2025, https://my.clevelandclinic.org/health/diseases/22370-mageirocophobia.

Scholars have long endeavored to explain this peculiar prohibition about a young goat. It's clear from the repeated commands in Exodus that this law pertained to festival rituals. Immediately preceding Exodus 23:19 are these two commands: "Do not offer the blood of a sacrifice to me along with anything containing yeast," and "The fat of my festival offerings must not be kept until morning" (v. 18). In Genesis 9:4, God gave Noah and his family the initial prohibitions on eating meat containing blood: "You must not eat meat that has its lifeblood still in it."

Why is consuming the blood of animals an issue for God? The shedding of blood was intended for sacrifice and the forgiveness of sins. Such is the case in Leviticus 17:10–12 (NIrV), where God says:

> "Suppose someone eats meat that still has blood in it. It does not matter whether they are an Israelite or an outsider. I will turn against them if they eat it. I will separate them from their people. The life of each creature is in its blood. So I have given you the blood of animals to pay for your sin on the altar. Blood is life. That is why blood pays for your sin. So I say to the Israelites, 'You must not eat meat that still has blood in it. And an outsider who lives among you must not eat it either.'"

My coauthor, Eric Bargerhuff, observes elsewhere, "The animals that were sacrificed were not sufficient to atone for *human* sin; only a sinless human could do that, and therefore those sacrifices were short term, a type of a better sacrifice to come."[2] Thus the sufficiency of animal sacrifice for the permanent atonement of sins was merely temporal.

Moving to Deuteronomy 14:21, the prohibition seems to include the mixing of milk with meat. Rabbi Zev Farber explains that "Jewish

---

2. Eric J. Bargerhuff, *The Most Misused Stories in the Bible: Surprising Ways Popular Bible Stories Are Misunderstood* (Bethany House, 2017), 127, italics in original.

law forbids: 1. Cooking meat and milk together; 2. Eating meat that was cooked with milk; 3. Receiving any benefit from such a mixture." Farber believes the prohibition meant nothing beyond a literal interpretation of "do not cook a kid in its mother's milk."[3]

Eugene Merrill sees the prohibition as linked to ancient cultic ritual, which God detested:

> Exactly what this means has been much debated, but it clearly has to do with a religious or cultic ritual so abhorrent to the Lord that it is mentioned twice previously as a summary statement of that which is illicit to Israel as a special people. . . . It is reasonable to conclude that the boiling of a young goat in its mother's milk was part of a Canaanite festival ritual that so epitomized that depraved cultus that it came to symbolize all that was evil and detestable in it. Both uses of the prohibition against it in Exodus are in festival contexts and, indeed, this is the case here in Deuteronomy as well, though here the festival instructions follow rather than precede it (Deut 14:22–29). Its position in Deuteronomy is to allow it to serve as a framing device matching the prohibition of 14:1.[4]

Others explain that "the prohibition may involve a nursing animal (which may have mother's milk in its stomach), or the possibility that the milk might contain blood and would thus contaminate the meat."[5]

When it comes to food rituals, the Jewish people remain tethered to many Old Testament laws to varying degrees. As an example, Genesis 32:32 reads, "Therefore to this day the Israelites do not eat the tendon attached to the socket of the hip, because the socket of

---

3. Dr. Rabbi Zev Farber, "Prohibition of Meat and Milk: Its Origins in the Text," TheTorah .com, accessed February 14, 2025, www.thetorah.com/article/prohibition-of-meat-and-milk -its-origins-in-the-text.

4. Eugene H. Merrill, *Deuteronomy*, New American Commentary (B&H, 1994), 238–39.

5. John H. Walton and Craig S. Keener, eds., *NIV Cultural Backgrounds Study Bible* (Zondervan, 2016), note on Deuteronomy 14:21, p. 320.

Jacob's hip was touched near the tendon." According to kosher laws, "the prohibition applies to any combination of goat, sheep, or cow's meat cooked with goat, sheep, or cow's milk. However, the Torah does not forbid the meat of non-kosher animals (e.g., pork), wild animals (e.g., venison), or fowl with milk."[6]

Since context is king, we must look carefully at the previous sentence in Deuteronomy 14:21: "You are a people holy to the LORD your God." In fact, Deuteronomy 14 in its larger context emphasizes the holiness of God's people. The big picture with regard to all ceremonial food laws handed down by the Lord has to do with his great concern for holiness among his people. Ken Gore explains, "The prohibition, therefore, reminds [the Israelites] to avoid anything that would prevent them from following the Lord completely."[7]

What does this verse mean for believers today? Whether the ritual is referring to cultic practices, food laws, or something different altogether, its essential teaching is that we are to do as God says and stay away from behaviors seen as unholy by a holy God. The "do not cook a young goat in its mother's milk" prohibition may be linked to Paul's instructions to the Corinthians about eating food sacrificed to idols (1 Corinthians 8). Paul minimizes the significance of consuming specific foods: "Some people are still so accustomed to idols that when they eat sacrificial food they think of it as having been sacrificed to a god, and since their conscience is weak, it is defiled. But food does not bring us near to God; we are no worse if we do not eat, and no better if we do" (vv. 7–8). Paul reminds the Corinthian believers that with the knowledge they have, they are to demonstrate wisdom and care

6. "The Torah (Shemos 23:19) Writes," OU Kosher, accessed February 14, 2025, https:// oukosher.org/halacha-yomis/the-torah-shemos-2319-writes-that-you-shall-not-cook-a-- young-goat-in-the-milk-of-its-mother-in-his-commentary-on-the-torah-rashi-points-out -that-this-prohibition-appears-in-the/.

7. Ken Gore, "Please Explain the Commandment: 'Do Not Cook a Young Goat in Its Mother's Milk' (Ex. 23:19)," *Arkansas Baptist News*, November 21, 2019, https://arkansasbaptist.org /post/please-explain-the-commandment-do-not-cook-a-young-goat-in-its-mother-s-milk -ex-23-19/.

for new believers or nonbelievers and refrain from eating things that may cause others to fall.

While we may approach life with a legalistic emphasis, I believe there is a greater tendency to be nonchalant about sin and be licentious in what we choose to eat and drink. Many practicing Christians and even ordained ministers of the gospel partake freely of (and in some cases regularly get drunk on) alcohol, even posting photos of beer bottles and hard liquor on social media. Could it be that we have taken Christian freedom too casually and forgotten that we are to be witnesses to a nonbelieving world that Jesus is the Lord of all?

Holiness stems from our obedience to God in every part of life. If God commands us not to cook an animal in its mother's milk, we should obey him. If God prohibits consumption of meat sacrificed to idols, then we follow his instructions. What gets in the way of holiness? In *The Pursuit of Holiness,* Jerry Bridges writes this about why some Christians look and act more culturally than counterculturally: "*We do not take some sin seriously.* We have mentally categorized sins into that which is unacceptable and that which may be tolerated a bit."[8] Perhaps we have taken unjustified liberties when it comes to what we eat and drink. Maybe we've overindulged in food and drink and struggle with gluttony. Perhaps we sin by judging others for what they munch on or imbibe.

Teaching on this text calls for bold instruction on God's commands for holy living. Every congregation will have those who raise their hands and their fists in response to sermons or lessons on holiness. "Don't tell me how to live my life" is the common chorus of teetering Christians or unconvinced unbelievers. Deuteronomy 14:21 is not so much about recipes as it is about God's desire that his people be holy. I confess that I struggle daily with holiness. I'm not always eager to live a holy life. I both combat sin and cave into sin. Yet just

---

8. Jerry Bridges, *The Pursuit of Holiness* (NavPress, 2006), 5, italics in original.

because I fall daily doesn't mean I should stop striving for holiness in all aspects of life.

We invite God's people into a paradigm-shifting philosophy of life—a life of pursuing holiness. If God expects his children to be like him—to be holy—then "whether you eat or drink or whatever you do, do it all for the glory of God" (1 Corinthians 10:31). We are not off the hook when we preach and teach Old Testament passages, especially those in the Pentateuch. While some may claim we cherry-pick what we want to say, we can make the case that here in Deuteronomy 14:21 (and in the related Exodus passages), the consumption of food is a holy act unto God, and therefore we shouldn't take our food practices lightly. The Milwaukee-based Jerusalem Christian Center, a ministry committed to educating others about our Jewish-biblical roots, writes, "By enforcing a certain diet as acceptable for His people, God effectively separated them from the surrounding nations who had no issue with eating whatever food they could find. Although other nations who did not know God behaved in this manner, God's children were held to a higher standard."[9]

It's no wonder, then, that Jesus seeks a higher calling for those who claim to be his followers in the twenty-first century. Those who profess faith in Christ cannot look like everyone in the world. We are to be different and thus become difference makers in this life. As Jesus taught, "Be perfect, therefore, as your heavenly Father is perfect" (Matthew 5:48), even in the mundane matter of what we put on our dinner plates. In doing so, we seek to glorify God our Father.

---

9. "Holiness: Worship in Our Diet," Judeo-Christian Clarion, accessed February 14, 2025, https://judeochristianclarion.com/brochures/worship-in-our-diet/.

Principles for Reflection

1. In every part of our lives, represented most basically by what we consume and what we wear, God calls his people to be holy and set apart for him.

2. The application of this passage is in what God has and has not commanded us to do. We are commanded to obey whatever the Lord tells us to do—an obedience that leads to holiness.

3. We should not fixate on legalism, but at the same time, we can acknowledge that reverence for God's Word is often absent in Christian circles today. Too often, we rely heavily on God's grace to the exclusion of following his directives. Are we participating in sinful activities that God would disapprove of? If so, the preacher/teacher can give guidance by naming some of the cultural idols that captivate the affections of our hearts and our communities and turn us away from our commitment to holiness.

CHAPTER 8

WHERE IS GOD IN THE BOOK OF ESTHER?

Esther 1–10

MATTHEW D. KIM

Because the pages of the Bible contain the story of God, it's hard to fathom that any book of the Bible would fail to include mention of at least one member of the Godhead. As many teachers and preachers know, the book of Esther is such a book. If God seems nowhere to be found in this book and we don't know with certainty who the human author is, what, then, is the point of Esther? Debra Reid suggests, "On the one hand it appears to be a simple historical account. On the other it is a carefully crafted piece of literary genius."[1] Moreover, Reid speculates whether this book is about one Jewish heroine, Esther, or about a people (Jews and Persians).

Many pastors have preached sermons on Esther and taught the story to their congregations. If it's true, which it is, that all of

---

1. Debra Reid, *Esther: An Introduction and Commentary*, Tyndale Old Testament Commentaries (InterVarsity, 2008), 19.

Scripture teaches us about Jesus (Luke 24:27), how does this truth hit home theologically and practically when preaching or teaching from a book like Esther in which God's name is not specifically mentioned? Like Fuller Seminary professor Chloe Sun, we may raise certain theological questions such as, "What is the nature of God as revealed in texts that don't use his name? How do we think of God when he is perceived to be absent? What should we do when God is silent or hidden?"[2] What can Esther teach us about the triune God?

We're dealing with the biblical genre of historical narrative. The book of Esther recounts the story of God's deliverance of the Jews from their adversaries. We might consider it a bolstering chronicle to remind and embolden future Jewish readers to cling to the faithfulness of their God, who sustained and rescued his people in a foreign land during the reign of King Xerxes.

The book of Esther presents an evangelistic bent toward introducing Gentiles to Jewish traditions. Jewish festivals typically need some explanation in a preaching/teaching series, such as Purim, the one mentioned in Esther 9:20–32. David Horrell helpfully explains, "That the book of Esther both presumes and positively accepts the possibility of such conversions seems clear, however, not least from the declaration that the feast of Purim will be celebrated by the people, their offspring, and 'those who have joined themselves to them' . . . (Esth 9:27)."[3] What we find interesting here is that Esther, a Jew, ministers in a foreign land. She is introducing non-Jews to Jewish feasts.

The book of Esther is a classic underdog story of God using "the least of these" to be primary players in his kingdom work. While Haman was plotting to exterminate the Jews, God placed Esther and Mordecai in opportune situations to be used for Jewish deliverance.

---

2. Chloe T. Sun, *Conspicuous in His Absence: Studies in the Song of Songs and Esther* (InterVarsity, 2021), 2.

3. David G. Horrell, *Ethnicity and Inclusion: Religion, Race, and Whiteness in Constructions of Jewish and Christian Identities* (Eerdmans, 2020), 264.

Esther and Mordecai unyieldingly worshiped God alone and did not bow down to mere mortals——even powerful ones like Haman (Esther 3). The refusal to pay homage to Haman caused a vitriolic outrage against all Jews in the entire kingdom of Xerxes (v. 6). As a result, we see Esther and Mordecai receiving God's favor in a strange land among strange people. The marginalized become royalty when God acts on their behalf.

Whenever we preach or teach on Old Testament narratives, we face the danger of majoring in the minors. Tangential, noncritical interpretations get us only so far. For example, a preacher/teacher may focus on female beauty as a theme, since the author refers to both the beauty of Queen Vashti and the physical attractiveness of Esther, who wins the heart (or lust) of the king. Interestingly, both books of the Bible named after women, Esther and Ruth, record the fact that their female characters are physically desirable.

King Xerxes was clearly superficial in his selection of a bride. Physical appearance seemed to be the most important quality for this ruler: "'Let a search be made for beautiful young virgins for the king. Let the king appoint commissioners in every province of his realm to bring all these beautiful young women into the harem at the citadel of Susa. . . . Then let the young woman who pleases the king be queen instead of Vashti.' This advice appealed to the king, and he followed it" (Esther 2:2–4). If this passage is preached in a hypersensitive manner on outward appearances, it may end up being the most self-critical and insecurity-inducing sermon series for every woman in the audience.

A second narrative temptation or rabbit trail is to spiritualize or allegorize Haman and the evil in humankind. In his introductory preaching course, the late Haddon Robinson warned of the temptation preachers and teachers face to do just this. Our finite human minds often assign good and evil roles to the people mentioned in historical narratives. We would be in danger of misinterpreting or inappropriate allegorizing to connect characters in Esther with evil or good here.

A third faulty point of focus may be alluding to other passages of

Scripture. Esther 1:22 reads, "He [King Xerxes] sent dispatches to all parts of the kingdom, to each province in its own script and to each people in their own language, proclaiming that every man should be ruler over his own household, using his native tongue." I hear allusions here to Pentecost in Acts 2 and John's vision in Revelation 7.

Fourth, we may be tempted to overemphasize beauty in Esther because of our appearance-enslaved culture. Society's flood of cosmetic surgeries stems from an obsessive desire to be wrinkle- and blemish-free. Our human situation is such that we can't stave off the inevitable bodily decline that comes with aging. We hear echoes of a "Miss Universe" beauty pageant or a reality show like *The Bachelor* throughout the book of Esther. Is physical beauty important to God? Must a person be physically stunning to do God's work? Does God use attractive people more significantly than nonattractive people? We find ourselves wondering the same thing Heather Creekmore wonders: "I wonder why God would put a story in the Bible where a woman had to make herself as beautiful as possible to accomplish his purpose. Doesn't that seem counter-intuitive to everything we've been taught about what God values?"[4]

Fifth, we may resort to eisegeses and take verses out of context. The best-known verse in Esther (and one of the better-known in the whole Bible) is Esther 4:14: "Who knows but that you have come to your royal position for such a time as this?" Another well-known verse is "If I perish, I perish" (v. 16). Both verses speak to the *kairos*, or decisive, moment Esther finds herself in. Be careful of generalizing Esther's unique experience and applying it to everyone: "We are all made for such a time as this" or "If we perish, we perish." These statements are specific to Esther and her circumstances and not necessarily universal principles for all Christians everywhere.

What, then, can we legitimately teach and preach from the book

---

4. Heather Creekmore, "Esther: Beauty for a Purpose," Compared to Who?, January 9, 2017, https://comparedtowho.me/esther-beauty-for-a-purpose/.

of Esther? Surely this: God superintends his people. The superintending providence of God in human history is an overarching theme we can boldly present to people today. We see similar perceptions of God's mercy and sovereignty in Paul's letter to the Romans:

> So then he has mercy on whomever he wills, and he hardens whomever he wills.
> You will say to me then, "Why does he still find fault? For who can resist his will?" But who are you, O man, to answer back to God? Will what is molded say to its molder, "Why have you made me like this?" Has the potter no right over the clay, to make out of the same lump one vessel for honorable use and another for dishonorable use? What if God, desiring to show his wrath and to make known his power, has endured with much patience vessels of wrath prepared for destruction, in order to make known the riches of his glory for vessels of mercy, which he has prepared beforehand for glory—even us whom he has called, not from the Jews only but also from the Gentiles? (Romans 9:18–24 ESV)

While we sometimes question God's actions out of jealousy or curiosity, God makes it clear that he uses whom he chooses. In this narrative, his choices are Esther and Mordecai. Why? We don't know for sure. But we can teach a willing spirit to be used by God in ways that honor him and fulfill his purposes.

We also learn this from the book of Esther: God's plans cannot be thwarted. While the book of Esther could just as well have been named the book of Mordecai, it's significant that God used a woman to carry out his plans. At the end of the book, we see that Mordecai receives the honor that was due him: "All his acts of power and might, together with a full account of the greatness of Mordecai, whom the king had promoted, are they not written in the book of the annals of the kings of Media and Persia?" (10:2).

God calls us to be a voice for the voiceless. Esther spoke on behalf of the Jews, and Mordecai is celebrated for the same: "Mordecai the Jew was second in rank to King Xerxes, preeminent among the Jews, and held in high esteem by his many fellow Jews, because he worked for the good of his people and spoke up for the welfare of all the Jews" (Esther 10:3).

God is a God of reversals. Karen Jobes and Janet Nygren present a chiastic structure of reversals in the book of Esther.[5] We may think we are in control, but the truth is, God does a remarkable work of reversing human plans. Consider these reversals in Esther:

3:10	The king gives Haman his ring.	8:2	The king gives Mordecai the same ring.
3:12	Haman summons the king's secretaries.	8:9	Mordecai summons the king's secretaries.
3:12	Letters are written, sealed with a ring.	8:10	Letters are written, sealed with the same ring.
3:13	The Jews, even women and children, are to be killed on one day.	8:11–12	In self-defense, the Jews can kill their enemies in one day.
3:14	Haman's decree is publicly displayed as law.	8:13	Mordecai's decree is publicly displayed as law.
3:15	Couriers go out in haste.	8:14	Couriers go out in haste.
3:15	The city of Susa is bewildered.	8:15	The city of Susa rejoices.
4:1	Mordecai wears sackcloth and ashes.	8:15	Mordecai wears royal robes.
4:1	Mordecai goes through the city wailing loudly.	6:11	Mordecai is led through the city in honor.
5:14	Zeresh advises Mordecai's death.	6:13	Zeresh predicts Haman's ruin.

The next time you preach or teach on the book of Esther, I hope you'll find these principles helpful in your preparation—principles we

---

5. "Chiastic Structure of Reversals in Esther," in *NIV Study Bible*, ed. Kenneth L. Barker (Zondervan, 2011), 814. Adapted from Karen H. Jobes and Janet Nygren, *Esther: God Fulfills a Promise* (Zondervan, 2008), 74.

can preach to people in all generations: God is sovereign, and he uses unlikely people to carry out his mission.

Principles for Reflection

1. God delivers on his promise to fulfill his plans, often using unlikely choices to serve him in his work. God used Esther to protect and deliver his chosen people in a time of crisis.

2. While the story is more descriptive than prescriptive, we can take comfort in the fact that God can and will use us if we are willing to submit to him. Our journey may not look exactly like Esther's, but we can leave ourselves open to the possibility that God will call on us and others in our generation "for such a time as this."

3. The emphasis in Esther is not on physical beauty but rather on beauty of mind, heart, and character. God uses those who are moldable and teachable. May we as children of God reflect his image through godliness and moral living.

CHAPTER 9

DO WE HAVE PERSONAL GUARDIAN ANGELS?

Psalm 91:9–12; Acts 12:13–16

ERIC J. BARGERHUFF

D o we have personal guardian angels? This subject has fascinated believers over the centuries. The Bible gives a clear definition of angels, asking a rhetorical question: "Are they not all ministering spirits sent out to serve those who are going to inherit salvation?" (Hebrews 1:14 CSB). The clear implication is that these created heavenly beings play some sort of invisible role in ministering to the people of God who live by faith ("those who are going to inherit salvation").[1]

Though we are not told exactly *how* angels minister to us, the Bible

---

1. John Piper writes, "What Hebrews 1:14 says is that *all* the angels—*all* of them—are specifically sent 'for ministry' (Greek *eis diakonian*)—not ministry 'to' Christians, but ministry 'for the sake of' Christians (Greek *dia tous mellontas kleronomein soterian*)." ("The Surprising Role of Guardian Angels," Desiring God, April 4, 2017, www.desiringgod.org/articles/the -surprising-role-of-guardian-angels, italics in original). Piper's emphasis on "for the sake of" instead of "to" makes his point that angels minister to us in a general sense but not necessarily in a specific individual sense, like the idea of a personal guardian angel.

gives examples of angels who do a variety of activities. Theologian Millard Erickson summarizes some of their primary activities:[2]

1. Angels glorify and worship God (Isaiah 6).
2. Angels reveal and communicate God's message to humans (Luke 1:13–21, 26–38).
3. Angels minister to believers and protect them in accordance with God's will (Psalm 91:11–12; Daniel 12:1; Hebrews 1:14).
4. Angels ministered in relation to Christ's life and ministry on earth (Matthew 4:11).
5. Angels execute judgment on the enemies of God (Revelation 12:7–9).
6. Relatedly, an angel binds Satan during the millennium (Revelation 20:1–3).
7. Angels play a role in the reward of the righteous and the punishment of the wicked before the final judgment (Luke 16:22 [they carry Lazarus to Abraham's bosom]; Acts 12:23 [an angel strikes Herod dead for not giving glory to God]).
8. Angels announce and will be involved in the second coming of Jesus (Matthew 24:30–31; 2 Thessalonians 1:7).
9. Angels will gather the elect from the four corners of the earth at the second coming (Matthew 24:30–31).
10. Angels are said to be able to drive spirit horses and chariots of fire (2 Kings 2:9–12).
11. Angels are said to guard gates (Genesis 3:24; Revelation 21:12).
12. Angels bear witness to and long to know more about God's plan of salvation (1 Corinthians 4:9; Ephesians 3:10; 1 Peter 1:12).

---

2. Millard J. Erickson, *Christian Theology*, 3rd ed. (Baker Academic, 2013), 413–14. The list isn't meant to be exhaustive; it captures some of the more significant roles that Erickson highlights.

13. Angels are said to have administered and played a role in the giving of the law to Moses (Galatians 3:19).

Though they are active in ways we do not see and have a role in ministering to us today, the specific ways and methods of their daily activities with respect to Christians is still a mystery. Psalm 91:11–12, briefly referenced earlier in this chapter, assures us that they are busy: "He will give his angels orders concerning you, to protect you in all your ways. They will support you with their hands so that you will not strike your foot against a stone" (CSB).

The psalm gives the impression of a general sense of protection of God's people, but it does not go so far as to assign a personal guardian angel to each individual believer. Nor does it tell us what specifically we are being protected from, given the fact that we live in a fallen world where bad things happen to good people, even under God's sovereign plan. All it says is that there is general protection "in all your ways." I imagine we are protected every day from things we know nothing about.

But we do know, spiritually speaking, that Satan seeks to tempt us to destroy our testimony, relationships, and ministry. He accuses us and seeks to undermine God's will in multiple ways, even persecuting and targeting Christians with false teaching in attempts to deceive us. Despite all that, he cannot touch our souls or our salvation, for John tells us that God protects his children and keeps them safe, such that "the evil one does not touch him" (1 John 5:18 CSB).

Could it be that the means God uses to protect us from Satan are the angels referred to in Psalm 91? It is not only possible but highly likely. After all, it was the angel armies that protected the prophet Elisha and his servant from the Syrian (Aramean) armies in 2 Kings 6:8–23.

At times, however, God may sovereignly allow us to be tested. Take the story of Job, for example, in which Satan was permitted to afflict a righteous man under the guise of God's permissive will. Yet even in that scenario, God put limitations on what Satan could do to Job, and Job's salvation was not at stake, since no one can snatch us out of God's hand (John 10:28–29).

One of the more pressing questions is how to deal with the Acts 12 passage, where angels appear twice—once in freeing Peter from prison and later when the early church thought they encountered an appearance of "his angel" (Acts 12:15).

Herod Agrippa's persecution of the church had resulted in the death of the apostle James (John's brother). This pleased the Jews, whom Herod wanted to appease, so he also had Peter arrested and imprisoned. Fearing Peter's fate would be the same as James's, the early church prayed fervently for Peter (Acts 12:5). On the night before Peter was to face trumped-up charges and likely executed, an angel miraculously freed Peter from prison. Peter ran to the house of Mary (the gospel writer Mark's mother), where the believers were praying for Peter.

When Peter knocked at the door of the gate, a servant girl named Rhoda heard Peter's voice. But rather than let him in right away, she joyfully ran back to the praying believers, crying out that Peter was outside. They didn't believe her, but said, "You're out of your mind!" (What does this say about the level of faith we sometimes pray with? How relatable!) Rhoda insisted she was telling the truth, but the believers kept saying, "It's his angel" (Acts 12:15 CSB). Peter continued to knock, and when the church members finally opened the door, they were astonished. Their prayers had been answered, even in the middle of their doubting.

The Greek word *angelos* can be translated "messenger," as though Peter had a personal messenger sent to the home to deliver some news about him. But it's more likely that *angelos* here should be translated "angel." Since Peter was in prison, he wouldn't have had access to a messenger in such a hostile situation.[3] Furthermore, many Jews at the

---

3. It is also unlikely that this angel was the one who aided in Peter's release, since the text

time held a superstitious belief that each person had a personal guardian angel that would take on the form of the person they were sent to guard. Yet there is no biblical basis for this belief.

It is safe to say that this text does not provide definitive biblical evidence for guardian angels, especially since the person at the door was not an angel but Peter himself. The preacher/teacher of this text would do well to make it clear that whatever a particular culture believes doesn't necessarily mean something can be established as biblical fact or truth. We cannot rely on weak inferences, suspicions, conjecture, or superstition. Unless we have definitive evidence based on sound exegesis that establishes a biblical truth, the teacher or preacher must avoid speculating about things that do not meet that standard. To do so would be careless and misleading, which is how false teaching can emerge.

We must address one final text pertaining to a speculative belief in guardian angels. In Matthew 18:10, Jesus addresses the issue of childlike believers, or even children themselves: "See that you do not despise one of these little ones. For I tell you that in heaven their angels always see the face of my Father who is in heaven" (ESV).[4]

This passage has led some to believe that Jesus is teaching that each person has their own guardian angel. But closer examination does not support this belief. If these angels (note the plural) "always see" the face of the Father in heaven, it's hard to imagine that angels are at the same time personally ministering to select individuals on earth, since angels as created beings can only be in one place at one time.[5]

---

says the angel left, and the church wouldn't have known about any supernatural release from prison via an angel anyway.

4. I can vouch from experience that there are mature or theologically informed Christians who can easily despise other Christians (even children) who have a childlike or less theologically developed faith. Such pride is directly rebuked here by Jesus.

5. Similarly, biblical scholar D. A. Carson critiques the personal guardian angel viewpoint: "If ministering angels are sent to help believers, what are the angels in Matthew 18:10 doing around the divine throne, instead of guarding those people to whom they are assigned?" (*Expositor's Bible Commentary*, rev. ed. [Zondervan, 2017], 401).

What, then, are these angels doing? Are they worshiping God? If they are in the Lord's presence, surely they would be. Are they sitting in God's presence, waiting for a command to go down and serve believers? That's most likely. Wayne Grudem suggests, "Our Lord may simply be saying that angels who are assigned the task of protecting little children have ready access to God's presence."[6]

The thought is this: If angels are eagerly waiting in God's presence to receive a command to go down and minister to other believers or children, we must not despise "these little ones." They are inherently valuable to God, which is a fitting thought that precedes the parable of the lost sheep—the context for this verse.

The passage cannot be stretched to mean that every individual has a personal guardian angel. Everything in the passage speaks of angels in a plural, collective sense, while speaking of a general ministry to the "littles ones" in a plural sense as well.

In addition, Stephen Noll points out a potential theological conflict in the idea that each person has their own personal angelic intercessor who sits before God's throne: "Does this idea of a personal angelic intercessor conflict with the basic teaching that 'we have such a high priest, one who is seated at the right hand of the Majesty in heaven, a minister in the sanctuary and the true tent which is set up not by man but by the Lord'" (Hebrews 8:1–2)?[7]

Their role, then, must not be seen as interceding in prayer before the throne, but rather as worshiping and waiting on commands to be sent out to do ministry to "those who are going to inherit salvation" (Hebrews 1:14 CSB).

When we teach on the role of angels, we need to be clear about what we can and cannot prove, avoiding speculative and unwarranted conclusions based on mystical or experiential beliefs unsubstantiated

6. Wayne Grudem, *Systematic Theology: An Introduction to Biblical Doctrine*, 2nd ed. (Zondervan Academic, 2020), 519.
7. Stephen F. Noll, *Angels of Light, Powers of Darkness: Thinking Biblically About Angels, Demons, and Principalities* (InterVarsity, 1998), 171.

in the Bible. There is much we don't know about these unseen created beings, and we would do well to avoid an unhealthy fascination with them. They themselves would not want to steal any affection of our hearts from Christ.

Angels play a role in protecting (Psalm 91:11–12), keeping watch over (Daniel 12:1), and ministering to believers (Hebrews 1:14) in a general sense, as well as doing God's will as he carries out his plans for the world. But as most theologians rightly assert, we have no overwhelming biblical evidence to support the idea of personal guardian angels. We must be quick to identify what can be biblically verified. And we should go no further.

Principles for Reflection

1. The cultural beliefs or superstitions that provide context in some sections of the Bible are not derived from biblical truth. They are descriptive in nature and are not prescriptive for our lives today.

2. It is true that angels minister to us in a general sense, but there is no overwhelming evidence that each individual Christian has a personal guardian angel.

3. People you teach may have a testimony about an alleged encounter with an angel. Don't argue with them, even though there is no objective way to verify their story. Hebrews 13:2 reminds us that an angelic encounter is possible, but in the end, only God knows the truth about any encounter. Our speculation is not equal to absolute truth.

CHAPTER 10

DOES THE WOMAN CAUGHT IN ADULTERY BELONG IN THE BIBLE?

John 7:53–8:11

ERIC J. BARGERHUFF

W hat do we do with certain sections of the Bible that include
disclaimers, such as in the Gospels? My focus in this chapter
will be on John 7:53–8:11, but I'll begin with a brief discussion of
another large section that has an asterisk on it. Mark 16:9–20 contains a longer ending not found in the original gospel—a view widely
held by most New Testament scholars. The earliest and most reliable
manuscripts we have of Mark do not contain that section.

The style and structure of this section are different from the rest
of Mark. Early church theologians and historians do not acknowledge
it as authentic. Some of its themes seem to contradict other themes
highlighted in Mark's gospel, and some of its theology contradicts the
collective teaching of Scripture, where handling snakes and drinking
poison are not the kind of fruits that authenticate genuine believers

in Christ. I've concluded elsewhere that we should only read it to corroborate what is affirmed in other parts of Scripture, but "we should not derive any teachings of the Christian faith on the basis of verses 9 to 20 alone."[1]

Mark 16:9–20 was likely included by manuscript copiers who felt the gospel ended too abruptly, so they added it as a supplement (though not written by Mark or any other apostle). By the 1500s when Erasmus, a Dutch philosopher and professor of Greek, produced a full Greek New Testament text, this longer ending had been added, along with other manuscripts he had at his disposal. The Textus Receptus, as his assembly of manuscripts was called, became the basis for the King James Version translated into English—with a firmly established impact on Western Christianity.

Most English translations include a disclaimer in a text note that goes something like this: "The earliest manuscripts and some other ancient witnesses do not have verses 9–20."

We move now to the main focus of this chapter—John 7:53–8:11, the account of the woman caught in adultery. Here we find another disputed addition to the Bible that is widely held to be inauthentic. Norman Geisler and Thomas Howe provide a helpful summary of why this is the case:

> (1) The passage does not appear in the oldest and most reliable Greek manuscripts. (2) It is not found in the best manuscripts of the earliest translations of the Bible into Old Syriac, Coptic, Gothic, and Old Latin. (3) No Greek writer commented on this passage for the first 11 centuries of Christianity. (4) It is not cited by most of the

---

1. Eric J. Bargerhuff, *Why is THAT in the Bible? The Most Perplexing Verses and Stories—and What They Teach Us* (Bethany House, 2020), 158.

great early church fathers, including Clement, Tertullian, Origen, Cyprian, Cyril, and others. (5) Its style does not fit that of the rest of the Gospel of John. (6) It interrupts the flow of thought in John. John reads better if one goes right from John 7:52 to 8:12. (7) The story has been found in several other places in Bible manuscripts— after John 7:36; after John 21:24; after John 7:44; and after Luke 21:38. (8) Many manuscripts that include John 7:53–8:11 have marked it with an obelus, indicating they believe it is doubtful.[2]

The fact that this section has been found in other places in manuscripts has led New Testament scholar D. A. Carson to conclude that "the diversity of placement confirms the inauthenticity of the verses."[3] It doesn't even read like John's writing. Could it have been written by Luke or some other gospel writer? While we can't be 100 percent sure, we are nearly certain that John did not write it. Why, then, do we have it in our Bible? Like the Mark passage, it found its way into the seventeenth-century Textus Receptus.

Many manuscripts from medieval times include John 7:53–8:12, but these manuscripts date to nearly one thousand years after the gospel was originally written in the middle AD 90s. The earliest textual traditions convincingly undermine its inclusion because it is not there. Furthermore, it is highly unlikely that the church that recognized the closed canon of Scripture at the Synod of Carthage in AD 397 would have had this text in its list of authenticated Scriptures, since its first sighting as Scripture is found in a Greek-Latin text known as uncial D (fifth century AD), a questionable and unreliable manuscript that omits many passages and adds many passages to what is found in the

2. Norman L. Geisler and Thomas Howe, *The Big Book of Bible Difficulties: Clear and Concise Answers from Genesis to Revelation* (Baker, 1992), 414–15.
3. D. A. Carson, *The Gospel According to John*, Pillar New Testament Commentary Series (Eerdmans, 1991), 333.

earliest and most reliable Greek manuscripts that serve as the foundation for our modern-day translations of the Bible.[4]

Interestingly, this section is not covered in some commentaries today.[5] This is quite telling, and in his commentary on John, New Testament scholar Andreas Köstenberger emphatically declares that "the account was almost certainly not part of the original Gospel and therefore should not be regarded as part of the Christian canon. Nor does inspiration extend to it."[6] He regards it like apocryphal material, permitted to be read perhaps for edification but not recommended to be preached in churches. He argues in a footnote that studying this passage today, even for the sake of its effect on a reader, would not be wise:

> This judgment [that the passage should be incorporated into one's study of Scripture], however, is of doubtful merit in that it fails to consider the original and earliest readers of the Gospel (who would not have read the Gospel with this periscope), and in that it unduly neglects issues such as canonicity, inspiration, and biblical authority.[7]

---

4. *Britannica* provides an overview of this uncial: "D, Codex Bezae Cantabrigiensis, is a 5th-century Greco-Roman bilingual text (with Greek and Latin pages facing each other). D contains most of the four Gospels and Acts and a small part of III John and is thus designated D^{ea} (e, for *evangelia*, or 'gospels'; and a for *acta*, or Acts). In Luke, and especially in Acts, D^{ea} has a text that is very different from other witnesses. Codex Bezae has many distinctive longer and shorter readings and seems almost to be a separate edition. Its Acts, for example, is one-tenth longer than usual. D represents the Western text tradition. D^{ea} was acquired by Theodore Beza, a Reformed theologian and classical scholar, in 1562 from a monastery in Lyon (in France). He presented it to the University of Cambridge, England, in 1581 (hence, Beza Cantabrigiensis)." ("New Testament Canon, Texts, and Versions: Uncials," *Britannica*, accessed February 14, 2025, www.britannica.com/topic/biblical-literature/Uncials).

5. See for example, Kent Hughes, *John: That You May Believe*, Preaching Through the Word Commentary (Crossway, 1999). Hughes completely omits this section in his commentary.

6. Andreas J. Köstenberger, *John*, Baker Exegetical Commentary on the New Testament (Baker Academic, 2004), 248. Though not part of any biblical manuscript, the story, or a version of it, is found in the *Apostolic Constitutions* (circa AD 375–380), and therefore would argue that the story itself is rather old, even if not recognized as Scripture.

7. Köstenberger, *John*, 249, note 10.

Köstenberger argues that there is more at stake in preaching and teaching it than simply the lessons that can be learned from the 7:53–8:11 story itself.[8] Could preaching or teaching it set a bad precedent, and perhaps mislead people into thinking that it is authentically inspired Scripture? I would not go that far, especially if the preacher or teacher explains the disclaimer that is found in almost all Bible translations.

In his five-volume commentary on John, James Montgomery Boice urges us to be cautious in how we treat this passage, even though he sees it as a genuine story found elsewhere, though perhaps not from the apostle John's pen. He nevertheless goes on to suggest that the reason it may have been omitted was that it "might have been used by enemies of the gospel to suggest that Christ condoned fornication," citing Augustine and Ambrose, who suggested that very reason.[9]

He further suggests that the story is true to Jesus' nature, "in accord at every point with his perfect holiness, wisdom, and deep compassion."[10] I agree with Boice on these two points. I think the story itself is an authentic encounter in the ministry of Jesus, and if understood properly in the context of sound biblical theology, it does not condone or dismiss adultery and rightly portrays the character of Jesus. Am I willing to say with 100 percent certainty that it should be recognized as canonical and inspired Scripture that has authority over us? No, I cannot, and I'm not sure any biblical scholar could ever say that.

Skeptics may say, "Well, if you crack the door open, some other

---

8. D. A. Carson has a different opinion: "There is little reason for doubting that the event here described occurred, even if in its written form it did not in the beginning belong to the canonical books. Similar stories are found in other sources." (*John*, 333–34.) He then goes on to comment on the passage, contra Köstenberger.

9. James Montgomery Boice, *The Gospel of John: Christ and Judaism (John 5–8)*, An Expositional Commentary (Baker, 2005), 603. The fact that Augustine and Ambrose, who lived in the fourth century, knew of this story, even if it hadn't made it into the biblical manuscripts they were using, suggests its potential authenticity as a story about an adulterous woman's encounter with Jesus.

10. Boice, *John*, 603.

stuff is going to come in with it." Not if you are careful. No false teaching will enter our thinking if we teach the story correctly and use Scripture to interpret Scripture—a principle of interpretation we referred to earlier. In my book *The Most Misused Stories in the Bible*, I argue that as long as we don't use the phrase "let any one of you who is without sin be the first to throw a stone at her" (John 8:7) as a shield for sin that seeks to excuse ourselves from accountability for it, we can go on to proper applications of the passage.[11]

The Pharisees and the teachers of the law in the story intend to trap Jesus, and Scripture elsewhere affirms that was their pattern. Here they allege to have found a woman engaged in adultery, and perhaps she truly was, because Jesus seems to confirm she was sinning when he says, "Go now and leave your life of sin" (John 8:11). Interestingly, they didn't bring the man she was caught with to Jesus, which shows their hypocrisy.

The trap had everything to do with her punishment, since the law of Moses required her to be stoned (Leviticus 20:10; Deuteronomy 22:23–24). Since the Romans zealously guarded the right to apply capital punishment, the Pharisees figured that if Jesus were to suggest she be stoned, he would get in trouble with the Romans. But if Jesus dismissed her sin and didn't agree to her stoning, he would be accused of violating the law of Moses.

These religious leaders think they have him trapped. Jesus bends down and writes in the sand—what he wrote, we don't know. And then he speaks: "He who is without sin among you, let him cast the first stone at her" (my paraphrase). He did not refute the law of Moses. He did not make excuses for her sin. And he did not mess with the prerogative of the Romans to execute capital punishment. Brilliant!

The plan of her accusers is foiled, and they walk away. Jesus then turns to deal with the woman, asking if anyone has stayed to accuse

---

11. See my book *The Most Misused Stories: Surprising Ways Popular Bible Stories Are Misunderstood* (Bethany House, 2017), 56–61.

her. She responds, "No one, Lord" (John 8:11 CSB). And in keeping with John's theme that the Father has not sent Jesus into the world to condemn the world (3:17), Jesus says he does not condemn this woman. But this does not make light of or excuse her of the sin; it simply shows that she has an opportunity to receive grace in a season of grace, but if she rejects that opportunity, it will result in condemnation. Without true repentance and faith, a sinner will perish in their sin (8:24).

Therefore, though Jesus did not condemn her, he did not acquit her either, and he told her to go and sin no more. In other words, demonstrate true repentance by forsaking it from now on. The story is powerful and contradicts no known biblical or theological truths in Scripture. It characterizes the Pharisees and the teachers of the law—consistent with other parts of Scripture—as those who were determined to trap Jesus (especially through their use of the law, as well as their own hypocrisy). It does not shrug off the sin of this woman. And it portrays Jesus as the compassionate but firm preacher of repentance to Israel.

The preacher or teacher would do well to investigate other places where Jesus is confronted by the Pharisees and the teachers of the law who are out to trap Jesus in matters of the law (for example, Matthew 12:1–2) and who hypocritically condemn those they judge to be unworthy sinners (for example, Luke 7:39). The gospel account is replete with examples of Jesus' demonstrations of grace to sinners.

But the John 7:53–8:12 passage must never be used to stereotype all women (because men are equally guilty of this sin) or to rationalize sin by suggesting that Jesus does not condemn the woman for her adultery. He brings not wrath but mercy and commands her to stop sinning and turn to a new life, so ultimately her sin doesn't end in eternal wrath.

So is the Bible trustworthy? Absolutely. We believe it is inspired by God and without error in all that it affirms. Does this passage threaten that doctrine? No, because it does not contradict any sound theology and its ideas are consistent with what is taught elsewhere in the Bible about the Pharisees and the teachers of the law, the sin that humanity struggles with, the character and tone of Jesus, and the lesson that we must practice genuine repentance.

It is good to hold one another accountable for sin, bathed in a commitment to reconciliation as we hold out grace to those caught in the web of sin. This passage provides a perfect example in Jesus—the One who extends grace while calling people to repentance.

If you teach John 7:53–8:12, you can share doubts about its scriptural authenticity without dismissing the biblical truths it so beautifully affirms.

Principles for Reflection

1. When it comes to sections of the Gospels that have a text note saying they aren't found in the earliest manuscripts, you should proceed with caution. Use what the Bible affirms elsewhere to verify that which is theologically sound and to weed out anything that may be questionable.

2. You would do well to familiarize yourself with textual criticism. You will discover just how reliable and trustworthy the Bible truly is.

3. When teaching on John 7:53–8:12, make sure the audience knows that Jesus did not dismiss the woman's sin but rather called her to repentance. What he gave her was the gift of his grace, and every one of us can thank God for his grace, because we all deserve death.

CHAPTER 11

CAN WE LEARN WHAT HEAVEN LOOKS LIKE?

Revelation 21:1–8

MATTHEW D. KIM

We discussed the uncomfortable topic of hell in chapter 6, and now we move on to the other "permanent place." Do you believe there is a literal heaven and a literal hell? In other words, do you believe in an afterlife? For Christians, if we believe in a literal heaven and hell, then heaven is the place where we want to go when we die, while hell is the place we want to avoid. We often speak of heaven in earthly terms such as, "When I get to heaven, I'm going to _____." For me, I've always said, "When I get to heaven, I'm going to slam-dunk a basketball." Others might say, "When I get to heaven, I'm going to splurge on my favorite pint of mint chocolate chip ice cream every day and never gain weight."

All joking aside, when we speak of the eternal destination referred to in our text as "a new heaven and a new earth," or "the Holy City, the new Jerusalem," our limited minds simply can't comprehend it. Trying to explain apocalyptic literature is scary, foreign, and completely idealistic. Nothing in our imaginations can sufficiently describe the new Jerusalem. Perhaps that's why we hear such little teaching on it from the pulpit or in seminary classrooms. Many Christians hear so little about heaven that they only think about life on earth. Is there something more that can be said of a new heaven and a new earth and what it means for us in the here and now?

In this text, the apostle John saw a vision or revelation of the new Jerusalem as described in Revelation. The new Jerusalem (Greek, *Ierousalem kainen*) is found in only two texts: Revelation 3:12 and 21:2. New Testament scholar Robert Mounce writes, "Although a few writers take the New Jerusalem in John's vision to be an actual city, it is far better to understand it as a symbol of the church in its perfected and eternal state."[1]

The concept of heaven is confusing for all of us, since we've never been there before (though some claim they have seen glimpses).[2] Questions abound: Where is it? What does it look like? What will we do there? Will my loved ones be there? Are they there now? Will my dog or cat be there waiting for me?

The Old Testament also mentions a heavenly city. Isaiah 65:17–19 reads:

> "See, I will create
>   new heavens and a new earth.
> The former things will not be remembered,
>   nor will they come to mind.
> But be glad and rejoice forever
>   in what I will create,
> for I will create Jerusalem to be a delight

---

1. Robert H. Mounce, *The Book of Revelation*, rev. ed., New International Commentary on the New Testament (Eerdmans, 1977), 382.
2. Many contemporary authors have tried to make sense of heaven and to describe it. See Randy Alcorn, *Heaven*; John Burke, *Imagine Heaven*; Don Piper, *90 Minutes in Heaven*; Todd Burpo, *Heaven Is for Real*; Mike Fabarez, *10 Mistakes People Make About Heaven, Hell, and the Afterlife*; and Lee Strobel, *The Case for Heaven*.

and its people a joy.
I will rejoice over Jerusalem
    and take delight in my people;
the sound of weeping and of crying
    will be heard in it no more."

In the next verses (vv. 20–25), Isaiah provides additional details of what will not and what will take place in this new heavenly place:

"Never again will there be in it
    an infant who lives but a few days,
    or an old man who does not live out his years;
the one who dies at a hundred
    will be thought a mere child;
the one who fails to reach a hundred
    will be considered accursed.
They will build houses and dwell in them;
    they will plant vineyards and eat their fruit.
No longer will they build houses and others live in them,
    or plant and others eat.
For as the days of a tree,
    so will be the days of my people;
my chosen ones will long enjoy
    the work of their hands.
They will not labor in vain,
    nor will they bear children doomed to misfortune;
for they will be a people blessed by the LORD,
    they and their descendants with them.
Before they call I will answer;
    while they are still speaking I will hear.
The wolf and the lamb will feed together,
    and the lion will eat straw like the ox,
    and dust will be the serpent's food.

> They will neither harm nor destroy
> on all my holy mountain,"
> says the LORD.

The first note concerning this new heavenly place in the book of Revelation is found in 21:1: "Then I saw 'a new heaven and a new earth,' for the first heaven and the first earth had passed away, and there was no longer any sea." We can interpret this as evidence that there is a place now called heaven that will one day be replaced by "a new heaven." The earth in its present form will also be gone, and "a new earth" will be created by God. There will be no sea, as we know it.

Another announcement about this new heaven and new earth is found in the words spoken by the "loud voice" booming from the throne: "Look! God's dwelling place is now among the people, and he will dwell with them. They will be his people, and God himself will be with them and be their God" (Revelation 21:3).

In much of the Old Testament, particularly in the Pentateuch, we have abundant mentions of God's dwelling with his people, Israel. While we often ponder the aesthetics of heaven and what it looks like, more importantly we are reminded about who is there rather than what is there.

T. Desmond Alexander writes in *From Eden to the New Jerusalem*, "Good theology always has pastoral implications. Doctrine and praxis ought to be closely related."[3] Knowing that heaven awaits those who put their faith in Christ alone, we need not wait for heaven to experience heavenly realities.

In C. S. Lewis's sermon "The Weight of Glory," he writes these remarkable words:

> The Christian, in relation to heaven, is in much the same position

---

3. T. Desmond Alexander, *From Eden to the New Jerusalem: An Introduction to Biblical Theology* (Kregel Academic, 2008), 11.

as this schoolboy. Those who have attained everlasting life in the vision of God doubtless know very well that it is no mere bribe, but the very consummation of their earthly discipleship; but we who have not yet attained it cannot know this in the same way, and cannot even begin to know it at all except by continuing to obey and finding the first reward of our obedience in our increasing power to desire the ultimate reward.[4]

What Lewis suggests is that the Christian does not wait for heaven to live a sanctified life on account of one's ticket to paradise. Rather, the Christian who understands the richness of one's future reward lives for heaven while on earth—as a fulfillment of one's pledge to discipleship. At the same time, Christians live with an eye toward their heavenly home.

While we anticipate the imminent consummation of all things, when suffering and pain are no longer daily earthly realities, we face today, knowing we will one day see our precious Savior, Jesus Christ, face-to-face. This longing and remembrance will let us not get too low or too high. Our spirits can be realistic and yet brimming with optimism. What a wonderful, unimaginably glorious day that will be!

If the new Jerusalem far exceeds this life's current realities because God will dwell with us, isn't it a place we would invite others to join? As much as heaven is a place that lacks suffering, it's also a place uninhabited by nonbelievers. Thus, the onus is placed on us to share with others the good news of Jesus Christ so they can put their faith in him.

The new heaven and the new earth represent the new garden that replaces the old, fallen Garden of Eden. *The Eerdmans Companion to the Bible* explains, "Sustenance from [the Edenic tree of life and the life-giving water that flows from God's throne] reverses the curse of death, handed down to humanity through the disobedience of Eve

---

4. C. S. Lewis, *The Weight of Glory and Other Addresses* (1949; repr., HarperOne, 2001), 28.

and Adam. The entire scene blends the characterizations of Jesus as the light of the world, the true vine, and the source of living water."[5]

Central to this text in Revelation 21 is the word *new* (Greek *kainos*). It's the same term Paul uses in 2 Corinthians 5:17, where he speaks of Christians becoming a "new creation," a *kainos ktisis*. As children of God who will one day enter a new heaven and a new earth—the new Jerusalem—we can live now as new people in Christ. Sadly, too many professing Christians live like people who don't know Christ. Our central identity is found in being *kainos ktisis*. Preaching and teaching about heaven reminds us that we don't wait for heaven to live as heavenly beings. Just the opposite, in fact. God calls us to live as sons and daughters now, in keeping with the prayer Jesus taught us: "Your kingdom come, your will be done, on earth as it is in heaven" (Matthew 6:10).

I encourage you to teach and preach regularly (at least two times a year) about heaven. Remind your listeners what awaits Christ followers and how they can live for heaven in the present day. What does this look like? Instead of focusing on where heaven is, what we will do there, or even how beautiful it will be, we must help our people concentrate on the One they will be with in heaven. Encourage them to eagerly spend time with the triune God through discipleship and spiritually formative practices—praying, fasting, giving, listening and discerning, reading Scripture, meditating, actively obeying now instead of waiting for heaven's magical discipleship touch. We want to be in relationships with non-Christians and introduce them to Christ. We want to encourage fellow believers to continue in the faith and to never give up. We want to bless God and bless others while we live on this earth.

---

5. Gordon D. Fee and Robert L. Hubbard Jr., eds., *The Eerdmans Companion to the Bible* (Eerdmans, 2011), 736.

Principles for Reflection

1. Heaven is real, and it will be a jaw-dropping experience when believers in Christ get to their eternal home. God is waiting eagerly for his children to come home. Heaven's majesty and glory cannot be fully comprehended here. Yet we can do our best to encourage skeptics and nonbelievers to put their faith in Christ so that we can all enjoy the glory and majesty of our Savior together, no matter what life will look like in the new heaven and the new earth.

2. Spending regular moments reflecting on the new heaven and the new earth will motivate us to think and live Christianly while we journey through life on earth.

3. What questions do Revelation 21 and 22 raise? When you read this passage, does it stir up greater anticipation for your future heavenly home? What is the intersection and impact of the current earthly reality and the future heavenly dwelling for the believer? How does knowing we will one day enter paradise with Christ influence how we live today and how we treat planet Earth?

PART III:
TROUBLING

How to Teach Hard Truths

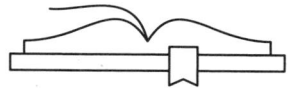

Here's the bottom line about Scripture texts that contain hard truths: God is holy, and he wants us to relentlessly pursue holiness. Every troubling text challenges us, primarily because it redirects our desires, pursuits, and lifestyles. Bible passages involving hard truths give clear principles for godly living. They demand obedience in attitudes and behaviors we don't naturally want to give up.

Teaching hard truths requires a balancing act between speaking lovingly and being direct and firm. Sin is an abomination to God. God expects his children to look like him and not like the world. When communicating hard truths, your tone matters. You can say hard things in loving ways. Each time you teach a troubling text, remember that your aim is not simply behavior modification. You are guiding people toward lives of freedom from a bondage of which they may not even be aware.

When teaching hard truths, patience is required. While the miraculous is possible with God, death to sin takes time—even a lifetime. Don't expect people to change overnight. As God is patient with us, we, too, need to be patient as we communicate hard truths, not expecting our listeners to be transformed immediately, while recognizing that we who pastor, teach, and lead also struggle to live holy lives.

CHAPTER 12

WHY WAS LOT SAVED FROM SODOM'S FATE?

Genesis 19:1–29

ERIC J. BARGERHUFF

The Old Testament character Lot is an example of a person who had a right heart toward God and yet struggled with worldliness and compromise. The nephew of Abraham, Lot is the textbook picture of one who at times showed great faith in and reverence for God and at other times lived dangerously close to the edge of destruction. James Montgomery Boice wrote, "Lot is an illustration of the worldly, half-hearted Christian. He had knowledge of God and wanted fellowship with him. But he wanted the world too, and in the end he lost almost everything he had."[1]

We may argue that a genuine believer would never do some of the things Lot did. He selfishly chose the best land for himself, his family, and his herds when Abraham gave him a choice. He lived on

---

1. James Montgomery Boice, *Genesis: A New Beginning (Genesis 12–36)*, An Expositional Commentary (Baker, 2006), 619.

the edge of and eventually inside the wicked city of Sodom, where he rose to prominence—not because of his righteous lifestyle but most likely because of his wealth and his tolerant attitude toward sin. In his eagerness to enhance his reputation as a hospitable person, he offered up his daughters for sex to the wicked homosexual men of the city in an effort to protect the two male visitors.

All these actions seem to indicate that Lot was anything but a righteous man in God's sight, but that would be a wrong assumption. Though he certainly had moments of "unambiguous moral weakness and poor judgment,"[2] as John MacArthur put it, he was still regarded by the apostle Peter as a man of faith who was mentally, emotionally, and spiritually torn and tormented over the "sensual conduct of the wicked" (2 Peter 2:7 ESV).

I often think that if certain highlights and lowlights of our lives were played back for all the world to see, we would be a little nervous about what others might point at. Peter probably would want to erase the gospel accounts where he opposed Jesus' agenda or the time he publicly denied knowing him three times. David would undoubtedly want to erase the stories of his selfishness, adultery, or murder from the public record for all time.

Yet Peter's boldness as Jesus' disciple allowed him to be the spokesperson for the group, and David's genuine faith gave him the reputation of being a man after God's own heart (1 Samuel 13:14). God used both men as authors of inspired Scripture.

The fact remains, "All have sinned and fall short of the glory of God" (Romans 3:23). None of us are perfect. Even those who are declared "righteous" in God's sight through repentance and saving faith still understand that the fallen flesh within us opens us to the potential of profound wickedness in moments of temptation and weakness. As the apostle Paul cried out in Romans 7, "What a wretched man I am! Who

---

2. John MacArthur Jr., *2 Peter & Jude*, MacArthur New Testament Commentary (Moody, 2005), 90.

will rescue me from this body that is subject to death? Thanks be to God, who delivers me through Jesus Christ our Lord!" (vv. 24–25).

Yet certain sins of true believers make us cringe, and Lot's shortcomings tend to grip us in an especially disgusting way—particularly with regard to his daughters. In Genesis 19, Lot is in yet another crossroads moment. The cities of Sodom and Gomorrah had become thoroughly corrupt and depraved, from the young to the old. Among Sodom's many sins, homosexuality became conspicuously prevalent such that the act of homosexual sex among men became known historically as the act of sodomy.

In Genesis 18, God had warned Abraham about this city's wickedness and the impending divine judgment, leading Abraham to intercede for his nephew and all other righteous people in the city. Initially asking God to spare Sodom if fifty righteous people were found, Abraham eventually negotiated the number down—if ten righteous people lived there, God would spare the city of his wrath (v. 32).

But when two temporarily incarnated angels entered the city for the purpose of destroying it, they were immediately intercepted by Lot, who was sitting at the city gate (a place of prominence in that culture).[3] It seems that when Lot met these men, he knew instantly in his heart that they were holy and pure in contrast to the men of his city. He obviously feared them, for we are told, "When Lot saw them, he got up to meet them. He bowed with his face to the ground and said, 'My lords, turn aside to your servant's house, wash your feet, and spend the night. Then you can get up early and go on your way'" (Genesis 19:1–2 CSB).

Clearly, Lot wanted to shelter these men from what he knew could be a humiliating encounter with the depraved wickedness of Sodom's men. But the two men refused at first, declaring that they

---

3. It would have been customary for leaders and prominent men to be seated at the city gate throughout the day, where the city's commerce and legal affairs would have taken place, much like what a downtown courthouse or community center would be like today, in which city officials and leaders participate in the business of the town.

would spend the night in the city square. But Lot insisted and eventually convinced the men to stay with him at his house in what would be seen as a generous act of hospitality. He set before them a feast, and they ate together before the time came for them to go to bed.

But the atmosphere soon turned ugly when men from all over the city, both young and old, surrounded Lot's house and demanded that he bring out his two visitors so that the men of the city might have their way with them, gratifying their sexually deviant passions. Lot confronted the mob, pleading with them to abandon their plan.

At this point, we might ask ourselves, *What were Lot's choices? Ethically speaking, what were his options?* There was no way he could have fought the men from all over the city. He was impossibly outnumbered. He might have continued to try to reason with them or maybe offer them money (since he was a prominent and wealthy man) to dissuade them. How about crying out to God in prayer in this moment of terror, as many other godly people have done in Scripture? Surely God had demonstrated his power to intercede. Or perhaps in a moment of fearless self-sacrifice, he could have offered himself to be abused instead of allowing his innocent and distinguished guests to be ravished by these evil men.

But to our shock and disgust, Lot chose none of these options. Instead, he offered his only two virgin daughters to the mob to satiate their sexual appetites with them instead of his visitors. The horror of his willingness to betray his children—his only daughters, those he is obligated to nurture, care for, and protect—is truly one of Lot's lowest moments of moral failure. Ken Mathews writes, "That Lot sanctions the rape of his daughters indicates a moral compass gone awry; he places hospitality above the protection of his children. It is difficult to conceive of such a custom that would put a guest's well-being over family. Such treatment by a father was despicable in the eyes of Israel. . . . For a moment it is Sodom that has taken up residence in Lot's soul."[4]

---

4. Ken Mathews, *Genesis 11:27–50:26*, New American Commentary (B&H, 2005), 236–37.

The evil men pressed him further. Lot was in trouble, since they refused his offer. He was pressed up against the door, but the angels inside opened the door and quickly pulled him back in. Lot had failed, yet this host of the two heavenly beings was bailed out as they supernaturally struck the mob with blindness. Spiritually blind and now physically blind, the predators were unable to find the door to break it down.

The angels warned Lot that he had better gather any other family members from the city and skedaddle, because wrath was coming down on that place in a hurry. Lot jumped into action. He found the two men who were engaged to his daughters, but they thought he was only joking about judgment. This was no joke. When morning came, the angels told Lot to take his wife and daughters and run. But Lot hesitated, once again showing a lack of faith. Yet God was gracious because Lot was Abraham's nephew (v. 29), and the angels led Lot and his family by the hand to a place outside the city. They were instructed to keep running and not look back.

Again Lot fussed, claiming he wasn't fast enough to run to the mountains. He asked to flee to the town of Zoar instead. By midday, Lot and his family reached Zoar and judgment fell. Hot, burning sulfur. The wrath of God descending from the sky. All-consuming fire, incinerating the two cities and all the fields surrounding them. Hell unleashed. No one was spared, not even the grass.

But Lot's wife disobeyed the command of the angels to not look back at what was left behind, and she supernaturally experienced a unique fate—transformation into a "pillar of salt" (Genesis 19:26). None of us gain any advantage by looking back at a previous life of sin, for we are called to press on (Philippians 3:13) to the new life ahead of us.

Later, Lot and his daughters left the city of Zoar out of fear that it would be judged too. They found shelter in a cave in the mountains. And in an ironic twist, Lot's daughters, who wanted to have children but acknowledged the absence of men due to God's judgment, ended up getting their father drunk and incestuously taking advantage of him. He who once offered up his daughters to sexual abuse himself faced humiliation. The women conceived and both gave birth—one to a boy named Moab, the other to a boy named Ben-Ammi, whose descendants—the Moabites and the Ammonites—became a group of people that would become Israel's Achilles' heel for years to come.

The story reminds us of many things. It emphasizes God's undeserved and unending grace. Lot is spared God's wrath. Lot's story teaches that even a little faith is better than no faith and that even those who possess faith have moments of great weakness. We falter. We fall. But God's grace is greater than all our sin.

Though Lot was a believer, in his weakness he had to be dragged along by God's angels. If we're honest, we all have times when we need to be guided toward God's good plan for us. In our own flesh we cannot please God. Praise God that he does not treat us according to what our sins deserve (Psalm 103:10–14).

The story also points us to our responsibility to protect the weak and vulnerable, a responsibility in which Lot failed miserably. Fathers have a sacred duty to protect their daughters, and yet many fathers fail in this high calling. But the heavenly Father watches out for his own, and he heals and embraces when others fail us.

Finally, we see here that God's wrath is not something to be trifled with. The phrase "Sodom and Gomorrah" will forever be linked with judgment, if only as a preview of the final judgment to come on an unbelieving world (Jude 1:7). But rest assured, justice will come (2 Peter 2:9–10). God sees. God knows. And in his perfect timing, he will set all things straight—if not in this life, then surely in the age to come.

Principles for Reflection

1. Lot did not nurture and protect his daughters the way a father should. In contrast, in Luke's gospel, a woman who had been bleeding for twelve years receive healing from Jesus when she reached out to touch his robe (8:43–44). She was a social outcast because of her condition, but Jesus stopped to address her, calling her a "daughter" of God because of her faith and telling her to "go in peace" (v. 48). Jesus' compassion and elevation of women to their rightful position as equally created in the image of God stand as a crucial biblical corrective to oppressive social structures and human perspectives like that of Lot, who undervalued the worth of his daughters.

2. Lot's story isn't particularly flattering to someone Peter would later call "righteous Lot" (2 Peter 2:7 CSB). From this, we learn that though we tend to assess a person's life on the basis of their actions, often quick to point out their faults and failures, we must remember that ultimately it is God who is the only one who knows and judges the heart. God's people will fail, to be sure, but God's grace covers all our sins—past, present, and future.

3. Certain sins have long-term consequences that can last beyond our lifetimes and affect future generations. Such was the case with the sins of Lot and his daughters, whose children born of incest brought forth ancestors who would be a thorn in Israel's side for years to come. Even what we consider private, or personal, sins (especially those of a sexual nature) can have a corporate impact.

CHAPTER 13

DO GOD'S PUNISHMENTS ALWAYS FIT THE CRIME?

Genesis 38:8–10

MATTHEW D. KIM

What happens if, God forbid, a man's brother dies and leaves behind a widow? According to Jewish tradition, he is to marry and procreate with his dead brother's wife. In recent years, Hunter Biden (son of former president Joe Biden) and Hallie Biden (the widow of Hunter's late brother Beau Biden) began an unusual relationship. Hunter and his first wife, Kathleen Biden, had divorced and parted ways. In time, Hunter and Hallie developed a relationship as they supported each other through Beau's death.[1]

The story of Onan in Genesis 38 reads like a script from a reality TV show in which the characters find themselves in disturbing family circumstances. The second-born son of Judah and a Canaanite woman named Shua, Onan was the younger brother of Er and the

---

1. Dan Merica, "Beau Biden's Brother, Widow in Romantic Relationship," CNN, March 2, 2017, www.cnn.com/2017/03/01/politics/joe-biden-hunter-beau.

older brother of Shelah. What do we make of Onan's story, and how do we communicate God's instructions about sexual intimacy and procreation? Or is there something else God wants us to understand from this text?

Here's the context: Er the firstborn marries Tamar, but God sees Er's wickedness and puts him to death (Genesis 38:6–7). We don't know what Er has done to deserve death, but his father gives instructions to Onan about Er's wife after Er dies:

> Then Judah said to Onan, "Sleep with your brother's wife and fulfill your duty to her as a brother-in-law to raise up offspring for your brother." But Onan knew that the child would not be his; so whenever he slept with his brother's wife, he spilled his semen on the ground to keep from providing offspring for his brother. What he did was wicked in the LORD's sight; so the LORD put him to death also. (vv. 8–10).

Genesis 38 narrates Judah's reckless desire to sleep with a roadside prostitute, not knowing that this woman, whose face is covered, is his daughter-in-law Tamar. This chapter provides the bizarre narrative of Judah and his illicit relations with Tamar, Er's widow, resulting in the birth of twins, Perez and Zerah. Verses 8–10 contain a substory within a grander plot involving Judah and Tamar. As noted by George Coats, "The sons [Er, Onan, and Shelah] function only as instruments for presenting the crisis of the story and heightening its tension."[2]

While the specific details about Onan's sin leave us wondering about why God would put Onan to death for that sin, as it turns out, Judah foolishly fulfills Onan's duty, what is referred to in the Jewish tradition as "levirate marriage." With roots in Deuteronomy 25:5–10, this ancient rite intends to continue the family lineage through

---

2. George W. Coats, "Widow's Rights: A Crux in the Structure of Genesis 38," *Catholic Biblical Quarterly* 34, no. 4 (October 1972): 461.

bearing an heir and protecting a widow's inheritance within her father-in-law's kin. A more familiar Old Testament text describing this custom can be found in the book of Ruth, which uses the concept of a kinsman-redeemer.[3]

If the author is more concerned about Judah and Tamar, what is the bigger purpose of including this odd episode regarding Onan? The stakes were high for Onan, who was instructed by Judah to procreate with his widowed sister-in-law. Since any children Onan had with Tamar would not be lawfully his, Onan "spilled his semen" on the ground to avoid insemination with Tamar (38:9). This was evil in God's eyes. Thus, Onan's punishment for his sin is death. What Onan did to displease the Lord is now referred to as the sin of onanism.

What biblical principle can we draw from this account? Is God's primary concern for the care of widows? Does this passage offer instruction on sex and sexuality? Is it about generational sin? Is it about fulfilling Jewish and family customs? I believe that an overarching metanarrative is Onan's deliberate disobedience of God's command to fulfill his familial duty of continuing offspring. Here the sin is connected to the consequences of Onan making an ongoing intentional choice not to impregnate Tamar and not to continue his brother Er's generational line. We might wonder about what appears to be the over-the-top severity of God's punishment of death. According to ancient tradition, noncompliance to levirate law typically did not warrant a death sentence. In such cases, the widow would ask the elders to convince the living brother to comply.[4]

However, as we know from other passages in Scripture, God does not take the life of anyone and everyone haphazardly. Is there something more to the story? What exactly did Onan do to circumvent the plan of God? Was his sin so grave as to demand his life? It seems to be a straightforward conclusion that Onan decides in his heart to defy

---

3. Much of this paragraph paraphrases Coats, "Widow's Rights," 462.
4. For more context, see Mark Brumley, "The Sin of Onan," Catholic Answers, July 1, 1991, www.catholic.com/magazine/print-edition/the-sin-of-onan.

the levirate marriage law. Thus God, in his holiness and sovereignty, takes his life. Through his disobedience, Onan also fails to care socioeconomically for his brother's widow.[5]

What does this text mean for us today, and how do we teach it appropriately? How would we as teachers and preachers explain the significance of this text? Is this story primarily about human sexuality, contraception, self-gratification, widow care, marriage and remarriage, or something else?

In this hypersexualized culture, we can easily fall prey to moralism and say this story is limited to prescribing divine boundaries and instructions for sex and human sexuality. For instance, some have erroneously argued that spilling one's semen on the ground is a reference to masturbation. Others contend that Onan's act is "the practice of ejaculating outside the woman's body ('withdrawal') as a means to avoid impregnation."[6] Thus, another possible theory stretching the current application might be that Onan's story is linked to the pro-life movement, or fertility, in general.

What does this text have to do with us? First, we are reminded of the holiness God demands from his people. God hates disobedience of any kind. Putting to death disobedient people is something that the Lord is acquainted with. In Leviticus, for example, Nadab and Abihu, the sons of Aaron and Elisheba, were struck down by the Lord for ignoring his command and offering "unauthorized fire" (10:1, see chapter 15 in this book). In Acts 5, the Holy Spirit put to death Ananias and Sapphira for their financial dishonesty. Onan's story is similarly remarkable and shocking. Yet as modern-day Christians, we seem quick to dismiss these accounts. God would never strike anyone down today, would he? We would be wise to remember that nothing is impossible with God and that he takes holiness seriously in every part of life.

---

5. John H. Walton and Craig S. Keener, eds., *NIV Cultural Backgrounds Study Bible* (Zondervan, 2016), note on Genesis 38:11, p. 84.

6. *NIV Cultural Backgrounds Study*, note on Genesis 38:9, p. 84.

Second, humans have not hesitated to define wickedness by their standards and not the Lord's. As a result of the fall recorded in Genesis 3, we have become "like God," looking to discern for ourselves what constitutes moral and immoral behavior. We have become the arbiters of moral judgment. The problem, as we see in the book of Judges, is that "everyone [does] as they [see] fit" (17:6). In God's economy of sin, he determines the hierarchy of sins, and we, his creatures, are not privy to such designations. Onan's story is a clarion call to take all sin—including sexual sin—as being wicked and despicable in the eyes of the Lord, even punishable by death. As Paul testifies in Romans 6:23, "The wages of sin is death." God makes the rules, not us.

Third, we must evaluate our view of contraception through the lens of God's sovereignty. Humans have adopted an anthropological view (making their own decisions and choices) instead of a scriptural view on procreation. We foolishly believe we can control procreation. Yes, it was God's original intention for a husband and wife to procreate. He commands, "Be fruitful and increase in number; fill the earth and subdue it" (Genesis 1:28). As humans challenge God's plan and design for traditional marriage and sexual relations within the boundaries of a covenantal marriage between one man and one woman for life, Christians must be reminded of God's desire for a married man and woman to procreate (as he grants the ability).

Finally, we must respond in obedience to God's desire for procreation. Mark Brumley explains from a Catholic perspective: "By acting contraceptively, Onan robbed sexual intercourse of its life-giving meaning and acted against the good of his potential offspring's life. Both his intent and his concrete actions were against life."[7] The blessing of God is found in sexual pleasure (within the covenant of marriage between a man and a woman), which leads to procreation (as God wills). God expects holiness in marital relationships.

Onan's story is not a throwaway story. God wanted us to know

---

7. Brumley, "Sin of Onan."

of his holiness and sovereignty over his entire creation. May we as sexual beings take God's holiness seriously and as his image bearers take inventory of our discipleship through holiness and obedience.

Principles for Reflection

1. God requires holiness and obedience from his children in all parts of life, including our sexuality, sexual identity, and sexual fulfillment, as well as in response to his mandate to reproduce and have offspring.

2. We are created to be holy and obedient to the Lord, even in our sexual desires, which can be experienced only through God's proper design and boundaries within the covenant of marriage between one man and one woman for life.

3. Sexual purity matters to the Lord in every stage of life, whether we are single or married. We are not bound, however, to the same onanic principle. The Lord does not ask us to marry our deceased sibling's spouse and procreate with them. Yet we can do our part to provide for our immediate family and family members (not in a sexual nature).

CHAPTER 14

ARE GOD'S RULES ARBITRARY?

Exodus 22:16–31

MATTHEW D. KIM

After receiving from God the Ten Commandments (Exodus 20), Moses describes various types of laws given to the Israelites. This specific portion of the law found in Exodus 22:16–31 has to do with Moses' instructions on the social responsibilities for people living in community. Particularly noticeable is the punishment of death and destruction for those who disobey God's laws in these ways:

- having sexual relations with virgins or premarital sex
- practicing sorcery
- bestiality
- sacrificing to other gods
- mistreating foreigners
- taking advantage of widows and the fatherless
- charging usury to the needy
- blaspheming God
- stealing offerings
- withholding firstborn sons and animals

- eating meat torn by wild animals

Why is God so violent in punishing those who disobey his laws? Why does he appear so arbitrary and cruel by requiring death? Are these sins any different from other sins? Old Testament scholar Douglas Stuart helpfully explains the context:

> No government welfare system existed in Israel. It was the responsibility of the covenant community—each Israelite, assuming the covenant was kept faithfully—to contribute his share of the welfare burden personally (rather than through taxes), to avoid personally any discrimination against the needy in any way, and to treat all those in need or of limited resources as brothers and sisters, virtual family members. Yahweh himself was the enforcer of this demand for fair treatment of all the "little" people anywhere in Israel (vv. 23–24, 27).[1]

As representatives of God himself, the Israelite community was expected to act on his behalf and care for all—especially those we typically call "the least of these."

We can carve out two main categories of social laws: (1) treatment of God and (2) treatment of neighbor. Embedded in these verses are actions and attitudes toward God and others.

First, how does God instruct the Israelites to treat him? God is supreme and expects unmitigated honor and worship. As Exodus 22:20 records, "Whoever sacrifices to any god other than the LORD must be destroyed." Verse 28 commands, "Do not blaspheme God." Then verses 29–30 demand, "You must give me the firstborn of your sons. Do the same with your cattle and your sheep. Let them stay with their mothers for seven days, but give them to me on the eighth day." Since everything belongs to the Lord, God expected his people

---

1. Douglas K. Stuart, *Exodus*, New American Commentary (B&H, 2006), 515.

to return to him whatever he asked of them. Withholding anything from the Lord, especially tithe offerings and even firstborn children, was unacceptable to God and considered acts of defiance.[2]

Second, longer expectations are spelled out for how we treat others—especially in situations where there is a hierarchy of position, power, or possessions. Those who have authority, position, power, or means to help others should not hoard or lord over those who don't. This includes the uneven power dynamics often seen in sexual relationships, treatment of foreigners or sojourners, and the exorbitant usury expected in granting of financial loans.

In the ancient Jewish world, writes Jannie Du Preez, "the law is maintained in the community through the protection of the weak, whose rights can easily be taken away from them. Thus the welfare of the community as community of the covenant is maintained."[3] It takes a radical paradigm shift for the Western mind to think in terms of the communal rather than the individual. Particularly when we go beyond the nuclear or even extended family, it's difficult to consider others in the community, to look out for their benefit, and to come to their aid. The Israelite community knew the expectations of Yahweh to care for others. Whether they followed the instructions is a different story.

While there are some overlaps as well as omissions, the teaching here resembles the Ten Commandments (with greater specificity) that Moses carried down from Mount Sinai just two chapters earlier in the narrative, but in reverse order. The Ten Commandments begin with reverence and honor of God and end with reverence and honor of people.

The sheer volume of possible teaching or sermon material is daunting. What would I teach and what would I leave out? One could justifiably preach or teach an entire sermon or lesson on each of

---

2. Stuart, *Exodus*, 521.
3. Jannie Du Preez, "Social Justice: Motive for the Mission of the Church," *Journal of Theology for Southern Africa* 53 (1985): 37.

these sins. We may want to lay the groundwork for two overarching observations—how to revere the Lord and how to revere others. Scott Rae classifies three distinct crimes or violations in this section: "(a) violations against the sanctity of life . . . (b) violations against the source of life, primarily sexual sins . . . and (c) violations against the purity of the worship of God."[4]

Another way to view these and other Israelite laws is through the lenses of God's holiness through honesty and his justice through action. Both themes flow through both Testaments. Beginning with holiness through honesty, it seems clear from these violations that a dishonest heart and mind lead to dishonest gain. When it comes to any of these unlawful acts, an honest person will strive for holiness by pursuing the highest good of one's neighbors.

It's clear that justice matters to the triune God and therefore requires Christlike action. Jesus takes caring for the destitute and disabled personally. His ministry oozed social justice on many levels. He took immediate action to help others and did not take advantage of them in the process. He was always looking out for the good of others (unlike the corrupt Pharisees and religious rulers of the day).

Much debate goes on today over whether Christians have responsibilities to care for others and work to overturn evil, dishonest systems that perpetually push down the downtrodden. These days, when we hear the phrases *social action* or *social justice*, our minds go to the views of people on the extreme ends of the political spectrum, whether liberal or conservative. Synonyms for a *liberal* include *left-winger, radical,* or *progressive,* while a *conservative* is often seen as a *right-winger, reactionary,* or *traditionalist.* The former are said to champion social justice with an agenda, and the latter seem to neutralize or downplay its importance. But why do we, like Pilate, wash our hands of the responsibility to act with social welfare as a guiding

---

4. Scott B. Rae, *Moral Choices: An Introduction to Ethics,* 4th ed. (1995; repr., Zondervan Academic, 2018), 267.

principle (Matthew 27:24)? If Christians do not care for others, why would anyone else?

What is clear from this passage in Exodus and many others is that social action, or social justice, is not antithetical to the work of the gospel. In fact, we may argue that social justice is the natural byproduct of being Jesus' disciples. Acting justly doesn't save us, but it is an instinctive response for those who are saved. In many ways, these Old Testament social laws are summarized by the two greatest commandments—love God and love neighbor (Matthew 22:36–40). Author David Platt makes this strong claim:

> The gospel is the lifeblood of Christianity, and it provides the foundation for countering culture. For when we truly believe the gospel, we begin to realize that the gospel not only *compels* Christians to confront social issues in the culture around us. The gospel actually *creates* confrontation with the culture around—and within—us.[5]

A third conspicuous, or elephant-in-the-room, topic is God's endorsement of the death penalty or capital punishment. According to God's playbook in Exodus 22:16–31, anyone found guilty of one of these crimes is to be executed.

Does each crime or violation mentioned in our text have the same weight today as in the past? To some degree, yes. As we know, breaking the law comes with legal consequences. For instance, committing sexual crimes often has uniquely severe penalties, such as having to register your name in the community and state where you live as a sex offender or sexual predator. You are flagged in your neighborhood permanently. We don't have the same types of mandates for other social sins, such as lying, slander, or gossip.

When it comes to sins leading to death, we must wrestle with the

---

5. David Platt, *Counter Culture: Following Christ in an Anti-Christian Age*, rev. ed. (Tyndale Momentum, 2017), 1, italics in original.

fact that in the Old Testament, sin always led to death—in most cases the death of an animal sacrifice. Romans 6:23 reminds us, "The wages of sin is death, but the gift of God is eternal life in Christ Jesus our Lord." Sin leads to death in all cases. The question for us is this: Why does God permit capital punishment for certain sins, and why do we as a society do that as well?

Many people today have become tolerant of sins of all kinds. Premarital sex is no big deal. *Sexual sins are private sins that don't affect anyone else*, we think to ourselves. David Platt said, "One of the easiest ways to assuage guilt is to convince ourselves that our moral standards are impractical or outdated. . . . We attempt to remove our guilt by redefining right and wrong according to cultural fads."[6]

One sign of a maturing disciple is whether they hate what God hates and love what God loves. I confess this is no easy task. My sinful nature gets in the way. But even in the earliest of human history, we hear God say to Cain, "If you do what is right, will you not be accepted? But if you do not do what is right, sin is crouching at your door; it desires to have you, but you must rule over it" (Genesis 4:7).

In *Just Discipleship*, Michael J. Rhodes shares this testimony about what awakened him to God's call for Christians to engage in social change:

> At some point, our church invited Dr. John Perkins to speak. The moment he opened his mouth, you knew Perkins loved Jesus and loved his Word. He was just like us!
>
> But he pointed out all this stuff in Scripture I'd never paid attention to, stuff that had never crossed my discipleship radar. Stuff like God's overwhelming love for the poor, his care for the ethnic outsider, his passionate commitment to justice. Perkins showed us that to be serious about Scripture, to be serious about *discipleship*, we had to be serious about poverty, racism, and injustice.

---

6. Platt, *Counter Culture*, 10.

Not because of some liberal agenda or to "keep up with the times."
Because "the Bible tells us so"!

This changed my life.[7]

We have a choice every second of every day, in every interaction, to choose holiness over sin, justice over injustice. Of course, the more we spend time with the Lord and get to know his heart, the easier it is to know how to love our neighbors well. We have the instruction manual in the person of Jesus, who perfectly modeled how to act justly toward marginalized and socially outcast persons.

As we take our cues from the Savior, we depend on the Holy Spirit to guide and empower us. The pursuit of holiness and justice requires supernatural power. We can't manufacture the holiness or the heart of justice God calls us to so that we act for the good of others. But we can read Bible passages like Exodus 22 and realize that social action is not unbiblical because it includes the word *social*. Rather, it is the call given to all disciples—to love and pursue hard after God, who wants his people to act as his hands and feet in a hurting world.

Principles for Reflection

1. God created us to love him and to love our neighbors. A crucial expression of our love is seen in how we treat others by way of social justice and engagement.

2. Justice is the heartbeat of God and of Christianity. We are commanded to love and care for our neighbors as we care for ourselves and our families.

---

7. Michael J. Rhodes, *Just Discipleship: Biblical Justice in an Unjust World* (IVP Academic, 2023), 4, italics in original.

3. We are called to feed the hungry, speak up for the voiceless and marginalized, and be first responders for anyone in need. When God calls us to respond, we must act wisely and promptly.

CHAPTER 15

IS PROPER WORSHIP A LIFE-AND-DEATH MATTER?

Leviticus 10

ERIC J. BARGERHUFF

I am wholeheartedly convinced that on this side of heaven, we will always have a woefully inadequate view of the horror of human sin before a holy God. But when the day comes when we see him face-to-face, the stunning reality and profound nature of the cross of Christ will grip us with the glory of God like never before. In that moment, we will more fully comprehend the price he paid for the offense of our sin because we will be awestruck by his holiness. It will undoubtedly lead us into never-ending worship.

Worship is something God delights in. It is also something we were made for. And when we think, feel, and act according to God's design, he is glorified. In the Bible one cannot help but notice that God takes worship with the utmost seriousness. He has always wanted his people to worship him "in the Spirit and in truth" (John 4:24). Worship must come genuinely from the heart and must be based on the truth of God and who he is as revealed in Scripture.

In both Old and New Testaments, it is worth noting that God is also particular about *how* he is worshiped. In Corinth, Paul was stern toward a church whose worship services had descended into chaos. Their celebrations of the Lord's Supper were divisive and full of drunken revelries. Their regular gatherings for worship were a free-for-all, with everyone doing their own thing without any sense of direction or order, and Paul made it clear that "everything is to be done decently and in order" (1 Corinthians 14:40 CSB).

Similarly, the Old Testament priests had abundant instructions on how Yahweh wanted to be worshiped among the Israelites from their time at Mount Sinai and into the future. When the book of Exodus concludes, Moses has erected a tabernacle, and God's glory and presence has filled it. Instructions on *how* the Israelites were to worship comes in the book of Leviticus.

In Leviticus, we see that God prescribes many unique laws and rituals for the way he desires them to worship him. These rituals required the obedience of God's people and were designed to reveal spiritual truths about God, as well as the spiritual needs of the Israelites. The offerings and sacrifices were designed to lead the people into thanksgiving and worship as well as provide temporary atonement for sin.

In Leviticus 6–7, God is specific about the roles the priests were to play and the many ways they were to carry out the various offerings required. Throughout the instructions given to Moses, the holiness of God surfaces as a reoccurring theme—a holiness designed to remind them that they, too, were to be set apart from sin and for God.

As chapter 8 begins, Aaron and his sons are consecrated as priests, and the role of the priesthood is put into service among the Israelites for the first time. To be sure, the patriarchs offered sacrifices to the Lord, but the priesthood was established for a specific ministry among all God's people. The priests were to represent the people before God, and their ministry of intercession and sacrifice foreshadowed many spiritual realities that would ultimately find their greatest fulfillment in our Lord Jesus himself.

Christ, like the priests of old, intercedes for us (Romans 8:34; Hebrews 7:25) and represents us before the Father (Hebrews 9:24). But unlike the priests in the Old Testament, who were continually required to offer sacrifices, Jesus is *himself* the final *sacrifice* for sin (v. 26). He is the full and complete *atonement* for sin, the one and only *mediator* between man and God (1 Timothy 2:5), thus rendering the sacrificial system and the accompanying role of the office of the priesthood obsolete. For Jesus is the perfect High Priest who fulfills all of those roles.

But until that future reality came to fruition, the priests in Israel had a job to do—a sacred one at that. Throughout Leviticus 8–10, a common phrase leaps out time and again: "as the LORD commanded Moses." About this phrase, Gordon Wenham notes, "Because it is such a commonplace statement in the Pentateuch, we are apt to overlook it. But beginning with 7:38, this or a similar phrase occurs with remarkable frequency in these three chapters (8:4, 5, 9, 13, 17, 21, 29, 34, 36; 9:6, 7, 10, 21; 10:7, 13, 15)."[1]

The fact that God commanded and expected obedience underscores the serious nature of the priesthood. Therefore, when we encounter something done in disobedience, our first response should be, "Uh-oh."

True to form, sinful human beings found a way to pervert something sacred, as two of Aaron's sons do something God had *not* commanded them to do: "Aaron's sons Nadab and Abihu each took his own firepan, put fire in it, placed incense on it, and presented unauthorized fire before the LORD, which he had not commanded them to do" (Leviticus 10:1 CSB).

When you first read this, you may think to yourself, *Typical boys. They love to play with fire.* My mind takes me to the movie *Cast Away*, starring Tom Hanks, who was stranded alone on a desert island, and after numerous attempts to make fire, he finally succeeds and dances

---

1. Gordon J. Wenham, *The Book of Leviticus*, New International Commentary on the Old Testament (Eerdmans, 1979), 130.

around deliriously chanting, "Look what I've created. I have made fire. I have made fire."[2]

Now we are not exactly sure that was what they were doing. Nothing seems to suggest that they were playing around. Could it have been possible that these boys were drunk since the Lord adds an additional command in verses 8–9 that Aaron and his sons were to drink no wine or strong drink when they entered the tent of meeting? Again, we can't be sure. But whatever they were doing, the narrative makes it abundantly clear that God had not authorized it.

Interestingly, not but a chapter before, at the end of Leviticus 9, we see fire come out from the Lord to consume an offering presented by Aaron, and the people verbally respond with undoubtedly a mixed shout of terror and joy as they fall on their faces in worship. God had accepted the sacrifice and visually demonstrated his presence (v. 23—"the glory of the LORD") and his approval before all of them.

By contrast, shortly after that, the two oldest boys of Aaron venture out on their own and disobey the Lord's command concerning the burning of incense that he had set forth in Exodus 30:1–10, 34–38. And fire comes out again, but this time it does not consume an offering or connote any level of acceptance or approval; rather it consumes Aaron's two sons.

> Then fire came from the LORD and consumed them, and they died before the LORD. Moses said to Aaron, "This is what the LORD has spoken:
>
> > I will demonstrate my holiness
> > to those who are near me,
> > and I will reveal my glory
> > before all the people."
>
> And Aaron remained silent. (Leviticus 10:2–3 CSB)

---

2. Robert Zemeckis, dir., *Cast Away* (20th Century Fox, 2000), DVD.

The judgment of God falls, and they are burnt to a crisp. Here again is another example of why I don't think we truly comprehend the holiness of God. Our immediate reaction is that this seems to be especially harsh, but we see no complaint on Aaron's part. He is stunned. Gripped with fear. He can't even speak, and Moses has stated that this is a demonstration of God's *holiness* and *glory*, the two things that Aaron's sons seemingly disregarded.

God knows and sees all things. God's commands were violated. Aaron knew it, so he remained silent. He knew that all that the Lord does is right and true. Surely, he mourned in his heart, but he did not argue with God's assessment and actions and was not allowed to mourn publicly (v. 6).

We are reminded of a similar type of action in Acts 5. Ananias and Sapphira were executed by God before all the people for lying to Peter and to the Holy Spirit when they sold some land and brought to the disciples what they claimed was the entire amount they received. However, they retained some of the proceeds for themselves. That would not have been a sin had they chosen to make that known. But that's not what they did. They wanted everyone to believe that what they gave was all they received for the land, but God wouldn't let them get away with it. God saw, God knew, and God acted decisively.

Comparing Leviticus 10 and Acts 5, we see that God chooses to demonstrate his holiness and glory in unique ways in critical moments of redemption history. Herbert Wolf notes, "There [in Acts 5] it was the beginning of the church; in Leviticus, it was the inauguration of the priesthood. At these two crucial periods God let it be known that He demanded holiness and that sin brought judgment and death."[3]

The Leviticus account concludes with Moses taking over the scene while a stunned Aaron looks on.

---

3. Herbert Wolf, *An Introduction to the Old Testament Pentateuch* (Moody, 1991), 174.

Moses summoned Mishael and Elzaphan, sons of Aaron's uncle Uzziel, and said to them, "Come here and carry your relatives away from the front of the sanctuary to a place outside the camp." So they came forward and carried them in their tunics outside the camp, as Moses had said.

Then Moses said to Aaron and his sons Eleazar and Ithamar, "Do not let your hair hang loose and do not tear your clothes, or else you will die, and the LORD will become angry with the whole community. However, your brothers, the whole house of Israel, may weep over the fire that the LORD caused. You must not go outside the entrance to the tent of meeting or you will die, for the LORD's anointing oil is on you." So they did as Moses said. (10:4–7 CSB)

The dead boys were carried away, and Aaron and his two remaining sons were instructed to keep themselves together (no customary outward signs of mourning with disheveled hair or torn clothes were allowed). They were to stay inside the tent while those outside were allowed to mourn. Further, it would have not been appropriate for Aaron, as the high priest, to defile himself by touching dead bodies (see God's later command in Leviticus 21:1–12), and this prohibition was extended to his remaining sons as well. God told them to stay put. The people would outwardly mourn with and for them.

The bar has now been set. God takes worship seriously. And undoubtedly a reverential fear of the holiness and glory of God came upon all the people. As Wenham reminds us, "The whole nation was called to be holy, but how much more responsibility rested on the priests whose duty was to perform sanctifying rituals and to teach people the way of holiness."[4]

This brings us to many helpful applications. Certainly, this story presses on our conscience regarding how casual we have often approached worship in today's church. On this it is less about ritual,

---

4. Wenham, *Book of Leviticus*, 156–57.

and more about the heart. Remember that Jesus taught us that the Father seeks worshipers who will worship him "in the Spirit and in truth." Do we truly see God for who he has revealed himself to be in Scripture? And does it grip our hearts? Consider this. It gripped the demons in Mark 1:24 and Luke 4:34, where one demon shouts, "I know who you are—the Holy One of God!" Even a demon is acutely aware of and is stunningly afraid of the holiness of God in Christ. In contrast, we are God's children by faith, and we have nothing to fear (for fear has to do with punishment—1 John 4:18). But we should be no less gripped by the holiness and majesty of God in such a way that we, too, should be concerned with what kind of worship we offer up to God.

Is our heart right? Do we worship God the way Scripture teaches us to—being taught by the Word, singing psalms and hymns and spiritual songs with thankfulness in our hearts to God (Colossians 3:16)? Do we approach him in prayer on a regular basis (1 Timothy 2:8)? Are we sincere (Jeremiah 29:13)? Are we learning more how to pray according to his will (1 John 5:14)?

How about our songs? Are they theologically sound? Are they derived from a sound biblical theology of God? Are they more about him or about us and what we are doing? We can sing about the Christian life, but remember the object of our worship is God. Let us rejoice in the Father of the blessings more than in the blessings of the Father. And let all experiences we sing about be seen through the lens of Scripture so that we can interpret our experiences rightly.

Second, the man who leads and instructs God's people in the Word of God must be a man above reproach (1 Timothy 3:2). He must be seeking to live a holy and godly life before God and God's people. This is surely part of the reason Nadab and Abihu were struck down by fire, for they were embracing disobedience in a public sense, and it dishonored the holiness and glory of God and undoubtedly would have influenced the views and attitudes of God's people because they would likely imitate their leaders. You become what you behold.

This is why the Lord put spiritual qualifications in place through Paul in 1 Timothy 3 and Titus 1. The public ministry of the church and its leaders has a vital influence on the integrity of the message and those who listen to its messenger. And like it was in Leviticus, the reputation of God is often at stake, and the message of the gospel must be declared boldly, accurately, and without apology.

So let us approach the throne of grace with confidence (Hebrews 4:16), with a clear conscience (1 John 3:21), and worship the Lamb who is worthy in all his splendor and glory. Unlike what is sometimes mentioned in a few ill-informed worship songs today, we don't want the consuming fire of God to fall on us.[5] We want to worship him in the Spirit and in truth, so that our worship and our lives are a sweet-smelling aroma to God.

Principles for Reflection

1. We are to love God with all our heart, soul, mind, and strength. Worship is crucial to loving God as we worship him "in the Spirit and in truth." Therefore, *how* we worship involves both heart and mind and is to be done in a fitting and orderly way. Our worship, whether corporate or individual, should embrace a sense of reverence and awe as we seek to more fully understand the God we worship.

2. The holiness of God is an attribute of his character that has lost much of its meaning and impact on modern-day churches that approach worship casually with an emphasis on attracting crowds through entertainment and

---

5. For a fuller understanding of the consuming fire of God and its specific relationship to judgment, see chapter 17 titled, "What Is the Consuming Fire of God?"

emotional experience. Churches should evaluate each aspect of its corporate worship services and evaluate whether it is more about us or more about him. God must be the object and centerpiece of our worship.

CHAPTER 16

WHAT IS SO IMPORTANT ABOUT KEEPING THE SABBATH?

Numbers 15:32–36

MATTHEW D. KIM

Christians have mixed feelings about the fourth commandment: to remember the Sabbath day by keeping it holy. Some resist legalism and refuse to make keeping the Sabbah an absolute command, while others, at least in principle, accept that God commanded his people not to work on the seventh day. I grew up in a church where keeping the Sabbath and worshiping on Sunday were highly legalistic and shame inducing for lawbreakers. Not only did my parents' church expect Sunday worship attendance, but we were also not supposed to shop on Sundays or eat at restaurants. The irony was that not studying on Sundays was never explicitly forbidden because we were expected to do well in school and go on to big and better things. But it's clear from Numbers 15 that in the Old Testament, breaking the Sabbath had life-and-death consequences.

Right before our passage, Moses speaks to the Israelites about unintentional sins, or sins of omission. Since these sins were done unknowingly, the penalty was less severe than others mentioned in Numbers. Numbers 15:27 reads, "If just one person sins unintentionally, that person must bring a year-old female goat for a sin offering." A few verses later, we read that a person who gathered wood on the Sabbath day (v. 32) was to receive the penalty for this sin, which was the death penalty. At the Lord's command, "The man must die. The whole assembly must stone him outside the camp" (v. 35).

If death was the lawful punishment for a wood gatherer on the Sabbath, aren't all of us doomed? The Sabbath was a big deal in the Old Testament. And it's also important today, even though many have minimized it. Ultimately, picking up wood led to this Israelite's premature death. Why was his punishment so severe for breaking the Sabbath? And what can we learn from his negative example? Breaking the Sabbath had severe repercussions back then, but in this chapter, I remind you that failing to realize the magnitude of breaking the Sabbath may be doing us more harm than we can imagine.

What is the Sabbath, and why is it so important to the Lord? From the beginning of creation, God saw fit to rest on the Sabbath day and consecrated it as holy. Genesis 2:2–3 reads, "By the seventh day God had finished the work he had been doing; so on the seventh day he rested from all his work. Then God blessed the seventh day and made it holy, because on it he rested from all the work of creating that he had done." As we know, God didn't rest on the Sabbath because he was tired. God doesn't get tired or weary.

It was a long time before God reminded the Israelites of the Sabbath's prominence in their lives. The Ten Commandments continue the creation narrative's emphasis on keeping the Sabbath—on resting from work and centering our lives on worship:

> Remember the Sabbath day by keeping it holy. Six days you shall labor and do all your work, but the seventh day is a sabbath to the LORD your God. On it you shall not do any work, neither you, nor your son or daughter, nor your male or female servant, nor your

animals, nor any foreigner residing in your towns. For in six days the LORD made the heavens and the earth, the sea, and all that is in them, but he rested on the seventh day. Therefore the LORD blessed the Sabbath day and made it holy. (Exodus 20:8–11)

The key takeaways from the fourth commandment are these: refrain from work for a day, and make the day holy, or set apart. The Sabbath reminded the Israelites of their bondage in Egypt and how God freed them from oppressive work.[1]

In our day, we have lost the gravity of observing the Sabbath. In his influential book *The Sabbath*, the late Jewish theologian Abraham Heschel spoke eloquently of how Judaism teaches us to be "attached to holiness in time, to be attached to sacred events, to learn how to consecrate sanctuaries that emerge from the magnificent stream of a year. The Sabbaths are our great cathedrals." More broadly, Heschel wrote, "Judaism is a *religion of time* aiming at the *sanctification of time*."[2] He explains further:

> The meaning of the Sabbath is to celebrate time rather than space. Six days a week we live under the tyranny of things of space; on the Sabbath we try to become attuned to *holiness in time*. It is a day on which we are called upon to share in what is eternal in time, to turn from the results of creation to the mystery of creation; from the world of creation to the creation of the world.[3]

Heschel's elevation of holiness experienced through human beings setting time apart as both holy and creative captures the essence of the Sabbath commandment. By Sabbath keeping, we are becoming sanctified as we embody creativity.

---

1. See Scott B. Rae, *Moral Choices: An Introduction to Ethics*, 4th ed. (Zondervan, 2018), 80.
2. Abraham Joshua Heschel, *The Sabbath: Its Meaning for Modern Man* (Farrar, Straus and Giroux, 2005), 8, italics in original.
3. Heschel, *Sabbath*, 10, italics in original.

We must try to make sense of the Sabbath not from our own limited vantage point but from the perspective of the Lord. I suspect this incident of wood gathering wasn't the first time in Israelite history that someone broke the Sabbath. Yet I wrestle with why the punishment for this individual was so severe. Simply put, Sabbath breaking was a blatant sin in the Old Testament, as it is today, even though we have minimized its significance and consequence. In its study note on Numbers 15:32–36, the *Life Application Study Bible* reads, "Stoning a man for gathering wood on the Sabbath seems like a severe punishment, and it was. This act was a deliberate sin, defying God's law against working on the Sabbath. Perhaps the man was taking advantage of everyone else while they were at home resting, in addition to breaking the Sabbath."[4] It's not the act of gathering wood that's the issue, correct? It's what gathering wood on the Sabbath signifies.

It's crucial to have a sound theology of Sabbath and not selectively interpret its meaning. Our grace-oriented culture shies away from legalistic Sabbath keeping, but the boundaries created by God are for our good. How, then, do we teach and preach about the Sabbath in today's world? What does observing the Sabbath mean in our day?

First, Sabbath signifies our dependence on God alone. Specifically, to refrain from work one day a week is an act of faith that communicates, "I depend on God alone to provide for all my needs." A contemporary example of a Christian who follows the Sabbath principle is Truett Cathy, founder of Chick-fil-A, whose website reads, "Our founder, S. Truett Cathy, made the decision to close on Sundays in 1946. He knew what it was like to work seven days a week in restaurants, so he saw the importance of letting his employees set aside one day to rest and worship if they choose. That's a practice we still uphold today."[5] Cathy understood that human beings were not created

---

4. *Life Application Study Bible*, note on Numbers 15:32–36, p. 219.
5. "Speaking of Sundays," Chick-fil-A, accessed March 4, 2025, www.chick-fil-a.com/about.

to work seven days a week and that God would ultimately honor his decision to give his employees a day off on Sundays.

Second, keeping the Sabbath isn't only about stepping away from work one day each week; most importantly, it's about worshiping God. Corporate worship is an act of reverence as God's people gather for worship and fellowship one day a week.[6]

Third, we need to pay attention to the New Testament teaching on Sabbath. Jesus says, "The Sabbath was made for man, not man for the Sabbath" (Mark 2:27). God created the Sabbath because he knows we need it. We may find ourselves asking, "Why do so many people want a four-day workweek?" Because we are finite beings who need time off from work.

Fourth, in Hebrews 4:9, the author encourages us to remember, "There remains, then, a Sabbath-rest for the people of God." Our reality today to receive Sabbath rest one day a week is a glimpse into our future, where we will find Sabbath rest in eternity. In weekly rhythms of rest, we prepare for our future reality.

Fifth, we keep the Sabbath because it helps us become others-focused. The purpose of a Sabbath day is not to sleep in or be lazy. Rather, as Mike Bennett explains, "The Sabbath is a day to bond with family, appreciate the creation and do good, perhaps visiting the widows and orphans (James 1:27). The Sabbath should be a delight, not by doing our own hobbies, interests and pleasures, but by honoring God and seeking to please Him and do His will (Isaiah 58:13–14)."[7]

Of these five benefits, we might pick a couple to share with those we preach to and teach. The original purpose, laid out by the Lord himself, is to keep the Sabbath as a day of rest. Some skeptics contend that Sundays are not Sabbaths for pastors or laypeople who serve the local church in various ways, or those who have essential service roles in the community that require them to work on the day of worship.

---

6. I will not argue whether the Sabbath is rightfully Saturday or Sunday in this brief chapter.
7. Mike Bennett, "Fourth Commandment: Remember the Sabbath Day," Life, Hope, and Truth, accessed March 4, 2025, https://lifehopeandtruth.com/bible/10-commandments/sabbath/.

If Sabbath were truly observed and respected and all work ceased, nobody would even be available to attend a church worship gathering.

The Sabbath is more than just going to church; though to worship God, we may expect to go to an actual building to worship alongside other believers. "What a sad commentary it is on North American spirituality," Marva Dawn writes in *Keeping the Sabbath Wholly*, "that the delight of 'keeping the Sabbath day' has degenerated into the routine and drudgery—even the downright oppressiveness—of 'going to church.'"[8] Dawn suggests that while New Testament Christians practice Sabbath through worship, the intention of Sabbath had a more wholistic meaning in Scripture. She gives a fourfold perspective on what it means to rest in accordance with the Sabbath. She envisions it as a form of ceasing, resting, embracing, and feasting. The Sabbath, Dawn writes, "creates in us a wholeness that is possible only when we live in accordance with this pattern of being graciously commanded by God."[9]

What gives us creative energy and the ability to create? Put differently, some use the language of how do we re-create ourselves? Rabbi Irving Greenberg says that the Sabbath "is more than a day of being, it is a day of becoming. Rest is more than leisure from work, it is a state of inner discovery, tranquility, and unfolding. . . . The Sabbath commandment is not just to stop working, it is actively to achieve *menuchah* (rest) through self-expression, transformation, and renewal. On this day humans are freed to explore themselves and their relationships until they attain the fullness of being."[10]

Daniel Ross Goodman quips, "Many have written about the Sabbath, but few keep it. . . . Greater than the almighty dollar is the Almighty deity. And greater than the finite value of quarterly profit is the infinite value of every human being—a value that can only be

---

8. Marva J. Dawn, *Keeping the Sabbath Wholly: Ceasing, Resting, Embracing, Feasting* (Eerdmans, 1989), x.

9. Dawn, *Keeping the Sabbath Wholly*, xi.

10. Irving Greenberg, *The Jewish Way: Living the Holidays* (Touchstone, 1993), 139–40.

nourished if we can assert our freedom from the market, for at least one day per week, and proclaim: *who I am is greater than what I earn.*"[11]

Just like any command or boundary instituted by God, the Sabbath and its call to rest from our work is a good thing. It also may be the very antidote to many troubles in this world—sleeplessness, worry, anxiety, depression, exhaustion, and more. A God who loves us will not tell us to do something that will harm us. Rather, the Sabbath is for our own benefit.

Principles for Reflection

1. God takes the Sabbath very seriously because it is beneficial to us, his finite creatures. He set a pattern for us to set apart the Sabbath day as holy.

2. We can trust that God will provide, even when we take time off for rest and recreation. We don't have to rely on our own strength to make money and be productive. God will take care of us and our families when we step away from our labor on the Sabbath.

3. We can live differently from a culture in which people are working endlessly. The Sabbath is not a suggestion but a requirement for our well-being. So, heed God's instructions and trust that God keeps his promises as Yahweh-Yireh, the God who provides. Find ways to proactively rest and enjoy God's creation and the creative spirit he has placed in you.

---

11. Daniel Ross Goodman, "Jewish Praise of Truett Cathy: Chick-fil-A Founder and Sabbath Observer," *Public Discourse*, September 18, 2014, www.thepublicdiscourse.com/2014/09/13811, italics in original.

CHAPTER 17

WHAT IS THE CONSUMING FIRE OF GOD?

Deuteronomy 4:24; 9:3; Isaiah 33:14;

Lamentations 2:3; Hebrews 12:29

ERIC J. BARGERHUFF

In chapter 15, I reflected on the deaths of Nadab and Abihu, two sons of Aaron the high priest, who were judged by God for offering "unauthorized fire." The Bible tells us that "fire came out from the presence of the LORD and consumed them, and they died before the LORD" (Leviticus 10:2). This was certainly a judgment for disobedience.

Furthermore, fire came out from the presence of the Lord to consume an offering that Aaron had sacrificed, and the people responded with what was undoubtedly a mixed shout of terror and joy as they fell on their faces in worship (Leviticus 9:24).

So in this one section of Leviticus alone, we see the consuming fire of God—one on an offering as a sign of God's acceptance, and one on two disobedient sons as a sign of disapproval and judgment. The question, then, is whether the consuming fire of God is a good thing or a sign of judgment throughout Scripture? Our answer depends on one thing—*context*, which is one of the most obvious keys to proper interpretation.

The *Dictionary of Biblical Imagery* gives a helpful summary of the many ways fire was used by people throughout Scripture: "Fire . . . is the servant of human beings. It cooks their food (Ex 12:8; Is 44:15–16; Jn 21:9), makes them warm (Is 44:15; Jn 18:18) and gives them light to see (Is 50:11; Mt 25:1–13). It can be part of a manufacturing process (Gen. 11:3) and can refine metals (Is 1:25; Mal 3:2–3). It also burns refuse (Lev 8:17)."[1]

Fire was also used in warfare, as in the conquest of Canaan by Joshua, who burned Jericho to the ground. It was also a form of capital punishment prescribed by the Lord for abnormally depraved sins such as incest (Leviticus 20:14) or the prostitution of a daughter of a priest (21:9).[2]

As we see throughout Leviticus, fire was used in the context of worship for ceremonial purification, burnt offerings, and the burning of incense: "According to Leviticus 6:8–13, the fire on the altar of burnt offering should be ever burning: the priests must not allow it to go out. It is a sign of God's continual presence."[3]

In another sense, fire was connected with many of the temporary appearances of God on earth known as theophanies. Moses encountered Yahweh in a burning bush in Exodus 3 and later on Mount Sinai, where the Lord had descended the mountain in fire (19:18). These theophanies often brought great fear to those who encountered them.

When Samson's parents encountered a "man of God" in Judges

---

1. The usages and metaphors for fire summarized here are taken from Leland Ryken, James C. Wilhoit, and Tremper Longman III, eds., *Dictionary of Biblical Imagery* (IVP Academic, 1998), 286–89. This quote is found on page 286.
2. Fire also came upon Achan and his family as a form of capital punishment for their disobedience in stealing the "devoted things" that were under the ban during the conquest by Joshua (Joshua 7:15, 25).
3. *Dictionary of Biblical Imagery*, 287.

13 who was announcing that they would give birth to Samson, a child who would deliver Israel, they encountered none other than an angel of God, who in this context was God himself (a Christophany—a temporary appearance of a preincarnate Christ).

After Manoah and his wife received the news of the impending pregnancy, they wanted to dine with the incarnate angel, who declined their food but accepted their burnt offering. While the burnt offering took place, the flame went up toward heaven and the angel ascended in the flame. Falling on their faces, Manoah was afraid they would die because they had seen God. His wife said to him, "If the LORD had intended to kill us, he wouldn't have accepted the burnt offering and the grain offering from us, and he would not have shown us all these things or spoken to us like this" (Judges 13:23 CSB).

In addition to theophanies, angels themselves seem to be accompanied by fire. When Elisha opened the eyes of his servant in 2 Kings 6 to show him the protecting angels surrounding them, he was able to see "the hills full of horses and chariots of fire all around Elisha" (v. 17).

With all the references to fire throughout the Bible, though, the fire that comes from God is the subject of our inquiry. When fire comes down on a sacrifice of some type, it is usually a sign of approval, as was the case when Elijah offered a sacrifice to the Lord in his contest with the prophets of Baal on Mount Carmel (1 Kings 18:38; for other examples, see Leviticus 9:24; Judges 6:21).

Fire also came from God to lead the Israelites out of Egypt in a pillar of fire by night and a pillar of cloud by day (Exodus 13:21). The fire was there as a sign of God's presence and to guide them.

Fire was often used in a practical sense to refine metals, heating them until they melted and the impurities rose to the surface, where they were scraped off, leaving a liquid metal that then cooled into a purer form. This refiner's fire is also used to describe what God can do in his people (spiritually speaking) to cleanse and refine them to make them more holy. Malachi describes such a refiner's fire in the life of God's people:

> Who can endure the day of his coming? And who will be able to stand when he appears? For he will be like a refiner's fire and like launderer's bleach. He will be like a refiner and purifier of silver; he will purify the sons of Levi and refine them like gold and silver. Then they will present offerings to the LORD in righteousness. (3:2–3 CSB)

Similarly, the prophet Zechariah described Christ's second coming as a time when the Lord will cleanse and restore the hearts of his people Israel.[4] It will be like a fountain of cleansing (13:1) where idols and false prophets will be removed (v. 2), where two-thirds of the Israelites will ultimately perish due to unbelief (v. 8). And yet the remaining third will put their faith in Christ and will be restored, refined, and purified:

> In the whole land—
> > this is the LORD's declaration—
> two-thirds will be cut off and die,
> but a third will be left in it.
> I will put this third through the fire;
> I will refine them as silver is refined
> and test them as gold is tested.
> They will call on my name,
> and I will answer them.
> I will say, "They are my people,"
> and they will say, "The LORD is our God." (vv. 8–9 CSB)

---

4. Note that the text explicitly says that this fountain is for the "house of David" and the inhabitants of Jerusalem. Attempts to eclipse the narrative by seeking a spiritual fulfillment in the church alone stands in direct contrast to a literal, grammatical, historical hermeneutic in which Zechariah gives a specific prophetic promise to Israel to offer hope for their future.

This remnant of people will be saved because God will have poured "a spirit of grace" on them such that when they will look on "the one they have pierced, and they will mourn for him as one mourns for an only child, and grieve bitterly for him" (Zechariah 12:10). Finally, the book of Proverbs compares a refiner's fire to the way God seeks to test our hearts (17:3).

But there is an altogether different type of fire that falls on people, which is a fire of fierce judgment. It is the fury of God against sin (Isaiah 30:27), and it is often described as an all-consuming fire. In other words, it consumes and destroys. Nothing is left. Such fire fell upon the ancient cities of Sodom and Gomorrah, where burning sulfur fell from heaven, and God "demolished these cities, the entire plain, and all the inhabitants of the cities, and whatever grew on the ground" (Genesis 19:25 CSB).

We also see it in Numbers 16, where Korah incited a rebellion against Moses. The Lord opened a sinkhole to swallow corrupted families whose leaders had sinned against him, and fire came down to consume 250 leaders who had also rebelled. This all-consuming fire, along with a plague that killed 14,700 Israelites who complained against Moses, Aaron, and the Lord, makes it clear that it is not good when God's all-consuming fire falls on people.

The prophets are known for describing God's wrath as a consuming fire. Consider these profound judgments:

Concerning the Annihilation of the Assyrians

Look! The name of the LORD is coming from far away,
his anger burning and heavy with smoke.
His lips are full of fury,
and his tongue is like a consuming fire. (Isaiah 30:27 CSB)

A Pronouncement of Judgment in the End Times

Look, the LORD will come with fire—
his chariots are like the whirlwind—
to execute his anger with fury
and his rebuke with flames of fire. (Isaiah 66:15 CSB)

A Judgment Against Wicked Kings of Judah

It was uprooted in fury,
thrown to the ground,
and the east wind dried up its fruit.
Its strong branches were torn off and dried up;
fire consumed them. (Ezekiel 19:12 CSB)

Apostate Israelites Who Will Fear His Wrath

The sinners in Zion are afraid;
trembling seizes the ungodly:
"Who among us can dwell with a consuming fire?
Who among us can dwell with ever-burning flames?"
(Isaiah 33:14 CSB)

The Destruction of Israel's Enemies

"Understand that today the LORD your God will cross over ahead of
you as a consuming fire; he will devastate and subdue them before
you. You will drive them out and destroy them swiftly, as the LORD
has told you." (Deuteronomy 9:3 CSB)

A Warning to God's People and Call to Obedience

"Be careful not to forget the covenant of the LORD your God that
he made with you, and make an idol for yourselves in the shape of

anything he has forbidden you. For the LORD your God is a consuming fire, a jealous God." (Deuteronomy 4:23–24 CSB)

A Lament Toward God's People Heading into Exile

He has cut off every horn of Israel
in his burning anger
and withdrawn his right hand
in the presence of the enemy.
He has blazed against Jacob like a flaming fire
that consumes everything. (Lamentations 2:3 CSB)

In the New Testament, the writer of Hebrews warns the church that they should pursue peace and holiness, not immorality or irreverence. He mentions those from the Old Testament who did not escape God's wrath, even though they were warned. We are not to be like them, for we are a believing people who are "receiving a kingdom that cannot be shaken," and with thanksgiving we ought to "worship God acceptably with reverence and awe, for our 'God is a consuming fire'" (12:28–29).

With these texts in mind, we can safely conclude that the consuming fire does not apply to the true believer in Jesus Christ. The eschatological judgment of God that awaits those who persecute the church in the final days is described as God's "vengeance with flaming fire on those who don't know God and on those who don't obey the gospel of our Lord Jesus" (2 Thessalonians 1:8 CSB).

Why, then, do some Christian songwriters include the concept of consuming fire falling on *us* in some of their worship songs? The popular Christian music group Third Day wrote these words: "Yes, our God, He is a consuming fire. He reaches inside, and He melts down this cold heart of stone."[5] A quick online search will reveal sev-

---

5. Third Day, "Consuming Fire," track 7 on the album *Third Day*, Reunion, 1996.

eral other recognizable worship songs that use the phrase "consuming fire" or "all-consuming fire."

I believe the intent in writing songs like these is truly honorable. We want to be set apart for holiness and grow in righteousness while forsaking sin. But there seems to be a lack of theological clarity here and a clear confusion between the refiner's fire that purifies and transforms and the all-consuming fire of God's wrath that destroys.

I do not intend to ruin your favorite worship song or discredit the ministries of these songwriters. These are gospel-preaching ministries of our brothers and sisters. Yet I do want to call the church to a discerning, theologically informed, and exegetically sound approach to worship when it comes to the songs we sing in worship. This is one small example of an area where the church must do a better job of identifying worship songs that are me-centered (what I as an individual am doing), hyperexperiential, and theologically weak.

Our worship should be centered on God himself—who he is and what he has done, is doing, and will do. This is not to say we can never express in our worship songs who *we* are or what *we* are doing to love and obey him. I do not want to make any such sweeping statement. But I believe we tend to be out of balance when it comes to worship. Worship should be more about God and less about us, and we must make sure that what we are singing is sound.

Fire can be a beautiful thing (think of a fire in a fireplace). But it can be destructive as well. In Scripture, the concept of fire has multiple meanings and uses, depending on its context. It can light the way, cleanse and purify, or ultimately destroy, to name a few functions.

The adjectives that accompany the word *fire* are important. There is a big difference between a refiner's fire and a consuming fire of wrath. Therefore, I urge us to reflect theologically on what we sing and to focus on biblically derived lyrics and theology. As Paul aptly said to the church, "God did not appoint us to suffer wrath but to receive salvation through our Lord Jesus Christ" (1 Thessalonians 5:9).

Principles for Reflection

1. Fire throughout Scripture is seen in a variety of contexts—some beautiful, others disastrous. We would do well to understand how the Bible describes each reference to fire in its context.

2. Mistakes are often made when we extract a theme from the Bible's original context and use it in a way the author did not intend.

3. Many people first get their theology from what they sing rather than from what they learn in their study of Scripture. We would do well to reverse that order so our worship is theologically accurate, robust, and God-centered. When we do that, our worship songs will reflect sound doctrine.

PART IV: BIZARRE

How to Teach Weird Stories from the Bible

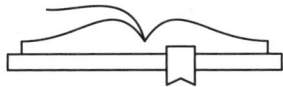

When reading weird Bible texts, we need to ask a crucial question: Why does this verse or passage seem so strange? Sometimes the weirdness of Scripture is simply the result of a different cultural context—because we are living in a different place and time. On other occasions, Scripture is bizarre because God's commands or ways are dramatically different from what we expect.

Teaching weird stories in Scripture helps us understand that we worship and serve a God whom we cannot conform to our own image. When God says go, we go. When God says stop, we stop. *Bizarre* does not have to mean "impossible" or "disposable." Rather, when we read peculiar texts, we should approach them like puzzles, seeking to fit the pieces together to learn why God chose to share these thoughts in his Word.

Whenever something or someone is bizarre, our tendency is to disengage or sidestep it or them altogether. Bizarre Bible texts are discipleship opportunities to address directly what God wants us to learn from him. Yes, to do so will take some discernment and perhaps even further study, but weirdness can serve as an opportunity for reflection. Ask yourself and your listeners, *Why is this weird, what makes it weird, and how can it be less weird?* Even the most bizarre Scripture texts can teach us things we need to learn and to live out in our lives.

CHAPTER 18

WHY DID ENOCH AVOID DEATH?

Genesis 5:21–24

ERIC J. BARGERHUFF

Anyone who knows some Bible trivia is aware that only two individuals never experienced death on earth. The most famous of them is the prophet Elijah, who according to 2 Kings 2 was whisked up to heaven in a whirlwind right before the eyes of his protégé and successor Elisha. His translation to heaven has been called a foreshadowing of the future rapture of the church as prophesied by the apostle Paul, who wrote that at some future point, the "dead in Christ" will be raised, and those who are alive will be "caught up" along with them to "meet the Lord in the air" (1 Thessalonians 4:16–17).[1]

Elijah never had to face death but entered glory as a transformed man who experienced immediate perfection and sanctification while relinquishing his earthly body as he stepped into the glories of heaven.

---

1. I believe it is best to interpret Paul to be describing literal events, since the whole context of 1 Thessalonians 4 is descriptive of literal events—the death and resurrection of Jesus (v. 14) and his future coming (v. 15).

He then took on some kind of heavenly, bodily form and appears again in the New Testament during the transfiguration of Jesus as recorded in Matthew 17, Mark 9, and Luke 9. Elijah has often been romanticized among the Jews as one of the most prestigious of prophets. He, along with the other pillar of the prophets, Moses, apparently discussed Jesus' future crucifixion (and likely resurrection and ascension) while up on the mountain.[2]

Elijah is not the only one to have never seen death. The other famous man "raptured" to heaven prematurely was a godly man named Enoch. We find him in the genealogy of Adam in Genesis 5 (prior to the flood), when human beings lived an unusually long time. In fact, Enoch's son, Methuselah, is said to have lived to the oldest age ever recorded in the Bible at 969 years.

But Enoch never had to face death. In a quick summary of his life in Genesis 5, we read, "Enoch was 65 years old when he fathered Methuselah. And after he fathered Methuselah, Enoch walked with God 300 years and fathered other sons and daughters. So Enoch's life lasted 365 years. Enoch walked with God; then he was not there because God took him" (vv. 21–24 CSB).

This Enoch is not the same Enoch we read about earlier in Genesis 4 (who was the son of Cain and the grandson of Adam). Rather, the New Testament book of Jude identifies him as being in the seventh generation from Adam (v. 14), and therefore from the line of Seth, a godly line of Adam's family tree.

Genesis tells us that after Enoch fathered Methuselah at age sixty-five, Enoch "walked with God" for three hundred more years. In other words, he had genuine saving faith in God, for his "walk," or

---

2. With Moses representing the Law and Elijah representing the Prophets, Luke's gospel says they were discussing Jesus' impending "departure" (Greek, *exodos*).

way of life, was pleasing to God and demonstrated a reverential fear for God and a love for righteousness. We know this, not only because the phrase "walked with God" in Genesis 5 implies it, but also because the New Testament provides more information about him. Enoch is one of the Old Testament saints privileged enough to be mentioned in the "Hall of Faith" chapter in Hebrews 11: "By faith Enoch was taken away, and so he did not experience death. He was not to be found because God took him away. For before he was taken away, he was approved as one who pleased God" (v. 5 CSB).

Enoch pleased God and was commended because of his faith. Genesis 5 says he walked with God, and "then he was not there because God took him." It wasn't as if he merely ran away and no one could find him, like some kind of alien abduction. He didn't fall into a sinkhole, never to be found again. Scripture confirms that God took him. This is not some euphemism for death. In fact, the Hebrews text states emphatically that he was taken by God in such a way that "he did not experience death."

Snatched away. Raptured to heaven, we might say. Nowhere to be found on earth any longer. To be sure, this was a supernatural event. In all of Scripture, only Elijah would share the same experience. But supernatural events happening in a supernatural book given to us by a supernatural God should not surprise us.

We are not told why God chose to do this. We are only told, "Then he was not there because God took him" (Genesis 5:24). However, when we turn again to the book of Jude, we learn even more about Enoch that can give us some grounds for conjecture.

Enoch is mentioned as someone who prophesied about the false teachers and apostate people of the present church age. Enoch would have understood apostasy well, since he lived in the years right before the flood when wickedness was running rampant and "every inclination of the human mind was nothing but evil all the time" (Genesis 6:5 CSB). Jude tells us that Enoch prophesied and preached about judgment:

It was about these [wicked people] that Enoch, in the seventh generation from Adam, prophesied: "Look! The Lord comes with tens of thousands of his holy ones to execute judgment on all and to convict all the ungodly concerning all the ungodly acts that they have done in an ungodly way, and concerning all the harsh things ungodly sinners have said against him." (vv. 14–15)

Jude quotes from a noncanonical, noninspired text known as the *1 Enoch*, a pseudepigraphal writing (a writing attributed falsely to an author to give it legitimacy). Christians do not regard this book to be inspired by the Holy Spirit—it is not Scripture—but according to D. A. Carson, apparently Jude "saw this text as preserving genuine prophecy" although "it does not necessarily imply that he thought all of *1 Enoch* was prophetic."[3] Therefore, since Jude, unlike the author of *1 Enoch*, was writing under the inspiration of the Holy Spirit, we can safely regard the section he quoted from *1 Enoch* to be accurate to what Enoch proclaimed in his day in Genesis 5.

The content of Enoch's prophecy is truly telling. With what many believe to be a view toward the second coming of Christ, Enoch prophesied that judgment would come to all who practice ungodliness. (In fact, he mentions the word *ungodly* four times.)

The Lord will execute judgment, something Enoch surely felt was imminent even in his day prior to the flood. But this judgment would not be merely floodwaters; the Lord himself, with his angelic hosts, would execute judgment on widespread ungodliness.[4] It is fascinating to consider that Enoch may have been the first human to foresee the reality of the second coming of Christ in judgment.

---

3. D. A. Carson, "Jude," in *Commentary on the New Testament Use of the Old Testament*, eds. G. K. Beale and D. A. Carson (Baker Academic, 2007), 1078. For other places where Enoch is mentioned in noncanonical books, see F. F. Bruce, *Hebrews*, rev. ed., New International Commentary on the New Testament (Eerdmans, 1990), 284–86.

4. Saints may accompany the Lord as well, since the word for "holy ones" can mean either angels or saints. But it is likely that the judgment will come from the Lord and his angels, since angels are often seen in biblical apocalyptic literature as those who will execute judgment.

Enoch prophesied about people who had no regard for God. We can safely surmise that in such an evil society, he would have faced opposition, since godliness naturally invites persecution from those who are evil (2 Timothy 3:12). Could it be that since Enoch was faithfully preaching and walking with God for so many years in such an evil world that God decided to reward him with a trip straight to heaven to avoid death at the hands of evil men? After all, right after the author of Hebrews mentions Enoch, the next verse reads, "Now without faith it is impossible to please God, since the one who draws near to him must believe that he exists and that he rewards those who seek him" (11:6 CSB).

Perhaps Enoch's translation to heaven was a unique way God chose to reward this man who had walked faithfully with him. While this is speculation, it's a rational one, with a couple principles worth noting: (1) God will come in judgment on the wicked, and (2) God is keenly aware of those who are his, who walk "by faith, not by sight" (2 Corinthians 5:7), who fellowship with God, who walk in his ways and please him. Since God has demonstrated that he has the will and capacity to spare at least two men from death (Elijah and Enoch), he will spare many others the same fate when he comes to rapture his church. Paul proclaimed as much in 1 Thessalonians 4:17.

So let us walk faithfully like Enoch, preaching the gospel of grace in our wicked world to any who have ears to hear as we long for the coming of the Lord, "who rescues us from the coming wrath" (1 Thessalonians 1:10). James Montgomery Boice pointed out, "Enoch was God's testimony to the fact that those who walk with God in this life will also walk with God in a better life hereafter, thanks to the future work of 'the Promised Seed.'"[5]

---

5. James Montgomery Boice, *Genesis: Creation and Fall (Genesis 1–11),* An Expositional Commentary (Baker, 1998), 289–90.

Principles for Reflection

1. The Bible asserts that there will be rewards for faithfulness (Matthew 25:21, 23) and that those who want to live godly lives will naturally face persecution and ridicule (2 Timothy 3:12). Though these rewards may be given only in the next life, faithful Christians will experience many spiritual blessings today as they walk in faith with a clean conscience before God.

2. Enoch's faithful life was talked about for generations afterward. The preacher/teacher would do well to press on the conscience of the listeners by asking what they will be known for after they are gone.

3. Readers should always seek out the full counsel of God when dealing with a particular person or topic. In this case, the New Testament witness in Hebrews 11 and Jude provides more insight into the Genesis 5 text and helps us avoid speculation about what Moses meant when he said simply that God took Enoch.

CHAPTER 19

WHY SHOULDN'T WE MIX FOOD, FASHION, OR FAITHFULNESS?

Leviticus 19:19

MATTHEW D. KIM

At times, the foreignness of the Bible is palpable to Western readers. We don't understand why certain topics are brought up together. This is often the case when we read Levitical laws. That's probably why, anecdotally speaking, Leviticus might be the number one most avoided biblical book, apart from perhaps Song of Songs or Revelation. What do we do with bizarre instructions?

For example, wisdom on how to approach farming and fashion design is not traditionally given in tandem in our world. This peculiar text in Leviticus 19:19 reads, "You shall keep my statutes. You shall not let your cattle breed with a different kind. You shall not sow your field with two kinds of seed, nor shall you wear a garment of cloth made of two kinds of material" (ESV). The act of mixing two different kinds of things seems to be forbidden in the economy of God, particularly in Old Testament texts.

In Leviticus 19, Moses expands on the law by declaring God's command of obedience and holiness. The Lord says to Moses, "Speak to the entire assembly of Israel and say to them: 'Be holy because I, the LORD your God, am holy'" (v. 2). Jesus repeats this statement in his Sermon on the Mount with slightly different wording: "Be perfect, therefore, as your heavenly Father is perfect" (Matthew 5:48).

Many of the details of expected obedience of God's people mirror the Ten Commandments, with variations and addendums. In other words, God expands the instructions on a deeper level. A contextual reading suggests that what God seeks of his people is obedience in treating others as we want to be treated (aka, the Golden Rule), and holiness so as to remain pure. In fact, the key verse that summarizes this chapter can be found in Leviticus 19:18: "Do not seek revenge or bear a grudge against anyone among your people, but love your neighbor as yourself. I am the LORD."

Keeping God's decrees is central to the teachings God gave Israel. The three specific instructions or commands in this text concern breeding cattle, sowing seeds, and using two or more materials for clothing. Before we go further, however, it's relevant to point out that these three instructions begin with an overarching command: "You shall keep my statutes." In God's sovereignty, these three instructions, while strange to us, are significant to the Lord. The issue is elaborated on in the rabbinic literature many times, informing the Israelites of God's prohibition against mixing in three major areas of life.[1]

The first is, "You shall not let your cattle breed with a different kind [*kilayim*]." An uncommon Hebrew word in the Torah, *kilayim* was used only in prohibitions.[2] The word *kind* can be interpreted,

---

1. See Dov Bloom, "What Is Kilayim? The Torah Prohibition Against Mixing Seeds or Species," Chabad-Lubavitch, accessed March 12, 2025, www.chabad.org/library/article _cdo/aid/3570273/jewish/What-Is-Kilayim.htm.
2. Bloom, "What Is Kilayim?"

not as intracattle breeding, per se, but rather interanimal breeding. "The Hebrew word here for 'kind' (*kilayim*) is not the same as that used in Genesis 1 for a created 'kind' (*min*)."[3] Thus, "the word 'kind' in Leviticus 19:19 would loosely correlate with 'types' or 'varieties' (which could cover different breeds or species)."[4] Whether this teaching is commenting on intra-animal breeding or interanimal breeding, clearly the mixing of animals is not allowed. Lashing was the punishment for those who mixed animals.[5] Commentator Arie Noordtzij suggests that because each plant or animal has its own "life principle," plants and animals were not to be mixed.[6]

The second prohibition is, "You shall not sow your field with two kinds of seed." Common logic would say the reason for this command is that future harvesting could be a challenge in separating out the two different kinds of vegetation. But is there more? Modern gardeners, like Madeline Buiano, inform us that certain seeds should never be planted next to each other, including, for example, beans and onions, tomatoes and potatoes, and lettuce and celery. Why? It can, Buiano says, "cause stunted growth, welcome pests, and change flavor."[7]

The third prohibition addresses mixing fabrics: "Nor shall you wear a garment of cloth made of two kinds of material." Benjamin Noonan explains that the Hebrew word here is "a lexical blend" where two Semitic words combine to form a new word, those being "ewe" (*ta'at*) and "goat" (*'anz/'inz*) and "originally referred to a mixture of sheep and goat wool but was subsequently generalized to designate

---

3. Karina Altman and Troy Lacey, "Does the Bible Forbid Animal Hybridization?," Answers in Genesis, August 5, 2022, https://answersingenesis.org/hybrid-animals/does-bible-forbid-animal-hybridization/.

4. Joel Tay, "Does Leviticus 19:19 Prohibit the Cross-Breeding of Horses and Donkeys?," Creation.com, updated January 29, 2022, https://creation.com/leviticus-19-19-horses-donkeys.

5. Maimonides, "Kilaayim: Chapter 9," Chabad-Lubavitch, accessed March 12, 2025, www.chabad.org/library/article_cdo/aid/986698/jewish/Kilaayim-Chapter-9.htm.

6. A. Noordtzij, *Leviticus*, Bible Student's Commentary (Zondervan, 1982), 201.

7. Madeline Buiano, "16 Vegetables You Should Never Plant Together: Gardening Experts Explain Why," Martha Stewart, updated May 5, 2025, www.marthastewart.com/vegetables-to-never-plant-together-8425391.

any mixed fabric, which is precisely what זנטעש [sha'atnez] means in Lev 19:19 and Deut 22:11."[8] In modern terms, we might think of a lexical blend as a hybrid word or a fusion of two different words, such as in English, where *guestimate* fuses "guess" and "estimate."[9]

What, then, is the interpretive and contextual significance of this lexical blend in Leviticus 19:19? Does this instruction follow in the succession of holiness codes, or is something else going on? Jason DeRouchie categorizes Leviticus 19:19 and Deuteronomy 22:9–11 into "distinctions from the pagan nations."[10] Some, like Nicholas Campbell, make the case that God's commands about fabric have nothing to do with holiness but rather "that mixed garments were reserved for the special social class of Levites."[11]

What do we make of these three commands? According to allegorical lore, a common interpretation maintained that since creation God has frowned on mixing and desired separation in the created order. We see a trend in creation in which God separates and ultimately creates two different kinds of humans—male and female in his image. "The problem," Nicholas Campbell reports "with this interpretation is mixing fabric does not create a hybrid. The elements remain separate even if they are next to each other."[12]

Some scholars connect this verse to the created order: "*Do not mate . . . plant . . . wear.* Such mixing symbolically violated the distinction God established in the creation order."[13] Others have misused similar texts to universalize the prohibition of mixing races and intermarriage. As twenty-first-century Christians, we recognize that God

---

8. Benjamin J. Noonan, "Unraveling Hebrew," *Journal of Biblical Literature* 135, no. 1 (Spring 2016): 95, www.jstor.org/stable/10.15699/jbibllite.135.issue-1.

9. Noonan, "Unraveling Hebrew," 98.

10. Jason S. DeRouchie, *How to Understand and Apply the Old Testament: Twelve Steps from Exegesis to Theology* (P&R, 2017), 55.

11. Nicholas J. Campbell, "Prohibited Mixtures: Mixed Clothing and Social Class," *Zeitschrift für die Alttestamentliche Wissenschaft* 134, no. 3 (September 2022): 303.

12. Campbell, "Prohibited Mixtures," 305.

13. Kenneth L. Barker, ed., *NIV Study Bible* (Zondervan, 2011), note on Leviticus 19:19, p. 184.

prevented intermarriage between Jews and Gentiles because of the pagan religions and practices of Gentiles.

What, then, is a more faithful reading of this text? First, the short of it is that since God prohibited mixing according to his sovereignty and foreknowledge, we must obey. End of story. However, the larger context may give us clues; for example, commentator James King West wrote, "Leviticus 19 has been called the highest development of ethics in the Old Testament."[14] Melinda Thompson explains God's high expectations for his people to live a holy existence. They were to be holy, commonly translated as "set apart" or "different" from their pagan neighbors.[15] One of the central ways God wanted his people to be holy, or set apart, is seen in the way they treated one another. God wanted every part of their lives to be unmixed, or different, from others. Mixing corrupts or taints animals, plants, and clothing.

What do we do now? The holiness code in Leviticus 19 in many ways provides an umbrella for modern readers. While we may not be overly concerned about agriculture or fashion trends, God has a biblical ethic for how we are to live daily. I don't believe there is a literal application for New Testament Christians in this verse. For Christians today, I don't believe God is restricting a literal mixing of animals/cattle, seeds/plants, and fabrics/clothing.

Synthetics are elements that have been synthesized or even syncretized. Both have the prefix *syn*, meaning "with" or "together." Synthesizing and syncretizing does away with a pure version. Consider Paul's warning to the Corinthians against syncretism: "Do not be yoked together with unbelievers. For what do righteousness and wickedness have in common? . . . For we are the temple of the living God" (2 Corinthians 6:14, 16).[16] Our quest for holiness is not

---

14. James King West, *Introduction to the Old Testament* (Macmillan, 1971), 156.
15. Melinda Thompson, "Reading Leviticus 19: Issues for Interpretations," *Restoration Quarterly* 57, no. 2 (2015): 96.
16. Rebecca McLaughlin makes this connection in *No Greater Love: A Biblical Vision for Friendship* (Moody, 2023), 137.

self-serving, self-justifying, or self-referential at all. Rather, we are called to be different as we point people to Jesus.

As Rebecca McLaughlin urges, "If you, like me, are a Christian, we should be completely clear that we will only worship the one true Creator God, revealed in Jesus Christ. At the same time, we should be willing to set aside our own cultural preferences to come alongside the nonbelievers in our neighborhoods, schools, workplaces, and families. We're not called to blend in or to check out, but to shine."[17]

Our Christian witness accompanies a commitment to our Christian doctrines. Future generations will not tolerate an insincere or stagnant faith that refuses to reach out to help others. In our hyperindividualistic culture, it goes against the grain to respond to the communal call to care for our neighbor as ourselves. We have difficulty caring for our immediate family members. Why would we bother to show care and hospitality to a stranger?

One way of "not mixing" is to lead the charge in caring for our communities. Too often we have forsaken the commandment to love our neighbor as ourselves and watched as nonbelievers, God's image bearers, care for other human beings simply because they know it's the right thing to do. The ability of Christians not to mix manifests itself in accepting the charge to be holy and thus join God in the work of social justice, care, and action.

J. W. Buck writes, "Jesus mobilized ordinary people to do God's work of justice in the world."[18] The words *activism, justice,* and *action* make some Christians feel uncomfortable. Rather than getting stuck in the semantics, let's rally around the concept that God seeks partners who serve as his hands and feet in a hurting world. Kingdom work requires the pursuit of holiness—a holiness that expands as a result of intentional discipleship and obedience to God's commands.

As we read texts like Leviticus 19:19, let us not conclude that this

---

17. McLaughlin, *No Greater Love,* 139.
18. J. W. Buck, *Everyday Activism: Following 7 Practices of Jesus to Create a Just World* (Baker, 2022), 25.

teaching on "not mixing" is an outdated Israelite ethic. Instead, may we receive it as a God-given charge to Christians to live different lives than nonbelievers. We can and should be difference makers in every facet of our lives, reflected in our unwavering obedience to God.

Principles for Reflection

1. Mixing substances of different kinds pollutes and dilutes what are ultimately created things. God's mandate not to mix substances is a call to be wholly different from the world. It's a command to remain pure and holy.

2. This teaching reminds us of the many gray areas in our lives that were originally black-and-white in nature. That is, through our disobedience, we have synthesized and syncretized the sacred and the profane.

3. God's charge to refrain from mixing applies to every command in Scripture where he calls his people to be set apart for him. Being the people of God means we will not dabble with ungodly things and be led astray. Each person will have areas in which they are tempted to disregard God's teaching. In our preaching/teaching of this text, we can call attention to various common struggles.

CHAPTER 20

What Does Eating Scrolls Have to Do with Proclaiming Truth?

Ezekiel 2:9–3:3

MATTHEW D. KIM

Though I committed my life to Christ at age thirteen, I always struggled with the idea of becoming an overseas missionary. Granted, not all Christians are called to such a ministry. However, my reasoning was superficial. I'm not the most adventurous eater. Some might say I have a spiritual malady of pickiness. Although I've expanded the horizons of my palate, it still isn't open to sampling the plethora of spices from around the world. I like what I like. Maybe you're the same way.

Given my selective taste buds, I wouldn't have done well to be the main character here—the prophet Ezekiel. The wider setting of this passage is the calling narrative of Ezekiel found in chapter 2. After we see that Ezekiel is ministering among a rebellious people in exilic Babylon, God changes his palate to enjoy eating scrolls.

In Daniel 1, the prophet and his three friends chose to discipline their taste buds and not eat the fine fare on the king's table. They chose to eat vegetables, and not the gourmet dishes from the king's kitchen. God honored Daniel and his friends for putting him first.

When God calls a person, he sometimes asks them to do bizarre things. Here is such a command. Why would God instruct Ezekiel to eat a scroll—a thinly rolled piece of animal skin with words of wisdom etched on both sides? Is this literal or figural in its meaning? What does that do for Ezekiel and for his missional assignment from God?

Brent Waters shares, "In our common callings and vocations, through which we love and serve our neighbors, we catch a glimpse of what a good life entails. Most importantly, it requires decentering ourselves."[1] He continues, "The admission 'I am *not* the center of the universe' seems obvious. The universe is vast, and assuming that it revolves around oneself is the height of folly. Nonetheless, we often act as if it does."[2]

Let's try to make sense of what's taking place. First, and most peculiar, what is the purpose of eating a scroll? As far as I know, the only other Bible person who eats a scroll is the apostle John, the author of Revelation. It's clear that the purpose of Ezekiel's eating of the scroll is related to the message that is to be prophetically shared with God's people—a message of mourning and lamentation. To prepare Ezekiel for this proclamation, it was necessary to eat the message. Meredith J. C. Warren provides helpful background here: "Hierophagy is the word I chose to describe this genre of transformational eating. . . . Hierophagy results in three specific types of transformations: (A) the binding of the eater to the place of origin of the food; (B) the transformation of the eater either in terms of

---

1. Brent Waters, *Common Callings and Ordinary Virtues: Christian Ethics for Everyday Life* (Baker Academic, 2022), 28.
2. Waters, *Common Callings*, 29, italics in original.

behaviour or physical appearance; and/or (C) the transmission of new knowledge."[3]

In life, God's people are called to serve him in various roles. Calling moments in the Bible can seem like a higher-than-thou experience, such as Moses' burning bush (Exodus 3) or Saul's encounter with the living Christ on the road to Damascus (Acts 9). For ordinary folks, the calling seems rather mundane and less sensational.

It is evident that God can call on whomever he pleases and ask them to prepare themselves in whatever fashion he wants. For example, the ministry of Jesus begins in the wilderness. Jesus' forty days of fasting physically and prayerfully is necessary preparation for launching his earthly ministry. In the same way, it could be said that Ezekiel's call to bring a message of repentance to his people required him to eat the scroll that contained words of judgment and mourning.

We learn from Ezekiel's encounter with the Lord that "Ezekiel must ingest the Lord's message that he is commissioned to bring to the exiles, so that it becomes, as it were, a very part of his being."[4] In *Eat This Book*, Eugene Peterson considers the metaphor of eating a book as "reading words rightly."[5] Peterson's use of the imagery of eating has a deeper purpose: "What I want to call attention to is that the Bible, all of it, is *livable*; it is the text for living our lives. . . . Eating a book takes it all in, assimilating it into the tissues of our lives. Readers become what they read. If Holy Scripture is to be something other than mere gossip about God, it must be internalized."[6]

Is eating a book, or eating a scroll, then, akin to swallowing, digesting, and receiving spiritual nourishment from God's Word?

---

3. Meredith J. C. Warren, "Food and Transformation in Ancient Mediterranean Literature," *Ancient Jew Review*, September 18, 2019, www.ancientjewreview.com/read/2019/9/18/publications-.

4. Kenneth L. Barker, ed., *NIV Study Bible* (Zondervan, 2011), note on Ezekiel 3:1, p. 1343.

5. Eugene H. Peterson, *Eat This Book: A Conversation in the Art of Spiritual Reading* (Eerdmans, 2009), 9.

6. Peterson, *Eat This Book*, 18, 20, italics in original.

Is that the proper way to interpret and apply this text for all New Testament believers? Is there more?

The act of eating the scroll appears to have direct connection to God's message preached through the prophet Ezekiel. The order of instructions is straightforward:

> "Son of man, eat what is before you, eat this scroll; then go and speak to the people of Israel." . . .
>
> Then he said to me, "Son of man, eat this scroll I am giving you and fill your stomach with it." So I ate it, and it tasted as sweet as honey in my mouth.
>
> He then said to me, "Son of man, go now to the people of Israel and speak my words to them. . . . But the people of Israel are not willing to listen to you because they are not willing to listen to me, for all the Israelites are hardened and obstinate." (Ezekiel 3:1, 3–4, 7)

These are God's commands to Ezekiel: eat, go, speak, eat, fill your stomach, go to Israel, and speak my words to them (knowing full well they won't listen). By consuming God's words in the form of these scrolls and lining his stomach with them, Ezekiel has God's words literally filling his body and soul to embolden him to speak a difficult word to a difficult people.

When you were a child, you probably took a stick of gum lined with paper and began to chew it. When the paper sticks to the gum, it eventually stands out in your mouth as a taste different from the chewing gum. Paper doesn't taste great. But the scroll (most likely animal hide) tasted sweet to Ezekiel, so sweet that it tasted like honey on his tongue.

The relationship between partaking of the scroll and the Word of God is clear. The scroll somehow represents God's Word literally and figuratively in terms of consumption. Most of us don't have a strong theology of the Word. God makes himself known through his Word.

J. T. English and Jen Wilkin explain, "We do not discover God. We don't stumble across Him or search Him out, but rather, He makes Himself known. He reveals Himself to us. We cannot know God unless He gives Himself to us in revelation."[7] By eating God's Word literally and figuratively, Ezekiel received God's revelation in practical and theoretical ways unexperienced by the Israelites in the exile. He tasted with his mouth and experienced in his heart the Word of the Lord in a novel, life-altering way never known by human flesh. His body and soul connected with the living Word.

Normally, we read God's Word with the sense of sight or perhaps the sense of hearing (listening to audio Bibles, for example). By eating the scroll, we approach God's Word with a different sense—the sense of taste. "Taste and see that the LORD is good," wrote the psalmist (Psalm 34:8). Some have said that the Bible's difficulty comes not so much in understanding it as in obeying it. Ezekiel's experience is clearly unique and only something he and the apostle John in Revelation are asked by God to do. If this esoteric, "eat this scroll" instruction is limited to the experience of two people in history, what does it have to do with us today?

One clear application may concern the simple act of obedience to anything and everything that God commands of his people. Ezekiel could have responded, "I'm not doing that. That's gross! I don't eat scrolls." There was no hesitation in Ezekiel's response to God's command to do something peculiar as his messenger. How often do we draw back when prompted by the Spirit to do something illogical or strange? We easily dismiss God's Word and give ourselves options for disobedience. We come up with any number of excuses not to say yes to God's Word. So Ezekiel is a positive example of simply doing what God commands. When we sense the Spirit telling us to do something, it's in our best interest to obey.

---

7.   J. T. English and Jen Wilkin, *You Are a Theologian: An Invitation to Know and Love God Well* (B&H, 2023), 65.

Second, on a more figurative level, Ezekiel found the words of God sweeter than anything this world had to offer. Jesus said, "Heaven and earth will pass away, but my words will never pass away" (Matthew 24:35). For the psalmist, the words of the Lord were sweeter than honey to his mouth (Psalm 119:103). The sad reality for many believers is that we fail to read and ingest the living Word. Many professing Christians don't read the Bible regularly, or ever.

May Ezekiel's vision call us to repentance and rededication to reading and eating the scroll—for sustenance and for life. Just as our stomachs crave sustenance, we ask the Spirit to give us the same hunger for God's Word. And God will give us the confidence to be proclaimers of his truth, no matter who we are and what message he calls us to share with others.

Principles for Reflection

1. God sometimes asks strange things of his people. Ezekiel's task to "eat this scroll" is a perfect example of an act of God that makes no sense to our finite minds. The question is whether we will still obey him and do as he says. By eating the scroll, Ezekiel experienced the power of God's Word in transformative ways that enabled him to lead the people of God in fresh and powerful ways.

2. God's Word is something many Christians today (including me) tend to take for granted. God can empower us to ingest his Word daily and allow it to become something sweet and savory on our tongues, which is a metaphor for our lives.

3. How are we doing with eating God's Word and delighting

in it? Are we starving from a lack of enjoyment of God's Word? Are we malnourished and leading others to similar starvation? Ezekiel's vision is a stark reminder that more than any earthly, temporal pleasure, only the delight of God's Word lasts forever.

CHAPTER 21

WHAT IS THE "BAPTISM FOR THE DEAD"?

1 Corinthians 15:29

ERIC J. BARGERHUFF

Occasionally the avid reader of Scripture will stumble across an idea or narrative that causes them to wonder, *What in the world is that?* What they read doesn't seem to fit any other theology they've learned from Scripture, and it causes them concern. These difficult passages are ripe for misinterpretation or even abuse from false teachers who wish to lead others astray from the truth that we are saved by grace through faith alone in the perfect life, sacrificial death, and subsequent resurrection of Jesus Christ from the dead.

Such is the case when we encounter Paul's discussion of the essential truths surrounding the resurrection of Jesus and its implications in 1 Corinthians 15. Paul is combating here some of the Greek philosophies or perhaps even the teaching of the Sadducees who erroneously taught that there was no resurrection of the dead, even though it was clearly taught by Jesus (Matthew 23:29–33;

Luke 20:34–37) and plainly alluded to in the Old Testament (Isaiah 26:19; 53:10; Daniel 12:2).

Even the Jews of Jesus' day understood there would be a resurrection of the dead, as Martha asserted about Lazarus, "I know he will rise again in the resurrection at the last day" (John 11:24).

The Greek dualistic philosophies popular around Corinth taught that all matter was evil and only the soul had the potential for good. They even denied that God could become human, and the apostles clearly saw this teaching as a threat (1 John 4:1–3), warning the church against it.

The Greek philosophers interpreted the idea of a new embodiment of the soul in the form of a resurrection as a preposterous thought, since death had released the eternal soul from the wicked body (Acts 17:32). This belief system later became known as Gnosticism.

It is amazing to consider that this line of thinking appeared to have slipped into the church, since a Christian is someone who believes in Jesus' resurrection from the dead. Paul was clearly dumbfounded by it too: "But if it is preached that Christ has been raised from the dead, how can some of you say that there is no resurrection of the dead?" (1 Corinthians 15:12).

Maybe they thought Jesus was raised but believers would not be. This made no sense to Paul, so throughout 1 Corinthians 15, he defended the biblical and apostolic teaching of the resurrection of the dead (notably Christ's) as essential to the gospel and our own faith and future hope as believers. Paul argues that Christ's resurrection guarantees our future resurrection as well. Otherwise, Paul said, what's the point? If there is no resurrection from the dead, then "let us eat and drink, for tomorrow we die" (v. 32).[1]

Now in this larger context, we come across a statement by Paul that on the surface should cause considerable head-scratching: "Now

---

1. As if to say, *We may as well live it up now if this is all we will experience in the body and there is no bodily form of life in the life to come*—an allusion to the exact saying in Isaiah 22:13.

if there is no resurrection, what will those do who are baptized for the dead? If the dead are not raised at all, why are people baptized for them?" (1 Corinthians 15:29).

Baptized for the dead? What could Paul possibly mean here? What spiritual advantage would there be for being baptized (as a proxy) on behalf of someone else in any sense, and even more so if they are dead? None whatsoever.

Since we use the Bible to interpret the Bible, and we believe the Bible is inspired by God, is without error, and does not contradict itself, we can make some assertions and clearly postulate what this passage is *not* teaching. In other words, we know what Paul does not mean.

First, he does not mean there is any saving value to baptism, since we are clearly taught in Scripture that we are saved by grace through faith and not by any works (Ephesians 2:8–9).[2] Baptismal regeneration is not biblical.[3] Further, he is not suggesting that the spiritual activity or works of a believer in the present could have spiritual benefits for or blessings on someone else who has already died, believer or otherwise.[4] The Bible teaches that "people are destined to die once, and after that to face judgment" (Hebrews 9:27). There are no second chances after death, and no one who is currently alive can change the spiritual position of someone who has already died.[5]

---

2. Baptism is an outward, public symbol of our identification with Christ and the cleansing that comes from our faith in his life, death, and resurrection.

3. For more on the unbiblical notion that we are saved by baptism, see my book *The Most Misused Verses in the Bible* (Bethany House, 2012), 133–38.

4. Contra the Mormon church, which believes we have a second chance to be saved after death and that proxy baptisms give those who have died in the afterlife the opportunity to accept or reject them and thus be saved by the work of the ordinance on their behalf (provided ordinances could save someone, which they cannot). For more on the teaching of the Mormon church on this topic, see "About Proxy Baptism and Confirmation," accessed March 14, 2025, www.churchofjesuschrist.org/temples/what-is-proxy-baptism?lang=eng.

5. This fact would refute the doctrine of purgatory as well, a heretical doctrine of Roman Catholicism that believes in an intermediary place where the dead go and suffer penitently for remaining sins to make them more suitable for salvation. Those alive can shorten their loved one's time in purgatory through prayers and the acquisition and purchase of indulgences offered by the church. This has no basis in Scripture whatsoever and undermines the

That's all well and good. It's good to emphatically state what Paul does *not* mean. No one is saved through water baptism, and the spiritual activities of a living person have no direct consequence on someone who is dead. But the question still looms large: *What* does *it mean then?* Were there actually people being baptized in hopes of influencing people who had already died? (Even if there had been, Paul would be *describing* the practice and not *prescribing* the practice for all the reasons just mentioned.) Commentator Gordon Fee wrote the following:

> There is no historical or biblical precedent for such baptism. The NT is otherwise completely silent about it; there is no known practice in any other churches nor in any orthodox Christian community in the centuries that immediately follow; nor are there parallels or precedents in pagan religion. This is a genuinely idiosyncratic historical phenomenon. For that reason, if in fact some were actually practicing such a baptism, we are left quite in the dark in all the essential questions: (a) *Who* was being baptized? (b) *For whom?* (c) *Why* were they doing it? And (d) *What effects* did they think it had for those for whom it was being done? It is quite impossible to give a definitive answer to any of these.[6]

---

sufficiency of Christ's substitutionary atonement for sin, thus rendering the cross ineffective. The Catechism of the Catholic Church states the following: "All who die in God's grace and friendship, but still imperfectly purified, are indeed assured of their eternal salvation; but after death they undergo purification, so as to achieve the holiness necessary to enter the joy of heaven. . . . The Church formulated her doctrine of faith on Purgatory especially at the Councils of Florence and Trent" (Catechism 1030–1031), accessed March 14, 2025, www .vatican.va/content/catechism/en/part_one/section_two/chapter_three/article_12/iii _the_final_purification,_or_purgatory.html. This concept of purgatory led to the unbiblical Catholic doctrine of prayers for the dead (Catechism 1032). Catholic believers are taught that "it is a holy and a wholesome thought to pray for the dead that they may be loosed from their sins" (Catechism 958), accessed March 14, 2025, www.vatican.va/content/catechism /en/part_one/section_two/chapter_three/article_9/paragraph_5_the_communion_of _saints.index.html.

6. Gordon D. Fee, *The First Epistle to the Corinthians*, rev. ed., New International Commentary on the New Testament (Eerdmans, 2014), 846–47.

So let's assume for a minute that this baptism was what they were doing. Why, then, wouldn't Paul emphatically rebuke them? Well, for starters, it would likely be because he didn't feel a rebuke was necessary since it was such an absurd notion. Assuming the absurdity, could Paul be saying that even such a strange notion would be meaningless if the dead in fact are not raised? It's possible but still too difficult to know for sure.

No shortage of ink has been spilled and conjecture made about what this passage teaches, and the preacher/teacher must acknowledge that. It would be disingenuous to simply brush over it and try to give a simple answer to the listener who is looking for answers.[7] So the teacher must model humility while making clear that any interpretation that contradicts other known and widely accepted theological truths is not an option.

When it comes to questions people ask, we sometimes have to reply, "I don't know." We can do our best to provide answers, but there are times when we simply can't. Some things in life are left within the counsel and wisdom of God. In our 1 Corinthians 15 passage, there is much to wonder about. But perhaps a preferred way to look at this is offered by G. G. Findlay in the *Greek Expositor's Commentary*:

> [Paul] is referring . . . to a much commoner, indeed a normal experience, that the death of Christians leads to the conversion of survivors, who in the first instance "for the sake of the dead" (their beloved dead), and in the hope of reunion, turn to Christ—e.g., when a dying mother wins her son by appeal, "Meet me in heaven!" Such appeals, and their frequent salutary effect, give strong and touching evidence of *faith in the resurrection*. . . . Paul designates

---

7. For a thorough discussion on the competing views and their strengths and weaknesses, see Anthony Thiselton's helpful summary in *The First Epistle to the Corinthians*, New International Greek Testament Commentary (Eerdmans, 2000), 1240–49.

such converts "baptised (sic) for the dead," since baptism seals the new believer and commits him to the Christian life.[8]

This interpretation makes the most sense and is the least problematic. The testimonies of Christians who have died can have a dynamic impact on those left behind, perhaps even leading them to Christ as well. As they testify to their already professed faith through water baptism, it communicates the idea that they, too, embrace the hope of the resurrection from the dead, the same kind of hope those faithful Christians who died before them had. In this sense you could say they were "baptized for the dead."

You never know the influence your faithful life to Christ will have on others. And if my faithful life causes someone to seek Christ long after I'm gone, then glory be to God! In Hebrews 11, the writer told us to consider the "great cloud of witnesses" so as to imitate their faith. And we do so, knowing there will be a reunion with them in the life to come.

When King David's baby died in 2 Samuel 12:23, David said, "Now that he is dead, why should I go on fasting? Can I bring him back again? I will go to him, but he will not return to me." David's hope was for a reunion. The apostle Paul suggested the same thing in 1 Corinthians 15:29. People are being baptized who have come to faith due to the influence of believers who have already died. In following Christ like their forefathers did, these new believers will be granted eternal life through faith and a subsequent resurrection from the dead.

---

8. G. G. Findlay, *The Expositor's Greek Testament*, vol. 2, ed. W. Robertson Nicoll (Eerdmans, 1951), 931, italics in original. Thiselton concurs and references Findlay in his commentary referred to in the previous footnote (p. 1248). The idea that baptism "seals" the believer must be understood not in a theological sense but rather in a social sense.

Principles for Reflection

1. Use Scripture to interpret Scripture. In this case, this principle helps us decide what a passage *does not mean.*

2. We don't always have a clear background for every cultural practice we find in the Bible. In those cases, we cannot speak emphatically about passages that are obscure to us today. Don't be afraid to exercise humility and simply say, "I don't know for sure, but here is a potential answer that is the least problematic."

3. Resurrection from the dead is a key aspect of the gospel that provides hope for our glorious future. Water baptism is a testimony to that fact, since we were raised with Christ spiritually in our conversion and will be raised up to Christ physically at his second coming. To be baptized for the dead vicariously is not a practice seen anywhere else in the Bible or in Christian tradition. Paul may be saying that even those who are carrying out a practice that has no effect at least believe in the symbol of baptism and the hope of resurrection associated with it. Or he may be saying that the testimony of Christians who have gone before them has an impact on people who are currently being saved, and since they longed for a reunion and shared in the hope of the resurrection, they were also being baptized. It would be like saying, "I believe what you believed, Grandma, and I'm doing this for you because it's the right thing to do."

CHAPTER 22

CAN WE EXPERIENCE THE THIRD HEAVEN LIKE PAUL?

2 Corinthians 12:1–6

ERIC J. BARGERHUFF

A t the end of Ecclesiastes, King Solomon says, "My son, be warned: there is no end to the making of many books" (12:12 CSB). He tells us that the sayings of the wise come from one Shepherd—namely, God (v. 11). Our source of truth lies in the revealed Word of God, not in the experience of human beings. Solomon's warning is not that we should never read or write new books, but that we can easily be caught up in the thoughts of other people and the ideas found in books more than the things of God.

Over the past several decades, the Christian marketplace has been flooded with books about near-death experiences, trips to heaven and back, and dreams and visions of the afterlife. Each one is full of the unsubstantiated experiences of people from all walks of life—from children to the elderly, neurosurgeons to hospice nurses, grade-schoolers to pastors, you name it. Countless books have been sold to people with an appetite for mystical, speculative, fanciful, and unbiblical experiences of heaven.

All you need is someone to say they had a "supernatural experience" of heaven of some type, write it down with all sorts of glowing details, add a few scriptural proof texts ripped out of their original context to back it up, and you are more than likely to have a bestseller that peddles ideas the Bible does not hold to or say is true. But in an effort to make these tales more believable, many of them add some mixture of biblical truth to convince the vulnerable reader of their absolute truthfulness.[1]

In his blistering review and rebuttal of the bestselling book *Heaven Is for Real* by Todd Burpo, Pastor John MacArthur clearly identifies the dangers that plague this type of fictional genre of books:

> I've given this prolonged critique of *Heaven Is for Real* not because it is the worst of the genre, but because of all the books in this category, it is most likely to be read and deemed harmless by the typical evangelical. It is *not* harmless. It denigrates the authority and sufficiency of Scripture; it confounds faith with superstition; it subtly elevates human experience to a higher level than the Word of God; it purports to reveal things about God and the heavenly realm that are not in Scripture; and it repeatedly insinuates that the testimony of someone who has been mystically enlightened can be a more effective stimulant to faith than Scripture alone.[2]

One might say that evangelicalism has been infiltrated with the dangers of modern-day subjective experientialism, where experiences have risen above the truth of Scripture as authoritative for life and practice. There is no doubt that experiences are a part of the normal Christian life. God shapes us profoundly through relationships, acts

---

1. One of the more poignant biblical rebukes of the modern trips-to-heaven genre comes from David Platt, who identifies several of the most popular "heaven books" and refutes their credibility with Scripture. See David Platt, "Heaven Is for Real," YouTube, April 25, 2014, www .youtube.com/watch?v=10pG_L48l9E.
2. John F. MacArthur, *The Glory of Heaven: The Truth About Heaven, Angels, and Eternal Life* (Crossway, 2013), 48.

of service, times of travel, worship in a community, seasons of prayer, set times of biblical study, and so forth. We cannot avoid subjective experiences. But these experiences are not the lens through which we gauge truth; rather, truth is seen through the lens of Scripture, through which all our experiences in life must be evaluated.

We must remember that one of Satan's biggest tricks is deception. He is a deceiver who disguises himself as an angel of light (2 Corinthians 11:14). Therefore, we must be like the Berean Christians in the book of Acts, who, when visited by Paul and Silas with the gospel, "received the message with great eagerness and examined the Scriptures every day to see if what Paul said was true" (17:11).

It has become obvious that when it comes to the issue of what is true and not true about heaven, the church is lacking in discernment. This, too, is one of Satan's strategies, as Randy Alcorn aptly notes:

> Revelation 13:6 tells us the satanic beast "opened his mouth to blaspheme God, and to slander his name and his dwelling place and those who live in heaven." Our enemy slanders three things: God's person, God's people, and God's place—namely, Heaven. After being forcibly evicted from Heaven (Isaiah 14:12–15), the devil became bitter not only toward God, but toward mankind and toward Heaven itself, the place that was no longer his. It must be maddening for him that we're now entitled to the home he was kicked out of. What better way for the devil and his demons to attack us than to whisper lies about the very place on which God tells us to set our hearts and minds?[3]

---

3. Randy Alcorn, *Heaven* (Tyndale, 2004), 10–11. Most scholars see the Isaiah 14 passage as a possible reference to the fall of Satan. In the passage, Isaiah is describing the judgment of God on the king of Babylon, but there seems to be more to the pronouncement than judgment on an earthly king. Wayne Grudem suggests, "This language of ascending to heaven and setting his throne on high and saying, 'I will make myself like the Most High' strongly suggests rebellion by an angelic creature of great power and dignity. It would not be uncommon for Hebrew prophetic speech to pass from descriptions of human events to descriptions of heavenly events that are parallel to them and that the earthly events picture in a limited way. If this is so, then the sin of Satan is described as one of pride and attempting to be equal to God

Therefore, our views about heaven must come from the divine revelation of Scripture itself. To go any further than that is pure speculation based on unverifiable experience, and it is likely to be deceptive experiences because the Bible reveals that the only four prophets and apostles who had visions or revelations of heaven were Isaiah, Ezekiel, Paul, and John.

Paul's experience as an apostle raises a question that has puzzled many readers. In 2 Corinthians 12:2, he talks about "the third heaven." The context is this: Paul is defending his life and ministry to the Corinthian believers who have fallen prey to many false teachers—called "super-apostles" by Paul (v. 11)—those who are not apostles but rather deceivers who hold to a false gospel. Paul was afraid the church would be "led astray" (2 Corinthians 11:3) by these men, who seemed to be capturing the minds and hearts of the Corinthians with their rhetorical skill, something Paul readily acknowledged he was not trained in (v. 6).

In a rare moment in Paul's writings, he strongly defends himself as a genuine apostle, resorting even to sarcasm and boasting, something he feels uncomfortable doing, such that he labels himself at times "a fool" for doing it (2 Corinthians 12:11). He acknowledges that the Lord has given him something to keep him "from becoming conceited," something Paul calls a "thorn in my flesh" (v. 7). No one knows exactly what he was referring to, but it may have been anything from a physical problem to the false teachers themselves that plagued his soul and gave his prayers such urgency.

To substantiate his right to boast, he refers to visions and revelations that he, as an apostle appointed directly by Christ (Acts 9), had received throughout his ministry.[4] Paul suggests that only true apostles receive these heavenly blessings—along with signs, wonders,

---

in status and authority. (Ezek. 28:11–19 also possibly alludes to Satan's fall.)" (*Systematic Theology: An Introduction to Biblical Doctrine*, 2nd ed. [Zondervan Academic, 2020], 534).

4. Other places where Paul refers to his visions and revelations include Acts 9:12; 16:9–10; 18:9; 22:11; 27:23–24; Galatians 1:12; 2:2; and Ephesians 3:3.

and miracles (2 Corinthians 12:12). He then gets specific about one of his visions:

> Boasting is necessary. It is not profitable, but I will move on to visions and revelations of the Lord. I know a man in Christ who was caught up to the third heaven fourteen years ago. Whether he was in the body or out of the body, I don't know; God knows. I know that this man—whether in the body or out of the body I don't know; God knows—was caught up into paradise and heard inexpressible words, which a human being is not allowed to speak. (12:1–4 CSB)

Notice a few things right away. Paul distances himself and talks about himself in the third person—"I know a man." But it is clear from the context that he is talking about his own experience, because referring to someone else's vision makes no sense if he is defending himself. Mark Seifrid notes, "It quickly becomes clear that it was Paul himself who received this vision."[5]

The vision happened some fourteen years earlier, where he was "caught up" (Greek, *harpagenta*—"snatched up") to the third heaven or, as he also calls it, "paradise." This is something God did to him, and he has difficulty understanding whether he was "in the body" or "out of the body" when it happened. But he states that God knows.

This third heaven is what we may understand to be the heaven today where Christ himself dwells. This is because in the biblical mindset, the first heaven is the atmosphere of the earth (where birds fly); the second heaven is what we know as outer space (where stars

---

5. Mark A. Seifrid, *The Second Letter to the Corinthians*, Pillar New Testament Commentary (Eerdmans, 2014), 438. Seifrid also notes, "His distancing himself from his own experience is not to be understood as a mere act of humility. It is a theological judgment that corresponds to the 'eccentricity' that he has expressed repeatedly in this letter: his sufficiency is not of himself but God (3:5–6); he bears the deadness of Jesus in his body in order that the life of Jesus might be manifest in him (4:10). This theology is summarized in his well-known statement in Galatians, 'I live, yet no longer I, but Christ lives in me.'" For more on why Paul may have used this technique in articulating this experience, see David A. Garland, *2 Corinthians*, New American Commentary (B&H, 1999), 510–12.

and planets reside); and the third heaven is the unseen inhabitation of God himself, the place where angels reside and to which departed saints have gone.[6]

Paul said his experience was extraordinary. He heard things he was forbidden to repeat—words that apparently were for him alone. Paul was not given permission to describe or elaborate anything about this experience, unlike Isaiah, Ezekiel, and John.

Therefore, the preacher/teacher of this Scripture passage should clearly define what the third heaven is, as previously described. But they should also make it plain that God himself is the one who gives the authority to relay truths about heaven that are consistent with divine revelation—the teaching of Scripture, which are the revelations inspired by the Holy Spirit (see 2 Peter 1:21). Anything that goes beyond this is unverifiable and quite likely fraudulent. John MacArthur goes even further:

> Those who demand to know more than Scripture tells us are sinning; "The secret things belong unto the LORD our God: but those things which are revealed belong unto us and to our children for ever" (Deut. 29:29)—[that is, written down and made Scripture] . . . The limit of our curiosity is thus established by the boundary of biblical revelation.
>
> The typical Christian today seems oblivious to the principles established by Deuteronomy 29:29 and 1 Corinthians 4:6 ("that you may learn . . . not to go beyond what is written"). In fact, people seem to be looking for spiritual truth, messages from God, and insight into the spirit world everywhere but Scripture.[7]

God is not giving us new revelation beyond the pages of Scripture. There are no prophets and apostles today who are authorized by God

---

6. The first two "heavens" can be clearly seen in Psalm 19:1–6, referring to the skies above (v. 1) and to outer space, where the sun exists (vv. 4–6).

7. MacArthur, *Glory of Heaven*, 39.

to communicate additional truth, as Joseph Smith of the Mormon Church claimed. Therefore, we should be reticent to use the words "God told me" or "God showed me" in the context of Christian conversation, unless we are discussing what we learned from the pages of Scripture itself.

Rather, I suggest we use phrases like "God has brought conviction to my heart about such and such," knowing that the impression must be tested against the truths of Scripture and affirmed by godly Christians. Our thoughts may even be wrong, amended, or tweaked according to later insight and understanding. Only Scripture is inerrant and infallible; we are not.

God does guide us through the inner promptings of the Holy Spirit as we read his Word and sense convictions about a course of action as we've been praying. He even uses the obvious instances of open and closed doors and the wisdom of godly believers to steer our paths. But everything must be tested by and in concert with the already revealed Word of God, and we cannot claim it as "new revelation" or as a "new word from the Lord." We shouldn't be looking for signs from God but rather should seek wisdom to discern our circumstances according to the principles of God's Word.

I once had a dream about the second coming of Christ. When I woke up, I wrote it down. While it was very encouraging, it was not some sort of divine revelation or prophetic word that God was giving me. Rather, it was my subconscious mind rehearsing and imagining something I already believed to be a biblical reality from the pages of Scripture. Our brains are mysterious and truly extraordinary, but we cannot claim that which is "beyond what is written" (1 Corinthians 4:6).

Therefore, let us stop buying books that claim to have some fresh revelation about what heaven is like. If we are believers, we'll get there soon enough. We have all we need to know for now in the pages of God's Word.

As an apostle, Paul was not given permission to disclose his visions of heaven. What makes us think, then, that people today who are not prophets or apostles have been authorized to talk and write about what they allegedly have seen and heard—and often for a hefty profit?[8]

Principles for Reflection

1. Many people have claimed to have received some sort of new revelation from God. Does God still guide us today? I believe he does, but he is not giving us any new Scriptures or revelations that hold the same authority as Scripture itself.

2. The Holy Spirit may prompt us with convictions of the heart, but even these need to be tested. They do not hold the same authoritative weight as Scripture itself, and any conviction must correspond to what Scripture teaches and not contradict it.

3. We should avoid "God told me" language, which can be a manipulative way to deflect opposition. Rather, we should say, "I am feeling a conviction or sense that God may be leading me this way," and then invite church leaders and fellow mature believers to pray alongside us to see if they sense the same leading. Remember that we discern God's will in the context of the Christian community in keeping with the already revealed Word of God.

---

8. I am well aware that my argument is commonly known as the cessationist argument concerning divine revelation. Godly and faithful Christians and scholars whom I love and highly respect hold differing views. Most of them, however, would likely agree that these alleged visions of heaven written down in books are also unverifiable and lack significant biblical support for what is described in their contents.

CHAPTER 23

WHAT IS THE SECRET WORD THE ENEMY COULD NOT SAY?

Judges 12:1–7

MATTHEW D. KIM

According to Dictionary.com, the English language has twenty-six hardest-to-pronounce words:[1]

1. Accessory
2. Anemone
3. Choir
4. Colonel
5. Coup
6. Epitome
7. Espresso
8. February
9. Hyperbole
10. Isthmus
11. Juror
12. Library
13. Mischievous
14. Murderer
15. Nuclear
16. Onomatopoeia
17. Remuneration
18. Rural
19. Schadenfreude
20. Scissors
21. Specific
22. Squirrel
23. Supposedly
24. Synecdoche
25. Vocabulary
26. Worcestershire

---

1. "Wrap Your Head Around These 26 Hard Words to Pronounce," Dictionary.com, November 16, 2021, www.dictionary.com/e/hard-words-to-pronounce/.

Now imagine you were in a dire, life-and-death situation where if you mispronounced a word, your life would end immediately. If you've ever learned a different language, you know your tongue doesn't easily roll in the required way. This is the scene in Judges 12:1–7, where forty-two thousand Ephraimite soldiers were killed immediately because they couldn't pronounce the word *shibboleth*. Why is this story in the Bible, and what is our response to it?

It seems rather arbitrary that *shibboleth* is used as the litmus test of whether one is a true Ephraimite. It's meaning is unclear, as it could denote "ear of wheat or (less likely) current of water."[2] In our lingua franca, it's the equivalent of being able to say po-**tah**-toe or po-**tay**-toe. One letter or one syllable off, and you're doomed.

The premise of using pronunciation as a test is to distinguish in-groups from out-groups, "one of us" from "one of them." For example, in 2017, a New Orleans resident challenged out-of-towners' ability, or in this case inability, to pronounce the street name Tchoupitoulas.[3] Similarly, born in the United States but growing up in the home of Korean immigrants, we second-generation American-born Koreans would often create shibboleths around the name *Jesus*. If you could say "Je-sus" and not "Je-jus," you were American. The latter pronunciation would immediately signal that you were born in Korea or had immigrated later in childhood. And in this Bible passage, for the Ephraimites, the ability to say *shibboleth* rather than *sibboleth* was the distinguishing trait to show in-group membership.

Let's go back to the beginning. Why was there such a fuss about pronouncing a certain word? Israel's judge at the time, Jephthah, was leading a battle against the Ephraimites at the fords of the Jordan (Judges 10:6–12:15).[4] The tribe of Ephraim was upset with Jephthah,

---

2. D. A. Carson, ed., *NIV Zondervan Study Bible* (Zondervan, 2015), note on Judges 12:6, p. 455.
3. "Tchoupitoulas," Wikipedia, accessed March 17, 2025, https://en.wikipedia.org/wiki/Tchoupitoulas_Street.
4. Steven D. Mathewson, *The Art of Preaching Old Testament Narrative*, 2nd ed. (Baker Academic, 2021), 61.

who hadn't invited them to partner in the fight. Jephthah was a mighty warrior of the Gileadites (11:1). The son of a prostitute, he was sent away without any inheritance and later recruited by the Gileadites to lead them against their foes, the Ammonites (v. 6). Whether or not Jephthah had a chip on his shoulder from his earlier familial rejection, it's clear he wanted a position of leadership. Ultimately, he decided to fight as their commander.

Later, in verses 30–36, Jephthah makes a foolish vow to the Lord: "If you give the Ammonites into my hands, whatever comes out of the door of my house to meet me when I return in triumph from the Ammonites will be the LORD's, and I will sacrifice it as a burnt offering" (vv. 30–31). Jephthah's daughter—his only child—was the one who came out to greet him after he returned. The daughter displayed extraordinary faith as she told her foolish father to fulfill his vow to take her life (v. 36).

This, then, is the background for Judges 12:1–7. Jephthah was a proud, insecure, and foolish person. While the Ephraimites were angry that he hadn't recruited them for military service, Jephthah pointed out that he had asked, but they had refused to help:

> The Ephraimite forces were called out, and they crossed over to Zaphon. They said to Jephthah, "Why did you go to fight the Ammonites without calling us to go with you? We're going to burn down your house over your head."
>
> Jephthah answered, "I and my people were engaged in a great struggle with the Ammonites, and although I called, you didn't save me out of their hands. When I saw that you wouldn't help, I took my life in my hands and crossed over to fight the Ammonites, and the LORD gave me the victory over them. Now why have you come up today to fight me?" (12:1–3)

Jephthah proceeded to take up arms against the Ephraimites. Ruthlessly, he used a linguistic test to mark out who would be killed.

Only those who could say *shibboleth* rather than *sibboleth* would be spared:

> The Gileadites captured the fords of the Jordan leading to Ephraim, and whenever a survivor of Ephraim said, "Let me cross over," the men of Gilead asked him, "Are you an Ephraimite?" If he replied, "No," they said, "All right, say 'Shibboleth.'" If he said, "Sibboleth," because he could not pronounce the word correctly, they seized him and killed him at the fords of the Jordan. Forty-two thousand Ephraimites were killed at that time. (vv. 5–6)

Speaking with an accent in the United States can be a source of shame. As someone born and raised in America, I speak in a standard Midwestern/Chicago accent, even though I am ethnically Korean and have Korean facial features. Whenever I leave the country or visit another part of the US, my American accent should convey both that I'm an American and that I didn't grow up in a region that has a noticeable dialect, such as in the South or the Northeast. That is, I don't have a Texas twang or flatten my *r*'s like a Bostonian (even though I've lived in both places).

Correspondingly, when I speak my broken Korean, most native Korean speakers don't understand me at first, even though I look like them. Why? Because I don't sound like them. My American version of the Korean language gives me away. Interestingly, speaking with an accent is also mentioned in Scripture, where Peter is outed by his accent, which signaled that he was an outsider (Matthew 26:73).

What do we do with this strange story about accents in the book of Judges? Is there a proper way to explain it for our listeners? The *NIV Cultural Backgrounds Study Bible* provides a bit more understanding:

> The Gileadites' plan to identify Ephraimites involves a dialectical contrast between a "sh" sound and an "s" sound. This is a case of differentiation in the pronunciation of the same sibilant in different regions.

To the Gileadites, the Ephraimite pronunciation of the two sounded exactly alike. Accordingly, whenever the Gileadites demanded that an Ephraimite say, "Shibboleth" (pronounced "thibboleth" by the Gileadites), he would have betrayed his origin by saying, "Sibboleth."[5]

In a sermon titled "What Is Your 'Shibboleth'?" one preacher provided this takeaway principle for his hearers: "If the Ephraimites had known in advance what the password was, they would have rehearsed it until they could pronounce it correctly." Really? Is this a principle we can apply to our lives in the days ahead? There must be more. The preacher continues:

What are the "Shibboleths" in our life? . . . The "shibboleths" in our lives are blemishes on our souls, sins that easily ensnare or beset us. Here are some, certainly not all, of the "Shibboleths" that might trouble us.

1. Selfishness
2. Envy, jealousy and covetousness (spiritual "Siamese triplets")
3. Greed
4. An untamed tongue
5. Bitterness
6. Slothfulness
7. Pride[6]

If a Shibboleth is a password to cross-cultural identification, how is it that a Shibboleth is also used to demarcate sin and sinful behaviors? This cannot be a proper understanding or application of the text.

---

5. John H. Walton and Craig S. Keener, eds., *NIV Cultural Backgrounds Study Bible* (Zondervan, 2016), note on Judges 12:6, p. 433.
6. Kenneth Trent, "What Is Your 'Shibboleth'?," Sermon Central, November 28, 2017, www.sermoncentral.com/sermons/what-is-your-shibboleth-kenneth-trent-sermon-on-ot-judges-95206.

Taking instead a character or narrative study approach, a preacher could focus on any of these groups or themes:

- the Ephraimites (the complainers who didn't get their way)
- Jephthah (the ruthless, foolish leader)
- the Gileadites (the heartless soldiers)
- the spiritual context of Judges 12 and the passages before it

As is true when we examine other passages that seem to permit genocide, the question we must ask here is this: "What is the point of God's allowing forty-two thousand people to die in one fell swoop?" What is God ultimately doing in and accomplishing through this story? Put differently, why did the biblical author include this story as part of God's revelation? What can we learn from this text?

Obviously, we shouldn't play linguistic games to differentiate ourselves from others so as to justify killing them. What, then? Another preacher took this angle as a principle to consider:

> Say hypothetically that the Ephraimites were completely right to feel wronged by Jephthah. Say that someone in the church did do something wrong. Paul tells us how we should consider such slights: "Be kind to one another, tenderhearted, forgiving one another, as God in Christ forgave you" (Ephesians 4:32). . . . Let us not walk according to bitterness and self-conceit as the Ephraimites and Jephthah did, which leads to death. But let us walk according to the One who is able to give life.[7]

Principlizing a narrative text is easy to do in both Testaments. We take a specific story and find a timeless principle or truth—a prescriptive application—to encourage the listeners to apply to their lives

---

7. Eric Hamilton, "Making a Mountain Out of Shibboleth," Mountain View Church of Christ, March 19, 2023, https://mountainviewchurchofchrist.org/wp-content/uploads/2023/03/20230326-Bulletin.pdf.

in the days and weeks ahead. While it's easy to highlight the negative actions of our characters, I wonder if God is doing something here that isn't so specifically character-focused.

The larger storyline in Judges 10–12 is the demise of the Israelites. Beginning in Judges 10:6, where Jephthah is introduced, the narrator explains: "Again the Israelites did evil in the eyes of the Lord. They served the Baals and the Ashtoreths, and the gods of Aram, the gods of Sidon, the gods of Moab, the gods of the Ammonites and the gods of the Philistines. And because the Israelites forsook the Lord and no longer served him, he became angry with them" (vv. 6–7).

One of the gods of Moab was Chemosh, who provided victory and protection in battle. Could the case be made that Jephthah is an example of how even the judges of Israel "did evil in the eyes of the Lord" (Judges 3:7; 4:1; 6:1; 13:1) and followed other gods? Didn't Molek, the god of the Ammonites, endorse child sacrifice as a practice (Leviticus 18:21)? Could we then make the argument that Jephthah was consciously or subconsciously influenced by the teachings of foreign gods, which led him to make the foolish vow to the Lord to sacrifice the first person—"his only child"—as a way of celebrating victory? Is it too far a stretch to say that Jephthah became a follower of neighboring gods, whether purposely or as a byproduct of living in a land where evil reigned, rather than a follower of the Lord?

While we don't know the precise motivation behind Jephthah's annihilation of the Ephraimites, we do know he didn't consult the Lord. He assumed that because the Lord had granted favor and victory earlier, he could do as he pleased along the way. During Jephthah's six years of commanding the Israelites, many thousands of lives were taken. This distinguishes the Judges 12 passage from others, like the story of the sin of Achan (Joshua 7) in which he took (more accurately, stole) from the Lord, or the story of the sin of Saul (1 Samuel 15) in which he failed to destroy all living things and kept the choice animals for himself. Both of these episodes were examples of proactive disobedience to the Lord.

More than a story about pronunciation and mispronunciation, the tragic story of Jephthah is one of being wise in his own eyes. Whether knowingly or not, he accepted the philosophies of other gods. He foolishly took the life of his only child without consulting God. He took the lives of forty-two thousand Ephraimites who had challenged his authority.

Even though God used Jephthah to move forward the story of the Israelites, his is still a harrowing story of disobedience and folly. This is what we want to draw our listeners' focus to—the implication of a life without God, a life that does not show dependence on the Lord.

Principles for Reflection

1. The lesson of Shibboleth is one that reflects the moral decay of the times. As everyone did as they saw fit and were wise in their own eyes, God's people did not consult him in every part of life. Here we see Jephthah's hubris in killing those from a different background without first seeking the Lord's will.

2. I'm not certain it was God's will for forty-two thousand Ephraimites to die. Maybe it was; maybe it wasn't. Being wise in our own eyes encourages prayerless, self-centered lives of self-reliance. More than anything, God wants us to be dependent on him.

3. It can be important to take inventory of the areas of our lives where we have succumbed to self-reliance and personal wisdom rather than reliance on God and the pursuit of his wisdom. What are we doing that may seem good in our own eyes but is evil in the Lord's eyes?

PART V: MORALLY PROBLEMATIC

How to Teach Scripture Used to Justify Evil

The most difficult of all Scripture texts might be the morally problematic ones, and so we've saved them for last. You may have been asked—or you've asked—questions like, "How could a good God permit this to happen?" and its sister question, "How could a good God command this to happen as revealed in Scripture?"

Morally problematic texts are those in which what we deem as evil appears to be justified or even promoted—passages where God seems to allow or even command murder, lying, slavery, and other morally bankrupt beliefs, actions, and systems. In such cases, what is a preacher/teacher to do? Is our role to be an apologist for God, making sense of, and even making excuses for, his behavior?

No, we are not called to answer for God. God is who he is. He does not need defending. What we can do is set the stage for the passages that involve morally questionable actions. We do that by helping our listeners understand the biblical world, which often stands in stark contrast to the modern world. We share our exegetical nuggets to guide our people into the world of the Bible as best we can to help them distinguish between an apples-to-apples passage and an apples-to-oranges one. What God does, allows, or demands in morally problematic texts can be more effectively explained once the context is more accurately understood. We might also take this time to ask our people to pray that the Enemy would not succeed in luring us to distrust God and his Word about things that are impossible to fully comprehend.

CHAPTER 24

WHO REALLY HARDENED PHARAOH'S HEART?

Exodus 7:3; 14:4

ERIC J. BARGERHUFF

In the 1980s, the group Quarterflash produced a one-hit wonder about lost and broken love titled "Harden My Heart," which made it to number 3 on the Billboard Hot 100 chart in 1982. The painful but catchy lyrics proclaimed, "I'm gonna harden my heart, I'm gonna swallow my tears, I'm gonna turn and leave you here."[1] These lyrics suggest that a person is able to exercise purposeful control over their heart. Is that true?

We have all kinds of ideas and sayings about our hearts. Let's name a few of them:

- "She has a broken heart."
- "Bless your heart" (sometimes said in a patronizing tone).

---

1. Quarterflash, "Harden My Heart," track 1 on the album *Quarterflash* (October 1981).

- "I just lost something that meant a lot to me, and I am heartsick."
- "I'm going to take on this task with all my heart" (that is, "with as much energy, passion, and drive as I can muster").
- "Listen to your heart. Follow your heart wherever it leads you" (not always the best advice).
- "That person has a stubborn and cold heart."
- "God calls me to give thanks with a grateful heart."
- "The heart knows what it wants even when the mind doesn't."

These ideas merely scratch the surface of our quips and references to the heart. And perhaps one of the most famous quotes about the heart is attributed to Helen Keller, who wrote to Rev. Phillips Brooks that her teacher had explained to her, "The best and most beautiful things in this world cannot be seen nor even touched, but just felt in the heart."[2]

The human heart in Scripture is a complex thing. It is what we might call the soul/spirit of every individual.[3] It comprises our thoughts, emotions, memories, and essential conscious awareness, as well as our conscience and will. We are told throughout Scripture to guard it from the influence of a fallen world since it is the center of one's being and the source from which all actions flow (Proverbs 4:23).

Solomon told us that the reason we should guard our heart is because it is the wellspring of life (Proverbs 4:23). Much of who we are springs from our hearts. Jesus said, "Out of the abundance of the heart the mouth speaks" (Matthew 12:34 ESV), and "Where your treasure is, there your heart will be also" (Matthew 6:21).

But the dark side of the equation is that because we are born with

---

2. Helen Keller, "Letter to Rev. Phillips Brooks, June 8, 1891," in *The Story of My Life* (Grosset and Dunlap, 1902), 203.
3. I am a dichotomist, using the words *soul* and *spirit* interchangeably, as the Virgin Mary did in her song in Luke 1:46–47—as the Greek construction suggests. The words are in apposition to one another.

a sin nature, there is a profound problem with the human heart. In fact, the prophet Jeremiah tells us that apart from God's grace, "the heart is deceitful above all things, and desperately wicked: who can know it?" (17:9 KJV). The apostle Paul set forth the depths of the depravity of the fallen human heart in Romans 1:

> Though they knew God, they did not glorify him as God or show gratitude. Instead, their thinking became worthless, and their senseless hearts were darkened. Claiming to be wise, they became fools and exchanged the glory of the immortal God for images resembling mortal man, birds, four-footed animals, and reptiles.
>
> Therefore, God delivered them over in the desires of their hearts to sexual impurity, so that their bodies were degraded among themselves. They exchanged the truth of God for a lie, and worshiped and served what has been created instead of the Creator, who is praised forever. Amen. (vv. 21–25 CSB)

Because of humanity's love for sin, hearts become hardened toward the things of God. This catastrophic disposition separates people from God and is often linked to futile and worthless thinking and the desire for the sensual pursuits of the flesh. Paul warned the church about how new believers in Christ must separate themselves from that old way of thinking, feeling, and living:

> I say this and testify in the Lord: You should no longer walk as the Gentiles do, in the futility of their thoughts. They are darkened in their understanding, excluded from the life of God, because of the ignorance that is in them and because of the hardness of their hearts. They became callous and gave themselves over to promiscuity for the practice of every kind of impurity with a desire for more and more. (Ephesians 4:17–19 CSB)[4]

---

4. The writer of Hebrews issued similar warnings in Hebrews 3:8, 13, 15; 4:7.

A sinfully darkened heart is a hardened heart. Sin has a way of hardening it, which is why the writer of the book of Hebrews also warned the church to be proactive in their fellowship with one another and discerning about the things that affect the heart: "Encourage one another daily, as long as it is called 'Today,' so that none of you may be hardened by sin's deceitfulness" (3:13).

Therefore, we must be aware of the sin that so easily entangles (Hebrews 12:1) so we don't become desensitized toward the things of God (Psalm 119:70). Sinning is like pouring acid on spiritual sensitivity such that it eats away at and slows our progress in sanctification. Its effect is like the muffling of our ears and shading of our eyes toward God's Word and his will. When this happens, we lose sight of the glory of God and exchange it for idols—idols of our own making (Psalm 115:4); idols that do not speak (Jeremiah 10:5), see (Psalm 115:5), or hear (Revelation 9:20); idols that are worthless (Psalm 96:5); idols that do not and cannot save (Isaiah 45:20).

With all this in mind, we turn to the Old Testament and the puzzling topic of the hardening of Pharaoh's heart. The Lord's plan was to raise up Moses and Aaron to lead in the deliverance of God's people from more than four hundred years of slavery in Egypt. It was God's intent to put his glory and power on display in front of all Egypt and Israel.

No idol could compare to God's power. No leader could stand against him. The Lord would deliver his people with the kinds of signs and wonders you'd think would soften even the hardest of hearts. But not so for Pharaoh. His heart would remain hard, but the question is this: Did Pharaoh harden his own heart, or did the Lord harden it? The testimony of Scripture is that both ideas are true. But how do we explain this?

Let's first look at Pharaoh, who seemingly willfully rejected the God of Israel and all the miracles performed through the hand of Moses (the plagues). Throughout Exodus, there is ample testimony to his purposeful and willful hardening of his own heart.

Pharaoh's heart became hard and he would not listen to them, just as the LORD had said. (7:13)

The magicians of Egypt did the same thing by their occult practices. So Pharaoh's heart was hard, and he would not listen to them, as the LORD had said. (7:22 CSB)

When Pharaoh saw that there was relief, he hardened his heart and would not listen to Moses and Aaron, just as the LORD had said. (8:15)

This time also Pharaoh hardened his heart and would not let the people go. (8:32)

Pharaoh sent messengers who saw that not a single one of the Israelite livestock was dead. But Pharaoh's heart was hard, and he did not let the people go. (9:7 CSB)

When Pharaoh saw that the rain, hail, and thunder had ceased, he sinned again and hardened his heart, he and his officials. (9:34 CSB)

The cumulative testimony of these verses teaches us that Pharaoh's purposeful sin was connected to the hardening of his own heart (see especially 9:34 quoted above). His refusal to listen to Moses and Aaron and to accept the testimony of the power of God that was demonstrated in the plagues bore witness to his willful hardening to everyone around him. Even his officials joined in the hardening of their hearts.

Interestingly, the hardening of Pharaoh's heart became known even outside of Egypt. The book of 1 Samuel told of the plagues of tumors that fell upon the Philistines because they had captured the ark of the Lord. The Philistine priests and diviners are said to have recalled Pharaoh's disposition when he encountered the God of Israel, and they warned the Philistines, "Why harden your hearts as the Egyptians and Pharaoh hardened theirs? When he afflicted them, didn't they send Israel away, and Israel left?" (6:6 CSB).

The Philistines were perplexed as to whether these tumors were some random event (1 Samuel 6:9) or were indeed punishment from the God of Israel, but they were not willing to take the chance. They decided it was a wise thing not to harden their hearts like Pharaoh did and sent the ark away.

While Pharaoh is said to have sinned and hardened his heart, the Bible also makes it clear that behind all this was divine causation, that God also hardened Pharaoh's heart and sent the plagues as a form of judgment on him and all of Egypt and as a way of orchestrating the situation for the people of God.

First, it is said to be judgment on Pharaoh and all of Egypt for their sin and their refusal to recognize Yahweh as the only one and true God:

> I will harden Pharaoh's heart, and though I multiply my signs and wonders in the land of Egypt, Pharaoh will not listen to you. Then I will lay my hand on Egypt and bring my hosts, my people the children of Israel, out of the land of Egypt by great acts of judgment. The Egyptians shall know that I am the LORD, when I stretch out my hand against Egypt and bring out the people of Israel from among them. (Exodus 7:3–5 ESV)

Second, when the Lord told Moses of his mission, he emphasized the fact that he was in total control of the situation: "When you go back to Egypt, make sure you do before Pharaoh all the wonders that I have put within your power. But I will harden his heart so that he won't let the people go" (Exodus 4:21 CSB).

On the surface this may sound confusing. Why would Moses be motivated to go and do what God told him to do if God was going to harden Pharaoh's heart? Douglas Stuart comments:

The reader might at first blush think that God was here announcing to Moses that he was going to frustrate Moses' efforts. In fact, it was just the opposite. By indicating that he would control Pharaoh's resistance to the exodus, God assured Moses that he was totally in control of Pharaoh in every way, able to make him resist as long as necessary even during a buildup of increasingly painful plagues and then make him give up and let the Israelites go at a moment of his God's own choosing (which was already the essential message of 3:19–20).[5]

There is little doubt that God purposed to deliver his people, and the testimony of Scripture is that his plan will surely come to pass. As Isaiah rhetorically asked, "The LORD of Armies himself has planned it; therefore, who can stand in its way? It is his hand that is outstretched, so who can turn it back?" (14:27 CSB). Similarly, Job said, "I know that you can do anything and no plan of yours can be thwarted" (42:2 CSB).

God himself states that nothing can stop his sovereign will. In Isaiah we read:

> Remember what happened long ago,
> for I am God, and there is no other;
> I am God, and no one is like me.
> I declare the end from the beginning,
> and from long ago what is not yet done,
> saying: my plan will take place,
> and I will do all my will. (46:9–10 CSB)

Therefore, God has ordained not only the end but also the means when it comes to "the good pleasure of his will" (Ephesians 1:5 CSB). And the way he was going to deliver Israel from the Egyptians was

---

5. Douglas K. Stuart, *Exodus*, New American Commentary (B&H, 2006), 146.

through the judgment that was to fall on Pharaoh—a hardening of his heart.

What, then, do we do about the concept of free will here? Without getting into a long and contentious debate, let's remind ourselves of what we discovered earlier—that Pharaoh's sin is directly linked with his own hardening of his heart. He had ample opportunity to recognize the miraculous power of the one true God, but he refused. He made genuine choices.

Yet the testimony of Scripture is also true that God himself hardened Pharaoh's heart. That tension must be held together, even if it disturbs us. In the book of Genesis, Joseph's brothers willingly and purposefully sold him into slavery, but Joseph later said to them, "You planned evil against me; God planned it for good to bring about the present result—the survival of many people" (50:20 CSB).

We will always have a limited capacity to understand how God works at times. The teacher of this passage must not try to resolve the tension in such a way that makes God into either an omnicompetent responder who is subservient to the human will or the exact opposite kind of God—one who makes human beings into puppets. That's not how the Bible presents the realities behind these stories.

The fact is, our wills can be influenced. Paul said we were at one time "slaves of sin" (Romans 6:20 CSB), and no one can unequivocally say that sin never influences their life or choices. When you are a slave, you are not free in any sense. And yet we make genuine choices. Wayne Grudem provides a helpful overview of how Scripture speaks concerning this:

> Someone might object that if a choice is ordained (or somehow indirectly caused) by God, it may appear to us to be voluntary and willed by us, but it is *not a genuine or real choice* because it is not absolutely free. Once again we must respond by challenging the assumption that a choice must be absolutely free in order to be genuine or valid. If God makes us in a certain way and then tells us that

our voluntary choices are real and genuine choices, then we must agree that they are. God is the definition of what is real and genuine in the universe. By contrast, we might ask where Scripture ever says that our choices have to be free from God's influence or providential control in order to be real or genuine choices. It does not seem that Scripture ever speaks in this way.[6]

How many of us have looked back on our lives and remembered certain choices we made that were key in the journey that brought us to today? Yet is it not also true that in that same retrospective look, we can see God's providential hand working in ways that often mystify us? Ask your listeners to think about this when you preach/teach on this passage.

The fact is, God began a good work in us, and he will complete it (Philippians 1:6). Yet all along the way, we make choices that are genuine and real. I am just grateful that God can still work all things together for good even when I make foolish mistakes and stumble along the path (Romans 8:28). Knowing this, we respond by falling on our knees and worshiping God. What a wonderful God we have!

Pharaoh made a real choice, and he chose to harden his heart. God hardened it as well in judgment and to orchestrate the release of his people. In the end, the hardening of Pharaoh's heart (both by Pharaoh and by God) brought God glory. As hard as it is to understand, it is true. Pharaoh was accountable and responsible, and so is God, and in the end, it was not Pharaoh but God who received the glory for the hardening. The Lord himself says, "I will harden Pharaoh's heart, and he will pursue them. But I will gain glory for myself through Pharaoh and all his army, and the Egyptians will know that I am the LORD" (Exodus 14:4).

God has a plan for us, and it includes the choices we make and

---

6. Wayne Grudem, *Systematic Theology: An Introduction to Biblical Doctrine*, 2nd ed. (Zondervan Academic, 2020), 829–30, italics in original.

actions we take. It baffles me that even some of choices I make and things I do have been planned all along. To be sure, God is not responsible for the sin in my life—all of which is my choice. Yet he has mysteriously and sovereignly woven even my failures into his good plan for me. But if there is anything good in me, I know it has come from him, as well as the choices and actions I make. From my perspective, I freely make those choices while at the same time realizing that God had planned for me to do so. As the apostle Paul wrote, "We are his workmanship, created in Christ Jesus for good works, *which God prepared ahead of time for us to do*" (Ephesians 2:10 CSB, emphasis mine).

His ways are higher than our ways, and his thoughts are higher than our thoughts (Isaiah 55:9). I can't always understand, and sometimes it is a huge relief that I don't have to. I merely have to trust. He is the One who makes sense of it all in the end. *Soli Deo gloria.*

Principles for Reflection

1. God, who has control over evil, can use the free choices of evil people to accomplish his purposes. The most obvious example is seen in the cross, where the actions of evil people accomplished a divine purpose that God had planned before the foundation of the world.

2. Pharaoh made choices. He hardened his heart, and God hardened it as well. Pharaoh was culpable for his sin, but God is not. This is the way the Bible presents it, and it is therefore true. On this side of eternity, some things will always be a mystery, leaving us to face unanswerable conundrums.

3. People will make choices and take actions according to their own nature. The heart is influenced by sin, and so are our actions. Because of this, we must be born again (John 3:3) and given a new heart and a new spirit by God (Ezekiel 36:26). We must be rescued from our slavery to sin, and God is in the rescue business. Thank you, Lord!

4. Moses could confidently face Pharaoh, knowing God was in control and had a plan. In the same way, we can face evil and trust in God, even when life does not make sense to us. Everything in this world is under the providential hand of God.

CHAPTER 25

Is There a Double Standard on Virginity?

Leviticus 21:7, 13–15; Ezekiel 44:22

MATTHEW D. KIM

Conversations about human sexuality seem to be off-limits these days. We're not allowed to ask private questions about sexual history or call out sexual deviance. Whatever works for you is tolerated and even celebrated. Not so much for Old Testament priests or even New Testament Christians. God clearly has set boundaries for his children in the realm of sexual expression and fulfillment.

God had clear standards for Old Testament priests and high priests. You may be wondering, *What does this have to do with us today?*

Leviticus 21 contains various instructions and regulations for Aaronic priests. Becoming unclean or defiling oneself as a priest was forbidden. Verse 6 reads, "They must be holy to their God and must not profane the name of their God." And then comes verse 7: "They must not marry women defiled by prostitution or divorced from their husbands, because priests are holy to their God." Next, verses 13–15 read, "The woman he marries must be a virgin. He must not marry a widow, a divorced woman, or a woman defiled by prostitution, but only a virgin from his own people, so that he will not defile his offspring among his people. I am the LORD, who makes him holy." Ezekiel 44:22 describes a similar requirement for a high priest's marriage: "They must not marry widows or divorced women; they may marry only virgins of Israelite descent or widows of priests."

At a young age, I learned that Roman Catholic priests were forbidden to marry. However, Protestant pastors often marry and in most cases are expected to marry (to prevent sexual misconduct or the appearance thereof). According to this Leviticus passage, however, marriage seemed to be in the cards for all ordained priests.

A confusing description here ensues: Priests are permitted to marry, but they can only marry a virgin from their own family due to God's command of holiness. The passage never overtly states, however, that priests must be virgins themselves prior to this marriage. Perhaps that was the expectation. Yet a proper question a reader might raise is this: Is there a double standard on virginity for priests versus the chastity of the women they marry? Second, and more significantly, how does this teaching point to our ultimate and perfect High Priest, Jesus Christ?

To give some historical and religious context, all firstborn children in the line of Aaron were set apart for the work of priestly ministry. Being defiled in any way was unacceptable to the Lord. The priests were to lead the people in corporate worship before God and his people. There was never a question, though, as to whether or not a priest could marry. It was common for priests to marry in Levitical times:

> The Old Testament priests married. The first high priest, Aaron, clearly had sons, and it was from his biological line that the priests came (Exodus 28:1). The priests were prohibited from marrying a defiled or divorced woman (Leviticus 21:7), and the high priest was

required to marry a virgin (Leviticus 21:10, 13–14). But it is quite clear the priests were permitted to marry and produce children (Leviticus 21:15). Protestants still see the OT priests as corresponding to pastors because of the priests' teaching role in Israel (Deuteronomy 33:10; 2 Chronicles 17:7–9; 35:3; Nehemiah 8:7–9; Malachi 2:4–7).[1]

As a familial member of the Aaronic "priestly" line, a priest was called to the highest moral standards. Leviticus 21 explains various rules and regulations for the priestly order. As spiritual models for the community, the Lord gave Aaronic priests precise instructions on who they could not marry. Rabbi Israel Drazin gives helpful information:

> A kohen [or priest] may not marry a divorcee, a prostitute, or a dishonored woman (Leviticus 21:7). A kohen who enters such a marriage loses the entitlements of his priestly status while in that marriage.
>
> The Israeli rabbinate will not perform a marriage that Jewish law forbids to a kohen, although a foreign marriage would be recognized.[2]

This leads to the issue raised earlier. While the Old Testament is clear that high priests must marry a virgin (and from their own village/family), it says nothing about the high priest being required to be a virgin himself. In her book *Sexual Pollution in the Hebrew Bible*, Eve Levavi Feinstein notes, "The Hebrew term for pollution appears 286 times in the Hebrew Bible, and the term for purity appears 207

---

1. Zachary Garis, "The Immorality of Forbidding Clergy from Marriage," Knowing Scripture, March 7, 2023, https://knowingscripture.com/articles/the-immorality-of-forbidding-clergy -from-marriage.
2. Rabbi Israel Drazin, "Thoughts on the Torah Portion Tetzaveh, Priests, and Superstitions," San Diego Jewish World, February 28, 2023, www.sdjewishworld.com/2023/02/28/thoughts -on-the-torah-portion-tetzaveh-priests-and-superstition/.

times. Both terms are heavily concentrated in priestly literature."[3] Interestingly, Feinstein contends that "these texts suggest a conception of pollution based on the idea that women are the sexual property of men."[4]

Despite Feinstein's contention, there is no definitive requirement that high priests must remain virgins before marriage. At least, the Torah doesn't overtly say such a thing. It may have been a given, since the holiness codes of priests found in Leviticus 21 and 22 safeguard purity and holiness for priests and high priests as religious leaders in the community. This argument will not satisfy all readers or listeners. However, it doesn't negate the fact that the high priest and other regular priests needed to be holy, pure, and priestly in every aspect of their lives.

What does this passage mean for twenty-first-century Christians? The Reformation teaching of the priesthood of all believers has become solidified in our identity and purpose as New Testament believers. Yes, it's true that Levitical priests and high priests were required to do their best to be holy—which included the command that high priests would marry virgins (and I would submit, remain virgins themselves prior to marriage)—yet there must be more to what this passage can offer our listeners today.

The primary comparison I see is nothing novel. Despite all the codes of purity, no high priest could remain pure and holy. Therefore, as the author of Hebrews states, "If perfection could have been attained through the Levitical priesthood—and indeed the law given to the people established that priesthood—why was there still need for another priest to come, one in the order of Melchizedek, not in the order of Aaron?" (7:11).

---

3. Eve Levavi Feinstein, *Sexual Pollution in the Hebrew Bible* (Oxford University Press, 2014), 3.
4. Feinstein, *Sexual Pollution*, 8. This argument is a stretch and demonstrates a wide-swath, unhealthy kind of liberal feminism that does not take into full consideration the historical/religious contexts and overemphasizes the context of modern readers and liberal feminists (those who depart from biblical orthodoxy).

And this is our hope:

> Because of this oath, Jesus has become the guarantor of a better
> covenant.
>
> Now there have been many of those priests, since death pre-
> vented them from continuing in office; but because Jesus lives
> forever, he has a permanent priesthood. . . .
>
> Such a high priest truly meets our need—one who is holy,
> blameless, pure, set apart from sinners, exalted above the heavens.
> Unlike the other high priests, he does not need to offer sacrifices
> day after day, first for his own sins, and then for the sins of the
> people. He sacrificed for their sins once for all when he offered him-
> self. (Hebrews 7:22–24, 26–27)

In responding to our question about how the Leviticus passage
points to the ultimate High Priest, we see that what a high priest,
even one like Melchizedek, could not accomplish, Jesus did. We have
a Savior, King, and High Priest who remains unblemished and is the
perfect eternal sacrifice for the sins of the world. This is the gospel.
Jesus has accomplished everything for our salvation and for our right
standing before God. Rather than giving us license to sin, this truth
should embolden us to live in freedom and be as perfect and holy as
we can strive to be—yet ultimately knowing we struggle with imper-
fection due to our sinful nature. However, God's standard is for us to
pursue holiness in every part of life—even though we will never reach
perfection. That's what discipleship is all about.

Moreover, we can be affirmed in our identity as the bride of Christ
as we hear God's declaration: "I am jealous for you with a godly jealousy. I promised you to one husband, to Christ, so that I might present
you as a pure virgin to him"(2 Corinthians 11:2). Jay Carper explains:

> We are the bride of Christ, we are a nation of priests, and we are cit-
> izens of the Kingdom of God. We have been reborn into the nation

of Israel, wild olive shoots grafted into a cultivated tree. As citizens, whether physically circumcised or only spiritually, we are expected to behave ourselves as children of the King, not flaunting privilege, but obeying a higher standard.

Our ultimate purification is yet to come, but until we finally exchange these mortal, corruptible shells for eternal, incorruptible bodies, we must strive to live as pure as we are able, with the aid of God's Word and Spirit. We can't be perfect, but we can always be better than we are, one choice, one stop, one word at a time. It's the least we can do for our ultimate, heavenly High Priest and Husband.[5]

For the New Testament Christian, our priestly goal is continual sanctification. Perhaps more than in any other area of life (other than money), sexual purity and holiness are under continual challenge in all cultures. Holiness is a constant battle for all Christians, but let's take a moment to get practical for pastors and church leaders. We are living in a day of excuse-making. Pastors are not being held accountable for their sins (private and public). Instead of holding our pastors to a higher standard (James 3:1), we too often allow God's standards of holiness to slide. Instead of fearing an all-powerful God, we fear pastors and their power—that if we challenge our pastors, they'll go elsewhere and our church attendance will plummet.

This chapter reminds us that God's children are marked by obedience and purity in all facets of life, including sexual desires that fall outside of the God-given parameters. Let's resolve to be different from the world. We have a perfect High Priest in Jesus. Abiding in him provides every motivation to seek sexual purity, marital fidelity, and wholehearted dedication to him since we are the bride of Christ for whom he willingly died.

---

5. Jay Carper, "Bride, Priest, and Citizen," American Torah, October 12, 2021, https://americantorah.com/2021/10/12/bride-priest-and-citizen/.

Principles for Reflection

1. The Old Testament position of high priest has been fulfilled in the person of Jesus Christ, our Great High Priest.

2. Earthly priests and pastors will falter and fail us at times. That doesn't mean the office of pastor/priest is a free-for-all. Those in church leadership should aspire to holiness in all spheres of life, including their sexuality. Purity is expected for pastors/priests and for those in the priesthood of all believers.

3. We are not exempt from God's standards of sexual purity and virginity before marriage simply because we don't hold the position of pastor/priest today. Encourage one another to remain sexually pure before marriage and to be sexually faithful within the covenantal marriage relationship. Forgiveness in Christ is always available for those who earnestly repent and seek to follow God's ways.

CHAPTER 26

DOES THE BIBLE ENDORSE SLAVERY?

Deuteronomy 15:12–18

ERIC J. BARGERHUFF

Very few words in the English language are loaded with more emotional pain and horrific realities than the word *slavery*. An institution that has crossed millennia and cultures, slavery is well-documented in practically every season among most people groups. The idea of someone *owning* another person is diametrically opposed to the biblical truth that all people are created in the image of God and share equal value and worth in his sight.

Yet this has been the story of fallen humanity. The inherent evil of our sin nature has led to much suffering. To be sure, slavery is not simply a racial issue (though it often is), because people groups have enslaved members of their own race throughout the centuries.

Throughout much of history, slaves were seen as *property* instead of people. They possessed little to no rights. They were to do their owner's bidding without refusal, lest they be beaten or killed. It is true that some slaves had owners who were more lenient, and on rare occasions, some were even treated like family. But by far, the history of slavery is dark and is clouded with despair. The cruelty, destructiveness, and catastrophic impact of slavery is what most people think of.

The word *doulos* in the New Testament is rightly translated as *slave*. Most translations tend to soften the word by using the English word *servant*. But the word *servant* carries a slightly different connotation than the word *slave* in the sense that a servant could also be hired help, but a slave didn't have that status.

A significant question has been raised about the Bible that many unbelievers pick up on in their attempts to undermine Christianity: Why didn't Jesus and the apostles speak an outright condemnation of slavery as an institution in all their moral teachings in the New Testament? If human slavery is truly inherently wrong by virtue of the fact that we are all created equally in God's image (male and female), then why didn't they oppose it? Is their silence an implicit endorsement of some form of evil?

To answer this, we must understand a basic gospel principle. Jesus taught that the kingdom of God at this time "is not of this world" (John 18:36). The fallen world system will need to be destroyed and replaced in the future, but for now, the kingdom of God is a spiritual kingdom that awaits a future physical and material reality at the second coming of Christ. It is inaugurated now but awaits a fuller realization when this age comes to an end.

The implication of this reality is that Jesus and the apostles proclaim a message of repentance, faith, forgiveness, and the reign of God in the hearts of those who believe in Jesus. They did not want the gospel to be confused with a political or social reformation movement. Embracing such a movement would have had catastrophic consequences, leading people of that day to believe that Christians were just another rebellious group intent on upending Caesar and the Roman Empire.

Therefore, to directly attack a social institution such as slavery (even though such an attack would be justified) might have led people to miss the primary message—the forgiveness of sins and reconciliation with God. To be sure, Christianity was always seen by some as a threat to the authoritative institutions of that day, given the Christian claim that Jesus is Lord, not Caesar. But Christianity at its root was not a sociopolitical movement, even though it certainly had implications for society.

The calling, then, was to proclaim the good news to satisfy humanity's greatest need—to be born again and transformed by the power of the Holy Spirit—and to announce the reign of God through Christ in the hearts of those who believe, with all that it implied. The ramifications of this gospel are set forth in the teachings of Jesus and clearly spelled out by the apostles in the New Testament. These implications have moral, relational, and spiritual effects that can transform people and society one by one.

This, in turn, can change the way people think about God and every human being created equally in God's image. We may conclude, then, that though Jesus and the apostles did not attack slavery directly, their unique message of God's saving grace as seen in the life, death, and resurrection of Jesus would have an indirect impact on the institution of slavery by ushering in the message of peace with God and peace with one another—with direct implications on how people see each other and treat each other.[1]

This was precisely the thought Paul used when he wrote the book of Philemon. Philemon was a slave owner whose slave, Onesimus, had stolen money from him and run away. Through God's providence both Philemon and Onesimus (apart from each other) came to saving faith in Christ through Paul's proclamation of the gospel.

Paul, then, wanted to bring these new brothers in Christ back together in reconciliation, so he wrote this letter to encourage

---

1. It is not my intent in this short chapter to outline the differences between modern-day secular social justice and biblical justice as an implication of the gospel. For an excellent treatise on this topic, see Owen Strachan, *Christianity and Wokeness: How the Social Justice Movement Is Hijacking the Gospel—and the Way to Stop It* (Salem Books, 2021).

Philemon to forgive Onesimus and receive him back. Paul even offered to pay the restitution for the wrong that was done to Philemon by Onesimus prior to conversion (v. 18). But what is telling is that Paul notes that if Philemon receives Onesimus back, it would no longer be as a slave:

> Perhaps this is why he [Onesimus] was separated from you for a brief time, so that you might get him back permanently, *no longer as a slave, but more than a slave—as a dearly loved brother.* He is especially so to me, but how much more to you, both in the flesh and in the Lord.
>
> So if you consider me a partner, welcome him as you would me. And if he has wronged you in any way, or owes you anything, charge that to my account. (vv. 15–18 CSB, emphasis mine)

Paul demonstrates this same approach throughout his letters, where he teaches that all people are equal in Christ, no matter what their station in life is, and that each person, slave or free, has equal access to and worth in the light of the gospel. He spells this out clearly in his letter to the Galatians: "Those of you who were baptized into Christ have been clothed with Christ. There is no Jew or Greek, slave or free, male and female; since you are all one in Christ Jesus. And if you belong to Christ, then you are Abraham's seed, heirs according to the promise" (3:27–29 CSB).

Sadly, these verses in Galatians have been misused in all kinds of ways to wash out distinctions and roles. Paul is not disregarding ethnic heritage, gender, roles, or stations in life. He is doing quite the opposite; he is recognizing that even within all these distinctions, every person has equal access to and privileges for union with Christ and immersion into him through the spiritual baptism that happens at conversion.[2] He reiterates this same principle to the Corinthian

---

2. Paul is not referring to water baptism here, since water baptism does not save. We are saved

church: "For just as the body is one and has many parts, and all the parts of that body, though many, are one body—so also is Christ. For we were all baptized by one Spirit into one body—whether Jews or Greeks, whether slaves or free—and we were all given one Spirit to drink" (1 Corinthians 12:12–13 CSB).[3]

As the sanctifying work of the Holy Spirit takes effect in the hearts of people, the institution of slavery begins to fall quickly by the wayside among believers, who see each other as brothers and sisters in Christ, bought and owned by the blood of Christ and not by other human beings.

What, then, do we do with passages of Scripture such as Deuteronomy 15:12–18 that seem, at least on the surface, to endorse the institution of slavery among God's people, the Israelites, in the Old Testament?

> If your fellow Hebrew, a man or woman, is sold to you and serves you six years, you must set him free in the seventh year. When you set him free, do not send him away empty-handed. Give generously to him from your flock, your threshing floor, and your winepress. You are to give him whatever the LORD your God has blessed you with. Remember that you were a slave in the land of Egypt and the LORD your God redeemed you; that is why I am giving you this command today. But if your slave says to you, "I don't want to leave you," because he loves you and your family, and is well off with you, take an awl and pierce through his ear into the door, and he will become your slave for life. Also treat your female slave the same way. Do not regard it as a hardship when you set him free, because he worked for

---

only through repentance and faith. Water baptism follows as a symbol of the spiritual baptism and as a sign of obedience. For more on this, see my book *The Most Misused Verses in the Bible* (Bethany House, 2012), 133–38.

3. Note that Paul here regards the baptism of the Holy Spirit to be describing all that happens at conversion—and all believers have received this baptism. For more on this topic, see Wayne Grudem, *Systematic Theology: An Introduction to Biblical Doctrine*, 2nd ed. (Zondervan Academic, 2020), 942–66.

you six years—worth twice the wages of a hired worker. Then the LORD your God will bless you in everything you do. (Deuteronomy 15:12–18 CSB)

Doesn't this seem to suggest that God endorsed the institution of slavery among the Israelites? The answer to this is not so simple. The context of this section in Deuteronomy has to do with the releasing of people from debt. Moses had earlier established a sabbatical year *for the land*, which happened every seven years (Exodus 23:10–11; Leviticus 25:1–7). The landowners were allowed to sow in the fields and prune in their vineyards for six years, and then the land was to have a year of rest—all based on the Sabbath day principle, but here applied in years for the land.

Moses now applies this seven-year-rest principle to the cancellation of debts (Deuteronomy 15:1–2). This law of cancellation meant that anyone who owed a fellow Israelite money for a loan would have the loan canceled completely in the seventh year.[4] Sometimes during those previous six years a fellow Israelite would "sell themselves" into slavery to their debtor due to their financial inability to pay back the debt during those six years.

In the seventh year, regardless of the debt, they were to be released both from their service and their debt. But in keeping with the spirit of the way they were to be treated while in servitude, the owner of the slave was implored not to send them away empty-handed (15:13).[5] The

---

4. The exception was for foreigners, who often resided only temporarily in the land and were not bound by the Sabbath year principle with respect to land. "The debts of a foreign businessman—i.e., a foreigner but not a 'resident alien,' cf. [Deuteronomy] 14:29—were not canceled. This was because he did not let his land lie fallow or suspend his normal source of income for a year as the Israelites did" (John F. Walvoord and Roy B. Zuck, eds., *The Bible Knowledge Commentary: Old Testament* [Cook, 1983], 290). Note as well that the cancellation of debts did not have to correspond to the exact year of the land's resting; it was merely something that would happen after the six years of servitude, no matter when the servitude began.

5. For more on the treatment and release of Hebrew slaves, see Exodus 21:1–11. Christopher J. H. Wright remarks on the slave release law in Exodus 21: "Coming straight after the account of the exodus, the law of slave release stands at the very head of the law code—appropriately enough as the first law for a society of escaped slaves! (Exod. 21–23)." (*Deuteronomy*, New

owner was to give generously from their flock, threshing floor, and winepress. Christopher Wright notes that this generosity is rooted in God's blessings on his people:

> The motivation for this law is driven from a *theological* matter of principle (vv. 14b–15) and drawn from an *economic* matter of fact (v. 18). The theological reason focuses on present blessing and historical redemption. Give to him as the Lord has blessed you (v. 14b). This wonderful text, which could have fallen from the lips of Christ himself, perfectly sums up the reciprocal dynamic of obedience and blessing, of doing to others what God has done for you, that Paul also builds into his theology of Christian giving (cf. 2 Cor. 9:6–15). It is based on the historical motivation of the exodus redemption (v. 15).[6]

The culture and attitude concerning this type of servitude were in no way to be abusive or condescending toward the slave seeking to pay off debt. In fact, these slaves were to be treated like family, which in some cases became a reality, as verse 16 implies. So we must avoid importing the well-deserved disdain for the horrific nature of the modern-day history of slavery back into this text, lest we read it anachronistically.[7] In other words, we can't read a current negative idea back into an ancient text. The preacher/teacher of this passage must strongly emphasize that servitude among the Hebrews was different from the type of slavery that comes to our minds today.

Moses concluded the Deuteronomy passage with a reminder of the blessings of having someone work for you as a servant. When these

---

International Biblical Commentary [Hendrickson, 1996], 193).

6. Wright, *Deuteronomy*, 193.

7. A similar exegetical fallacy called "illegitimate totality transfer" is the idea of taking a meaning or concept from another part of Scripture and importing all of the meaning into another text with similar language or wording. Staying true to biblical theology demands that we understand words in their context and recognize that the author's use of those words may differ from what is being imported from somewhere else. Therefore, our negative experience and history of slavery should not be read back into Moses' text in Deuteronomy 15.

slaves were to be released, the owners had no reason to sulk or view it as some sort of hardship, because essentially the one who was working for you was "worth twice the wages of a hired worker" (v. 18 CSB). And upon the slave's release, the owner was assured of God's abundant blessing.

We must also consider another use of the word *slave* in Pauline texts, where he contrasts our lives before and after conversion to Christ. In Romans 6, Paul tells the church that he is going to use a human analogy to communicate a spiritual reality. In simple terms, he told the church that before their salvation, they were enslaved to sin. Sin held them in bondage as they offered themselves to impurity and increasing lawlessness (v. 19).

But now that they were "in Christ," they were no longer to submit themselves as slaves to sin, but instead to commit themselves to the obedience of righteous living and therefore, in a sense, become slaves to righteousness. We are now enslaved to God (Romans 6:22), bought and paid for by the blood of Jesus, and set free from the power of sin, no longer to be ruled by it. Paul described our lives as being "dead to sin" (v. 11). This doesn't mean we will become perfect in this life, but rather that sin will no longer serve as our master.

We are a new creation, set apart for God, alive to God, and no longer spiritually dead in our sins and transgressions (Ephesians 2:1). Enslavement to sin leads to death, but enslavement to God produces righteousness and fruit (Romans 6:19–22). As slaves to Christ, we have blessing, sanctification, and the promise of eternal life (v. 23).

Sinful slavery undermines the dignity of all God's children, created in his image, for no one has the right to own us but God himself. The ancient Hebrews may have enslaved themselves to work to pay off debts, but that was an altogether different type of slavery where the redemptive context of Israel's history must be considered. Slavery in that context and the relationship between owner and slave were designed to be much different from our negative concepts of slavery today.

Finally, anyone who teaches on this sensitive subject must be quick to point out a basic principle of biblical interpretation: *There is a difference between what the Bible describes as historical reality and what the Bible prescribes for moral behavior.* In other words, we must differentiate between the descriptive and the prescriptive.

In some sections of the Bible, the behavior of humanity in general (and even God's people) is inherently evil and worthy of God's judgment and wrath (see, for example, the book of Judges). This is some of the dark history recorded in the Bible. But describing history is altogether different from prescribing what truly is God's moral will. It was not God's will for Solomon to have many wives (Deuteronomy 17:17), but that's what he did. In describing Solomon's sin, the Bible was not prescribing it as a form of acceptable moral behavior.

Therefore, when it comes to slavery, obviously context matters. Human beings should never own other people against their will. We must reject slavery as an inherent evil because we ultimately belong to God. Only he has the right as our Creator to place a claim on us—and even more so for those who have faith in Christ. It is appropriate then that we joyfully identify as slaves of Christ (Ephesians 6:6) and no longer slaves to sin (Romans 6:17).

Principles for Reflection

1. The Bible describes slavery but does not endorse it.

2. Jesus and the apostles did not condemn slavery in their day because the gospel was not to be confused with a sociopolitical movement. The strategy for slavery's demise was to change the hearts of people one by one through the gospel.

3. We must not import the full meaning of a word (or words) in one context into another context if the author is using the word differently. Doing so results in an exegetical fallacy.

4. The Bible redeems the concept of slavery by giving it a new context and meaning for those who are in Christ, knowing that only God has the right to own us. He bought us with his blood. As slaves of Christ, we are blessed children of God, a part of his family with an eternal inheritance that awaits us.

CHAPTER 27

DID GOD COMMAND GENOCIDE?

1 Samuel 15

ERIC J. BARGERHUFF

When the apostle Paul wrote in Romans 12 about how to put faith into practice in various aspects of life, he instructed the believers that when evil was done to them, *they should not do evil in return* (v. 17).

Rather, they should be acutely aware of their actions, intentional about the things they do in front of people, and committed to making peace "as far as it depends on you" (v. 18) They were to be known as peacemakers—gentle, humble, and meek (strength under control). All of these qualities are found in Jesus' teachings on how to respond when evil is done to us and has everything to do with us being his followers—representatives and ambassadors of Jesus Christ.

To turn the other cheek (Matthew 5:39), as Jesus taught in the Sermon on the Mount, is one of the more difficult-to-practice responses when we are on the receiving end of evil. But this is our Savior's instruction. Romans 12:17–18 is Paul's application of this teaching as he explained what to do and what not to do in those circumstances. It may feel counterintuitive, but if we respond to evil *with evil*, we are not much better than the original perpetrator. We ought not to be known for our wrath.

In Paul's application of Jesus' nonreciprocating principle, he specifically instructs the church that Christians should not be in the revenge business.[1] He gives them clear direction and then cites an Old Testament Scripture originally given through Moses to the people of Israel (Deuteronomy 32:35–36). Paul writes, "Friends, do not avenge yourselves; instead, leave room for *God's wrath*, because it is written, Vengeance belongs to me; I will repay, says the Lord" (Romans 12:19 CSB, emphasis mine).

It is God's prerogative to execute justice in his perfect timing, using whatever means he deems necessary. God sees. God knows. He will avenge those who have been personally traumatized by evil. Therefore, in our interpersonal relationships, we are not to be known for retaliation and revenge. The Lord will bring about justice in his own way, and in the end, his wrath will bring justice to those who have done us wrong and refused to repent.[2]

This is not to say that in society there is no room for the punishment of evil, for God has delegated and appointed governing bodies with the authority to execute justice in a temporal sense (in contrast to the eternal sense, which belongs to God alone).

Our communities must have established systems to uphold some sense of morality so societies can function, which is why we have laws. Through God's common grace given to sinful humanity, he has appointed social structures to have authority and to be accountable for rewarding what is good and punishing what is evil to deter the

---

1. Most readers will likely be thinking of Inigo Montoya (played by Mandy Patinkin) in the famous movie *The Princess Bride*, who sought to avenge the death of his father by the "six-fingered man" (Count Rugen, played by Christopher Guest). As enjoyable and comical as that classic movie is, it is obvious that it does not stand as a model for Christian ethics.
2. Sometimes this justice comes in this life, but other times it awaits the life to come.

destructive effects, holding evil somewhat at bay. And so in the very next chapter, Paul writes these words:

> Let everyone submit to the governing authorities, since there is no authority except from God, and the authorities that exist are instituted by God. So then, the one who resists the authority is opposing God's command, and those who oppose it will bring judgment on themselves. For rulers are not a terror to good conduct, but to bad. Do you want to be unafraid of the one in authority? Do what is good, and you will have its approval. For it is God's servant for your good. But if you do wrong, be afraid, because it does not carry the sword for no reason. For it is God's servant, an avenger that brings wrath on the one who does wrong. (Romans 13:1–4 CSB)

God, then, *delegates* authority to carry out justice in the world in a temporal sense. Of course, when it comes to submitting to these authorities, we are bound to obey, unless they erroneously instruct us to violate the Word of God and our consciences (Acts 4:18–19). But in a general sense, we are called to obey those who have been given authority over us, for they have been established by God.[3]

One of the more difficult moments of the delegating of justice in a temporal sense is found in 1 Samuel 15. The context is this: Israel had rejected God as their king (1 Samuel 8:7; 10:19), wanting to be like all the other nations around them that had a king. Therefore God instructed the prophet Samuel to anoint Saul as king. He became the very first king of Israel, a tall, handsome man from the tribe of Benjamin who was entrusted with the mission of delivering God's people from their enemies.

His first victory came against the Ammonites, the wicked

---

3. Someone may want to argue that God would never establish a wicked ruler since he does not endorse wickedness. Clearly he does not endorse wickedness, but his plan may allow for a wicked ruler to exist because it is a form of judgment on society for its lack of repentance. Such was the case when Saul was named king of Israel in the Old Testament (see 1 Samuel 8:7).

descendants of Lot, who lived east of the Jordan River. These are the people who threatened to gouge out the eyes of the Israelites who lived in Jabesh-Gilead (1 Samuel 11:2). This victory sealed Saul's approval as king among the people.

The Israelites once again were engaged in a conflict, but this time with the Philistines. In the context of these skirmishes, Saul disobeyed the word of God that had come through Samuel (1 Samuel 10:8) by offering an unlawful sacrifice (13:8–10). This disobedience resulted in Samuel's announcement that Saul would lose his kingship over it (v. 14), although it wouldn't happen right away. David was to eventually ascend to the throne. But until then, the Lord still used Saul to defeat Moabites, more Ammonites, Edomites, and additional Philistines.

We then come to 1 Samuel 15, where the Lord spoke through the prophet Samuel, who delivered a message about Saul's next mission, and it was a tough one. When Israel had been liberated from Egypt, a group of people known as the Amalekites attacked Moses and the Israelites in a hard-fought battle eventually won by the Israelites under Joshua's leadership, in concert with Moses' intercession (Exodus 17:8–13).

But because of the ruthless attack of the Amalekites, God purposed to bring judgment on the entire people group for their heinous sin against God's people: "The Lord then said to Moses, 'Write this down on a scroll as a reminder and recite it to Joshua: I will completely blot out the memory of Amalek under heaven'" (Exodus 17:14 CSB).

God's pronouncement of judgment on the Amalekites was a severe promise. The holy God of Israel has every right to execute justice, much like he did in Noah's day, when he wiped out the people of the earth, with the exception of Noah and his family, whom he graciously chose to spare. Those who perished in the flood included everyone—men, women, children, and all the animals that Noah did not take with him on the ark. They died because God saw that "every inclination of the human mind was nothing but evil all the time" (Genesis 6:5 CSB). And thus God brought justice.

This same level of divine justice was destined for the Amalekites, not by a flood, but at the hands of King Saul and the Israelites. God chose Saul to be his agent of justice on a wicked people, and Saul received the word through Samuel:

> "The LORD sent me to anoint you as king over his people Israel. Now, listen to the words of the LORD. This is what the LORD of Armies says: 'I witnessed what the Amalekites did to the Israelites when they opposed them along the way as they were coming out of Egypt. Now go and attack the Amalekites and completely destroy everything they have. Do not spare them. Kill men and women, infants and nursing babies, oxen and sheep, camels and donkeys.'"
> (1 Samuel 15:1–3 CSB)

This sort of command disturbs us, as it seems to be an excessive act on God's part. Yet we're seeing things only from a human perspective, forgetting that our holy God has a right to bring justice to all sinful flesh—flesh that is sinful from the moment of conception (Psalm 51:5).

God had promised in Exodus to blot out the memory of the Amalekites—a promise that would come to fulfillment in his command to annihilate this wicked people group. This promise reminds us of God's command to Joshua and the Israelites on the verge of entering the promised land to destroy the Canaanites completely (putting them under *herem*—the "ban").

As hard as this story is to hear, we must remember that our holy God has the right to put every one of us under the ban, and the preacher/teacher must make that clear. This thought should cause us to fall on our knees in gratitude for God's patience with sinful people today and to worship him in deep humility for not putting us to death and sending us to hell. Instead, he gives all people everywhere the opportunity to repent and extends saving grace and eternal life to all who believe in him.

Unfortunately, Saul only half-heartedly obeyed the Lord's command. He struck down all the people but spared the life of Agag, the king of the Amalekites. Saul likely wanted to parade him in front of all Israel as a trophy so Saul could boast about his power and receive praise among his own people.

Saul and his army also refused to destroy all the animals as instructed by God: "Saul and the troops spared Agag, and the best of the sheep, goats, cattle, and choice animals, as well as the young rams and the best of everything else. They were not willing to destroy them, but they did destroy all the worthless and unwanted things" (1 Samuel 15:9 CSB).

To their way of thinking, the spoils of war could be used for their benefit, which would then increase Saul's popularity. When Samuel confronted Saul about this, Saul put on his best spiritual face, claiming they had kept the best of the animals in order to sacrifice them to the Lord. And yet weren't there enough high-quality sheep, goats, and oxen in Israel to offer acceptable sacrifices? Surely there were.

Once again, Saul's pride stood in the way of his willingness to obey God's command. Samuel reminded Saul, "To obey is better than sacrifice" (15:22). Saul then confessed he had sinned because he was "afraid of the men" (v. 24). In other words, his desire to gain the favor of the Israelites by letting them enjoy the plunder overrode his commitment to obey God's command.

He wanted to be a people-pleaser. But whenever we seek to please people rather than God, we forfeit our role as servants of God (Galatians 1:10). We elevate our pride and need for admiration over the will and glory of God. As for Saul, Samuel once again reminded him that his disobedience to the Lord would result in the loss of his reign (1 Samuel 15:26).

Samuel then finished the job, killing Agag with a sword (15:33). Yet we will find out later that Saul hadn't destroyed all the Amalekites but had only killed those they had found. Later in 1 Samuel, David faced the Amalekites in his raids (27:8), and they later returned to take David's family captive (30:1–3).

Disobedience had consequences, not just for Saul, but also for people in the years after Saul's lifetime. In the book of Esther, for example, we see that Haman, the man who sought to exterminate all the Jews, was a descendant of Agag—the king who Samuel had put to death. Even in this story in Esther, God acts to protect and save his people.

We can see God's wisdom in his command to Saul to destroy a people group that seemed to be demonically inspired to wipe out Israel—something God would never allow, even though Israel would pay a heavy price for its disobedience.

I recently saw a picture of terrorists and their children holding guns in the air, which reminded me of the potential for corruption in human beings—from oldest to youngest. Though no one is beyond the saving grace of God (consider the Ninevites who repented in the book of Jonah), it appears that some people will never repent and will inevitably face the justice of God, as in the case of the Amalekites.

Only God knows who those people are, and he has given no command today to wipe out a people group. Instead, he has given us a new command to take the gospel to all nations, so that "every tribe and language and people and nation" (Revelation 5:9) would turn from sin and put their trust in Christ, bring glory to the Lamb who was slain.

God has a right to bring about justice against sin in his way and in his time—either in this life or in the life to come. He has given authority to some to bring about temporal justice by the establishment of laws, but the ultimate authority to bring justice to someone in terms of their final destiny rests with him alone. In the Old Testament, God delegated his wrath to be carried out by his chosen people, who often failed in this mission. His purpose in pouring out wrath on these evil nations was to protect his people. Through it all, God found a way to protect them in spite of their disobedience.

But the mission has now changed, as the church, made up of both Jews and Gentiles, holds out to all people groups the message of grace and forgiveness. In this New Testament age, God has quenched his wrath for the sin of his people at the cross. For those who continue to love their sin unto death and reject God, he has stored up wrath for them in the future.

If there is one major truth the preacher/teacher needs to make clear, it is that God is holy and we are not. We should respond with profound gratitude for the grace that saves us from God's wrath, for every person now has the opportunity to be saved from the corruption of sin that infects each of us from the moment of conception. Because of God's love, we can be born again by the power of his Spirit and escape the penalty for sin that we deserve.

I am reminded again of how hard it is to comprehend the offensiveness of sin to a holy God. Yet the more we see God as holy, the more we will understand his right to bring justice and marvel at his amazing grace.

Principles for Reflection

1. Only God sees the heart, and he knows how vast the corruption of the human heart is. Therefore, as judge of the earth, he has the right to carry out justice at any time and to delegate that justice to whomever he chooses.

2. God's holiness is beyond anything we can comprehend on this fallen earth in our limited capacities. This should cause us to marvel at his grace and rejoice in the good news of salvation.

3. No government or people group today has received a divine command to exterminate a people group, as God commanded the Israelites to do in the Old Testament. No theocracies exist today, and therefore we who are committed to the gospel of peace must oppose genocide at every turn. There are "just wars," to be sure, but there is no command from God to put anyone under the ban.

CHAPTER 28

DOES GOD USE DEMONS?

1 Kings 22; 2 Chronicles 18

ERIC J. BARGERHUFF

One of the most difficult and profound truths for a Christian to come to terms with is that God can use evil for his glory and yet not be responsible for the evil itself. The Bible is filled with examples of this truth.

In Genesis, we find Joseph, who was betrayed, thrown into a pit, sold into slavery by his brothers, falsely accused, and imprisoned, only in the course of time to be made second-in-command in Egypt under Pharaoh, which allowed him to provide food for Israel. Though his brothers had done horrendously evil things to him, Joseph profoundly said in their presence, "Therefore it was not you who sent me here, but God" (Genesis 45:8 CSB). And later, "You planned evil against me; God planned it for good to bring about the present result—the survival of many people" (50:20 CSB).

The greatest example of God using evil without fault or blame is the cross of Jesus Christ. In God's preplanned and foreordained will (Isaiah 53), Jesus was crucified on a Roman cross at the hands of evil men. The apostle Peter clearly laid out where the blame lay when in his Pentecost sermon he boldly proclaimed these words:

"Fellow Israelites, listen to these words: This Jesus of Nazareth was a man attested to you by God with miracles, wonders, and signs that God did among you through him, just as you yourselves know. Though he was delivered up according to God's determined plan and foreknowledge, you *used lawless people* to nail him to a cross and kill him." (Acts 2:22–23 CSB, emphasis mine)

The sovereignty of God over all evil will always be a mystery to us, just as it was to Job during his time of intense suffering. Yet we know that things were happening in the heavenly realms during Job's test, and in the end, he passed the test. The fact that God used Satan to implement the test without being culpable for what Satan did teaches us that God can use evil without being blameworthy, for our God is holy and just (Isaiah 5:16; Revelation 16:5). And even during the time of Job's testing, God set boundaries over what Satan could do to him. Ultimately, God was and always is in control.

God can sometimes use Satan as an instrument of discipline or judgment. When Paul told the Corinthian believers to exercise church discipline on a professing believer who was practicing unrepentant sexual immorality and incest, he said, "Hand this man over to Satan for the destruction of the flesh, so that his spirit may be saved on the day of the Lord" (1 Corinthians 5:5). Paul wanted to put him out of the church—the realm of God's protection—so that he wouldn't influence other believers in the church. This would make him vulnerable to the attacks of the Evil One, in the hope that it would teach him a profound lesson—namely, that sin destroys people and relationships. Then by God's grace, the man might come to his senses and find the mercy needed to lead him back to right living that comes from genuine saving faith—the path that leads to everlasting life.[1]

Another example that has given pause to many people is a judgment

---

1. For more on the sin of this man and the discipline Paul commanded, see my book *Love That Rescues: God's Fatherly Love in the Practice of Church Discipline* (Wipf and Stock, 2010), 160–73.

pronounced by God on King Ahab of Israel, where God appeared to have recruited an evil spirit (perhaps Satan, though Scripture doesn't specifically mention him) to put a "lying spirit" in the mouths of Ahab's prophets to lead Ahab astray (1 Kings 22:22 CSB).

Here we have not just a remedial discipline, but a justifiably damning judgment on an evil Israelite king who refused to repent of his evil actions and was leading God's people astray into idolatry. The account is found both in 1 Kings 22 and 2 Chronicles 18.

God's people, the Israelites, were living in a divided kingdom at that time. The kingdom to the south was Judah (consisting of two tribes), with a godly king named Jehoshaphat. The northern kingdom was Israel (consisting of ten tribes), with a wicked, scheming, selfish, and idolatrous king named Ahab. His wife was Jezebel, who was also vicious and pagan and had ordered the murder of God's prophets, threatened Elijah, and influenced her husband to introduce Baal worship among God's people.

Having won a few battles against the Arameans, the prideful Ahab refused to acknowledge God's help and refused to kill the pagan king of Aram, as the Lord had commanded. He had also stolen a vineyard from a fellow Israelite because it was near his palace (thanks to Jezebel's murderous plot against its owner).

Later, Ahab asked the king of Judah to go with him into battle to gain back some of the land that the Arameans had not yet surrendered, even though it rightly belonged to Israel. Jehoshaphat agreed to help, but desired to inquire of the Lord first to see if this military action would have his blessing.

But instead of asking a prophet of the Lord, Ahab consulted the pagan prophets of Baal, who had made a regular practice of telling Ahab what he wanted to hear, which were essentially lies. They told Ahab to march against the enemy, and "the Lord will give it into the king's hand" (1 Kings 22:6).

Jehoshaphat, however, wasn't convinced: "Isn't there a prophet of the LORD here anymore? Let's ask him" (1 Kings 22:7 CSB). Micaiah was the true prophet of the Lord whom they should have consulted, but Ahab hated him because he prophesied only disaster and never good things to him. In other words, he never told Ahab what he wanted to hear, in contrast to the prophets of Baal.

The two kings waited at the gate of Samaria for the true prophet to come to them. While they were sitting there, the false prophets of Baal continued to butter them up with all kinds of false prophecies about Israel's impending victory. The messenger who had gone to get Micaiah tried to convince him to fall in line and echo what the other prophets were saying. But Micaiah responded, "As the LORD lives, I will say whatever the LORD says to me" (1 Kings 22:14 CSB).

When Micaiah arrived, the king asked him what to do, and the prophet told him to go ahead and march on to victory because God would be at his side. But apparently there was something in the way he said it that made Ahab suspicious. Micaiah may well have spoken in a sarcastic tone, as if he was mocking the false prophets, because Ahab didn't believe his answer: "The king said to him, 'How many times must I make you swear to tell me nothing but the truth in the name of the LORD?'" (1 Kings 22:16).

It is then that Micaiah prophesied defeat and Ahab's demise. In response, Ahab turned to King Jehoshaphat and said, "Didn't I tell you that he never prophesies anything good about me, but only bad?" (1 Kings 22:18). Micaiah proceeded to recount a vision he had about Ahab in which he saw the Lord seated on his throne with all his angels surrounding him. And then comes a set of verses that strikes us as remarkably odd:

> "And the LORD said, 'Who will entice Ahab to march up and fall at Ramoth-gilead?' So one was saying this and another was saying that.
>
> Then a spirit came forward, stood in the LORD's presence, and said, 'I will entice him.'

The Lord asked him, 'How?'

He said, 'I will go and become a lying spirit in the mouth of all his prophets.'

Then he said, 'You will certainly entice him and prevail. Go and do that.'" (1 Kings 22:20–22 CSB)

On the surface, this scene is troubling. Why would God, who is sinless and true, seemingly order a spirit of some type to deceive Ahab by putting lies in the mouths of Ahab's prophets? Does this mean God authors evil? This sounds a lot like the story of King Saul, where the Holy Spirit removed his empowering presence from Saul for his kingly rule, "and an evil spirit from the Lord tormented him" (1 Samuel 16:14).

To be sure, both Ahab's and Saul's situations are examples of God using evil as a means of his judgment on disobedient kings. The Lord himself is not the *agent* of deception; instead, a spirit (some have even suggested Satan himself, the "father of lies"—John 8:44) volunteered to put lies in the mouths of Ahab's prophets.

In the same way God permitted Satan to test Job, here he allowed a spirit to lure Ahab to his ultimate demise by using the mouths of pagan prophets who have already led both him and Jezebel astray. In Job's case, he was being tested; in Ahab's case, he was undergoing judgment. Remember that Micaiah, the true prophet of God, ultimately warned Ahab that defeat was inevitable. But as the story continued, Ahab refused to listen to him and threw Micaiah in prison and embraced the message of his false prophets (something he was accustomed to doing) and headed into battle. Paul House wrote the following:

> Therefore, this account portrays God giving Ahab a chance to respond to a true prophet, which is consistent with other similar, earlier opportunities (e.g., 1 Kgs 18:16–19:2; 21:17–29). . . . This account has some troubling aspects but can become less troubling

when read as part of the whole story instead of as an isolated tradition separate from its canonical context.[2]

In other words, Ahab had opportunities to repent and turn his heart toward the one true God of Israel, but he refused. Instead, he "did more evil in the eyes of the LORD than any of those before him" (1 Kings 16:30). God is essentially allowing evil to run its course as a form of judgment (much like what we see Paul describe in Romans 1). Ahab rejected the true prophets of the Lord and even called Elijah the "troubler of Israel" (1 Kings 18:17).

Ahab and his wicked wife, Jezebel, were hostile toward God and all his prophets. He "exchanged the truth about God for a lie" (borrowing Paul's terminology about descent into sin in Romans 1:25). He loved the language of lies, and so God gave him over to what he loved as a form of his judgment, even using an evil spirit to whisper self-flattering prophecies about a "victory" that would actually end in his death.

As the story continued, Ahab and Jehoshaphat marched into battle, and Ahab tried to disguise himself so as to deflect attention. He must have thought the Arameans would first go after the one who looked like a king. But a random arrow *just so happened* to get launched in Ahab's direction, striking him in a gap in his armor. Ahab ended up dead, and the dogs licked up his blood.

And so the prophecies of both Elijah (1 Kings 21:19) and Micaiah (22:17) come true, which is the test of a true prophet of God as established by Moses (Deuteronomy 18:22).

For the preacher or teacher, it's important to parse the idea that God ordains a world in which evil exists and can even use it for his divine purposes (for example, discipline, testing, or judgment, to name a few), but he is never the author of evil itself in a way that makes him

---

2. Paul R. House, *1, 2 Kings*, New American Commentary (B&H, 1995), 238.

culpable or guilty of it. This is the assertion of the Bible itself from a God who is "holy, holy, holy" (Isaiah 6:3).

When God brought judgment on his people for their apostasy and idolatry, he raised up a wicked Babylonian king named Nebuchadnezzar to destroy the people and the land, carrying the Israelites into exile in a foreign land for seventy years. Yet God calls Nebuchadnezzar "my servant" (Jeremiah 25:9; 27:6; 43:10). In other words, God used him as *an instrument and the agent of his judgment.*[3] Here God uses *evil men* to exact punishment on those who were supposed to be his people but who have walked away from God and what is true.

God's judgment on people and nations can come in many forms. We live in a fallen world where evil happens every day. But one fact remains: "God is good, all the time; all the time, God is good." How he uses evil to accomplish his sovereign purposes will always remain a mystery, and the preacher/teacher, Bible study leader, and discipler must be humble enough to admit that God's ways are higher than our ways.

There are some things we will never understand in this present age. But we must trust God and know that he has the right to exact his judgment by any means he chooses. He is not blameworthy for either the existence of evil or the use of it. For as we mentioned earlier, at the cross of Christ, it was the will of the Lord to crush him (Isaiah 53:10), and he used the hands of evil men to do it so that our sins would be judged and forgiven once and for all.

I have one final illustration to share. We can all agree that war is one of the great evils in the world, though it's necessary at times to protect the lives of the innocent. In the summer of 2011, I traveled to Hiroshima, Japan, on a short-term mission trip, where I met an older Japanese woman who was a believer (which is rare, since just over

---

3. The story of King Nebuchadnezzar is a fascinating one. This evil, ruthless king is used by God to chasten Israel. Later, after God chastened him, he came to saving faith in the God of Israel (Daniel 3:28–40; 4:34–37).

1 percent of the people in that area at that time were Christians).[4] As a young girl, she had survived the blast of the first atomic bomb in August 1945, while the rest of her family died.

When I talked with her, she said, "I praise God for the bomb," which took me by surprise since she had lost her family. In a quiet voice, I asked her to help me understand. She went on to explain that as time progressed, General Douglas MacArthur (the supreme commander of the Allied powers) permitted the shipment of food, engineers, and supplies of all kinds to assist in the rebuilding of Japan.

Among the people who came to help in the rebuilding were several American missionaries. It was through those missionaries that she heard the gospel and came to saving faith in Christ. None of that would have been possible, she told me, if it hadn't been for the bomb. I sat with her in stunned silence. Words were failing me. In the end, all I could say was, "To God be the glory." God knows how to bring beauty from ashes, and in this case, it came from tongues that told the truth.

Principles for Reflection

1. When we have a fully developed view of the doctrine of God, we can use our understanding of who God is in his holiness to help us interpret narratives where the story has any potential to impugn the character of God. We know that God would never do anything to compromise his holiness, and thus culpability for evil must always lie in his fallen creatures. In other words, we allow Scripture and its implications to help us interpret Scripture in hard-to-understand places.

---

4. "Table: Christian Population as Percentages of Total Population by Country," Pew Research Center, December 19, 2011, www.pewresearch.org/religion/2011/12/19/table-christian -population-as-percentages-of-total-population-by-country/.

2. Never underestimate God's ability to work "for the good of those who love him, who have been called according to his purpose" (Romans 8:28). He can bring forth dynamic fruit for his glory out of the most tragic situations. Since all of us go through painful times, the preacher/teacher must be ready with illustrations of God's restorative, redeeming power in order to bring hope and peace to those who are hurting.

CHAPTER 29

ARE SOME SINS WORSE THAN OTHERS?

1 Corinthians 6:9–11

MATTHEW D. KIM

Are some sins worse than others? As finite humans, we tend to create our own systems of measurement of sin. While all sin is detestable in God's eyes, is there a gradation of sins according to Paul? The text in 1 Corinthians 6 raises the question: Are there any sins that may disqualify a believer from entering the kingdom of God? At first reading of Paul's warning to the Corinthians, it seems clear there are sins that prevent a person from entering heaven:

> Do you not know that the unrighteous will not inherit the kingdom of God? Do not be deceived: neither the sexually immoral, nor idolaters, nor adulterers, nor men who practice homosexuality, nor thieves, nor the greedy, nor drunkards, nor revilers, nor swindlers will inherit the kingdom of God. And such were some of you. But you were washed, you were sanctified, you were justified in

the name of the Lord Jesus Christ and by the Spirit of our God.
(1 Corinthians 6:9–11 ESV)

About the Corinthian church, Jerry Bridges observes in *Respectable Sins*, "The church at Corinth was all messed up, both theologically and morally. They were proud and fractious; they tolerated gross immorality, sued each other in court, flaunted their freedom in Christ, abused the observance of the Lord's Supper, misunderstood the purpose of spiritual gifts, and were confused about the future resurrection of believers."[1]

Paul asked the Corinthians in verse 9 a rhetorical question: "Do you not know that the unrighteous will not inherit the kingdom of God?" The assumed answer is, "Yes, we Corinthians should know this." Yet what does Paul mean by "the unrighteous"? Translated also as "wrongdoers," the Greek word *adikos* means "acting in a way that is contrary to what is right; unjust; crooked."[2] In the ancient world, it was quite common for an orator or author to list out human vices.[3] In Paul's list, he begins with an emphasis on sexual sins—the sins of those who practice sexual immorality, idolatry, adultery, and homosexuality.

Corinth was a leading ancient epicenter of sexual deviance. Similar to today's society, Corinthian society viewed hypersexuality and seeking out sexual satisfaction as normative. Some Corinthian philosophers advocated for sexual union with prostitutes "to relieve one's appetites . . . so long as one was not 'controlled' by it; other philosophers argued that "one should have intercourse only for procreation, not pleasure."[4] The teachings of the philosophers stood in stark contrast to what Scripture envisions for God's people with regard to sexual integrity. Sexual immorality meant any engagement

---

1. Jerry Bridges, *Respectable Sins: Confronting the Sins We Tolerate* (NavPress, 2007), 1.
2. Frederick William Danker, ed., *A Greek-English Lexicon of the New Testament and Other Early Christian Literature*, 3rd ed. (University of Chicago Press, 2000), 21.
3. John H. Walton and Craig S. Keener, eds., *NIV Cultural Backgrounds Study Bible* (Zondervan, 2016), note on 1 Corinthians 5:10–11, p. 1989.
4. *NIV Cultural Backgrounds Study Bible*, "Prostitution and Sexual Immorality," p. 1990.

in sexual relations outside of the original design of a covenantal marital relationship between one man and one woman (Genesis 1:26–28).

The term *homosexuals* first found its way into English Bibles in 1946, according to religion professor Heather White.[5] Interestingly, she notes how previous translations of the same Greek word in the King James Version were defined as "effeminate" and "abusers of themselves with mankind." Seven commonly cited teachings or references regarding homosexuality are the Sodom account in Genesis 19:4–8; Leviticus 18:22; 20:13; Romans 1:26–27; 1 Corinthians 6:9–10; 1 Timothy 1:9–10; and Jude 1:7.

About the 1 Corinthians 6 passage, BibleRef.com explains:

> The words translated as "practice homosexuality" in the ESV include two Greek words: *malakoi* and *arsenokoitai*. Respectively, these indicate the passive and active participants in same-sex sexual behaviors. . . . In short, this is one of the New Testament's clear indications that homosexual actions—not temptations themselves, but behaviors—are deeply and unmistakably sinful. Embracing such behavior shows a deep rejection of God, just as much as would idolatry or cheating in business.[6]

Interestingly, in 1 Corinthians 6:10, Paul shifts the focus of unrighteous behavior to moral defiers such as thieves, the greedy, drunkards, revilers, and swindlers. Notice that Paul doesn't elevate sexual sin as being worse than these other moral sins. They are, in fact, named side by side in the same sentence. As Paul writes in verses 9–10, "Neither the sexually immoral, nor idolaters, nor adulterers, nor men who practice homosexuality, nor thieves, nor the greedy, nor drunkards, nor revilers, nor swindlers will inherit the kingdom of God" (ESV).

---

5. Heather White, *Reforming Sodom: Protestants and the Rise of Gay Rights* (University of North Carolina Press, 2015), 1.

6. "What Does 1 Corinthians 6:9 Mean?," Got Questions Ministries, accessed March 17, 2025, www.bibleref.com/1-Corinthians/6/1-Corinthians-6-9.html.

What complicates matters, however, is that in the previous chapter, Paul appears to instruct the Corinthians to disassociate from such sinners: "I wrote to you in my letter not to associate with sexually immoral people—not at all meaning the people of this world who are immoral, or the greedy and swindlers, or idolaters. In that case you would have to leave this world" (5:9–10). He continues in verse 11: "But now I am writing to you that you must not associate with anyone who claims to be a brother or sister but is sexually immoral or greedy, an idolater or slanderer, a drunkard or swindler. Do not even eat with such people." The reason is that Jewish readers would have excluded people who sinned in such ways from their community.[7]

While God does not seem to elevate sexual sin in this passage over moral sins, we find in Scripture more severe language when it comes to sexual immorality. For instance, God says in Leviticus 18:22, "Do not have sexual relations with a man as one does with a woman; that is detestable." The word *detestable* can also be translated as "confusion, violation of nature, or the divine order."[8]

Similarly, God uses strong words to describe his feelings toward divorce in Malachi 2:14–16, coupling his hatred for divorce and violence directed toward the other:

> You ask, "Why does he not [accept our offerings]?" Because the
> LORD was a witness between you and the wife of your youth, to
> whom you have been faithless, though she is your companion and
> your wife by covenant. Did God not make them one, flesh with
> spirit in it? And what does the one desire? Godly offspring. So look
> to yourselves, and do not let anyone be faithless to the wife of his
> youth. For I hate divorce, says the LORD, the God of Israel, and covering
> one's garment with violence, says the LORD of hosts. So take
> heed to yourselves and do not be faithless. (NRSVue)

---

7. *NIV Cultural Backgrounds Study Bible*, note on 1 Corinthians 5:11, pp. 1989–90.

8. Francis Brown, Samuel Rolles Driver, and Charles Augustus Briggs, *Enhanced Brown-Driver-Briggs Hebrew and English Lexicon* (Clarendon, 1977), 117.

Many evangelical denominations maintain a high level of reverence for the institution of marriage, particularly when it comes to homosexual behavior and LGBTQIA+ issues in culture and in the church. That is, since God prohibits same-sex unions and sexually deviant behavior that includes homosexual practice, many churches do not ordain practicing homosexuals to vocational ministry. While we don't have space to provide a full-orbed discussion about gay ordination and other similar matters, I'll offer a quick sidebar.

One of my primary concerns has to do with the way some interpreters of Scripture have elevated experience over accurate exegesis and hermeneutics. For example, the Human Rights Campaign posted an article titled "What Does the Bible Say About Homosexuality?" and made this argument: "To further complicate the argument against same-sex relationships, Scripture doesn't suggest that respecting biblical authority means Christians should reject experience as a teacher."[9] In doing so, they make the case that homosexual behavior is permissible because homosexuals have enjoyed positive experiences in such relationships. The article concludes with these glowing commendations of homosexuality:

> As it stands today, there are millions of faithful Christians around the world who have come to recognize the work of God in and through the relationships of LGBTQ+ people. As New Testament Scholar Daniel Kirk has pointed out, Christians today would do well by the tradition of the apostles and our current witness in the world to recognize that theological abstractions aside, God has already clearly embraced LGBTQ+ people into full communion, and it is now the church's responsibility to simply honor that reality and *rejoice* (Luke 15).[10]

---

9. Myles Markham, "What Does the Bible Say About Homosexuality?," Human Rights Campaign Foundation, accessed March 17, 2025, www.hrc.org/resources/what-does-the-bible-say-about -homosexuality.

10. Markham, "What Does the Bible Say?," italics in original. For more on this, see Robin

The world and even those in the church now celebrate what was once considered unrighteous behavior in the first century. Whether issues pertaining to sexual immorality or any other version of immorality, we as a culture and a church are more and more tempted to minimize sinful behaviors.

Let's get to the heart of the issue for the 1 Corinthians 6 passage. Paul does not seem to be emphasizing here the specific list of sins. Rather, he seems to be arguing that the Corinthian believers who have experienced spiritual regeneration ought not to continue in this list of sinful behaviors (one and all). He is reminding the Corinthians in rhetorical fashion that while they may have practiced these immoral ways in the past, these sins should not remain part of their spiritual identity and practice as new creations being transformed into Christ's image. Notice especially verse 11: "And that is what some of you were. But you were washed, you were sanctified, you were justified in the name of the Lord Jesus Christ and by the Spirit of our God." The darkness has been overcome for those who live in the light of Jesus Christ.

In my childhood and teen years, much of what I was taught by Christian pastors and teachers is that God's grace is available to all sinners, and this is absolutely true. But another message was communicated regularly as well—namely, that we must at all costs avoid sexual immorality, especially homosexual attraction and behavior. For many pastors and teachers, sexual immorality in the form of lust, pornography, masturbation, fornication, premarital sex, and many other such sins were forbidden and seemingly deemed unforgivable by God.

What 1 Corinthians 6:9–11 teaches is that *all sins* are an abomination to God. Does it literally mean that those who have committed any of these sins will be denied entrance into heaven? No, I don't believe that's true. However, it is true that those who have been redeemed in Christ will not pursue continually and regularly these practices that

---

Scroggs, *The New Testament and Homosexuality: Contextual Background for Contemporary Debate* (Fortress, 1983).

are unacceptable in God's eyes. We live to please the Father, Son, and Holy Spirit. As 1 Corinthians 6 summarizes in verse 20, "You were bought at a price. Therefore honor God with your bodies."

Principles for Reflection

1. Sin is something humans take lightly but the Lord takes very seriously. Sin is so despicable in God's sight that it warranted the death of his Son on the cross. All sin is detestable to God.

2. We seem to be allergic as a Christian church to any semblance of legalism. The nonchalant attitude we often have toward sin can quickly cause Christians to backslide. The more we disengage from our own sinfulness, the easier it becomes to fall away from our faith and our heavenly Father.

3. May we go back to the basics of the Christian faith. The reality is that we are made to be holy beings who will hate sin and love the ways of God. All sin is an abomination to God. In every part of our lives, including our sexuality and sexual behavior, may we pursue holiness and righteousness—honoring God with our bodies, minds, and actions.

CHAPTER 30

WAS PAUL A RACIST?

Titus 1:12

MATTHEW D. KIM

There seems to be a societal expectation that Christians are to be nice people who don't swear, smoke, or engage in stereotyping others. The third *s* is the subject of this chapter. In the book of Titus, the apostle Paul writes to Titus, another of his young protégés, who was pastoring on the island of Crete. Paul calls Titus his "true son in our common faith" (1:4). The purpose of the letter, as Paul clearly spelled out, is to exhort Titus to "appoint elders in every town, as I directed you" (v. 5), as well as to safeguard sound doctrine and to encourage his people to be "eager to do what is good" (2:14). And in Titus 1 Paul disparages Titus's ministry context, describing the inhabitants of Crete as "always liars, evil brutes, lazy gluttons" (1:12).

What's going on here with the name-calling? How do we make sense of the apostle Paul's seemingly insensitive, derogatory, and even racist comment in Titus 1:12? Is this comment or observation permissible or even tolerable? Does that mean Christians can also follow suit and regularly practice name-calling and stereotyping? What could

Paul possibly mean here? Is the application that we, too, can pigeon-hole others?

The apostle Paul sometimes seems like a maverick to whom social and cultural etiquette does not apply. Take this verse, for instance. He rattles off three labels within a particular ethnic/cultural context—that of the Cretans. On the island of Crete, where Paul likely planted at least one church, he quickly needed to do some spiritual intervention. The *NIV Faithlife Study Bible* tells us, "This letter addresses Paul's colleague Titus, urging him to bring order to the church on the island of Crete, oppose false teachers and appoint leaders (1:5)."[1] Situated southwest of modern-day Turkey, the island of Crete was the fourth largest in the Mediterranean Sea.[2]

Obviously, based on Titus 1:12, Paul did not hold the Cretans in high regard. The quote about Cretans being liars, brutes, and gluttons is attributed to a Cretan poet named Epimenides (sixth–fifth centuries BC).[3] Robert Yarbrough, in his commentary on Paul's letters to Timothy and Titus, explains that a probable source for Paul's generalization is taken from a third-century BC quotation: "Cretans are thieves from way back, pirates: they never think along legal lines."[4] Rather than qualifying his statement, Paul boldly confirmed it in verse 13 of chapter 1: "This saying [about them] is true."

Joseph DiLuzio of the classics department at Baylor University, noted that in that ancient culture, Cretans were known for their piracy:

1. John D. Barry, ed., *NIV Faithlife Study Bible* (Zondervan, 2017), note on Titus 1:1–4, p. 2015.
2. *NIV Faithlife Study Bible*, note on Titus 1:5, p. 2015.
3. NIV text note: *From the Cretan philosopher Epimenides*; see George W. Knight, *The Pastoral Epistles*, New International Greek Testament Commentary (Eerdmans, 1992), 298.
4. Robert W. Yarbrough, *The Letters to Timothy and Titus*, Pillar New Testament Commentary (Eerdmans, 2018), 495. See also Craig Keener, who attributes the quote to Callimachus's *Hymn to Zeus* (*IVP Bible Background Commentary: New Testament* [IVP Academic, 2014], note on Titus 1:12).

The Romans appointed M. Antonius "Creticus" to a special command in 74 BC to rid the eastern Mediterranean of pirates. Apparently, he . . . ended up plundering the very areas he was supposed to protect. Because of his incompetence, he was given the nickname "Creticus"—"Cretan"—as a mock honorific. . . . In the Odyssey, when Odysseus—the archetypal trickster—is lying to someone about his identity . . . he almost always says that he is from Crete.[5]

Yarbrough explained further about what Paul's purpose in stereotyping the Cretans might have been: "Social generalizations can be pernicious—today we call them stereotypes—but they can shed light on what is happening in a particular setting. . . . Paul apparently saw points of contact between their behavior and well-known motifs found in various literary sources of his day that reflected negatively on the social and personal character of Cretans generally."[6]

The *Faithlife Study Bible* offers another perspective that limits the scope of Paul's generalization to false teachers: "The Cretans gained a notorious reputation for their lack of moral integrity. Ancient writers popularized the verb 'to Cretanize' as slang for lying and cheating. Here Paul applies this well-known saying to the false teachers, using it rhetorically to make a point—not necessarily because he agrees with it being applied to all Cretans."[7]

Even if Paul had been using a Cretan stereotype to indict the false teachers on the island of Crete—his theological enemies—can we conclude that it's acceptable to label others? Moreover, by using a stereotype coined by a Cretan philosopher, is Paul doubly justified in his harsh generalization about Cretans? That is, since a Cretan said it, it must be true, and therefore it must be permissible to make the same declaration.

What might be a proper approach to stereotypes as we explain the

5. Email from Joseph DiLuzio on January 23, 2024.
6. Yarbrough, *Letters to Timothy and Titus*, 495.
7. *NIV Faithlife Study Bible*, note on Titus 1:12, p. 2016.

Titus passage and related texts? Stereotypes are sprinkled throughout both Testaments, often used in describing non-Jewish cultures and ethnicities. Take, for instance, Rebekah's clear disdain for Esau's idolatrous Hittite wives, Judith and Basemath (Genesis 27:46). Jonah ran from his call from God because he didn't want to preach a message of repentance to his enemies, the Ninevites, who were known as cruel and violent people (Jonah 1:3; 4:1–3). The Corinthians were characterized as sexually immoral people. In some cases, even God himself uses stereotypical language, such as in Habakkuk 1:6, where God answers Habakkuk's complaint without apology: "I am raising up the Babylonians, that ruthless and impetuous people, who sweep across the whole earth to seize dwellings not their own."

What else must we understand about labels? Patty Lane helpfully explains that stereotypes have three identifiers:

- from an outsider's perspective, that is, someone not from that culture
- restrictive or limiting
- accusative[8]

Lane continues, "Stereotypes originate with someone seeing members of another group. Often the observation is true of the few people observed and may even point out a positive quality, but to generalize that quality to all the members of the group creates a box, which limits the way in which others of that group will be seen. It allows people outside the group to decide who the others are without having to consider who that individual person is. Ethnic jokes and nicknames develop from these stereotypes."[9]

One of the blind spots we often have in church contexts is stereotyping our "own people," which is referred to by Lane as an archetype:

---

8. Patty Lane, *A Beginner's Guide to Crossing Cultures: Making Friends in a Multicultural World* (InterVarsity, 2002), 25.
9. Lane, *Beginner's Guide*, 25.

"An archetype is developed by an insider and is non-accusative and non-restrictive."[10] Archetypes or generalizations made by an insider can come out in our preaching and teaching when we state that all the members of our congregation think, believe, behave, interpret, and apply Scripture in exactly the same way. It has become second nature for us, to the point that we don't even realize we're doing it. This kind of generalization may go something like this: "At First Baptist Church, we are _____." And as we well know, stereotyping can also occur in hurtful ways when our congregations have a dominant racial/ethnic majority culture.

So should we avoid stereotypes altogether? What should we make of them when they appear on the pages of Scripture? Jesus is our model for how to evaluate the use of stereotypes. Stereotypes are typically negative in nature, where comments are made about something we dislike about another culture or another person. Jews held a common prejudice against the Samaritans, for example, since Jews considered them to be half-breeds (a mixture of Jewish and Assyrian). What Jesus does in the parable of the good Samaritan (Luke 10:25–37) is quite astonishing. Reversing a negative cultural/ethnic stereotype, Jesus commended a Samaritan person as a chief example of what it means to love our neighbor (v. 29). The half-breed became the hero of Jesus' story.

Preachers and teachers must oppose and seek to reverse negative stereotypes of other people and cultures. Whenever possible, use positive illustrations of all people, but especially ethnic minorities. As I stated in my book *Preaching with Cultural Intelligence*, it's important that an ethnic minority person be the hero of the story regularly.[11] We need to be intentional about changing the narrative of how we speak about people from different cultural backgrounds.

Years ago, I did research to prepare for teaching a course in

---

10. Lane, *Beginner's Guide*, 26.
11. See Matthew D. Kim, *Preaching with Cultural Intelligence: Understanding the People Who Hear Our Sermons* (Baker Academic, 2017), 115.

cultural exegesis for preaching. To my chagrin, I found copious collections of published cartoons perpetuating racism in the United States. In my search for examples of racism in this country's history, I saw one cartoon depicting a grimacing Black man holding a knife. The caption read, "Never relax." Another cartoon showed a fictional immigrant from Mexico named Pedro, who was expressing a litany of derogative stereotypes about him, his family in Mexico, his position as a manual laborer, and his assumed motives for being in the US. A third cartoon captured an exaggeratedly slant-eyed Chinese man wearing ancient Chinese clothing and carrying a wooden laundry washboard.[12] God forbid that in our preaching and teaching, we would perpetuate negative generalizations of others.

Conduct this thought experiment with me. Fill in the blank with the first word that comes to your mind:

All Presbyterians are _____.
All Methodists are _____.
All Baptists are _____.
All Muslims are _____.
All Hindus are _____.
All Mormons are _____.
All rich people are _____.
All poor people are _____.
All Republicans are _____.
All Democrats are _____.
All Independents are _____.
All White people are _____.
All Black people are _____.
All Hispanic people are _____.
All Asian people are _____.

---

12. See Matthew D. Kim and Daniel L. Wong, *Finding Our Voice: A Vision for Asian North American Preaching* (Lexham, 2020), 88.

All Arab people are _____.
All Native Americans are _____.
All men are _____.
All women are _____.
All teens are _____.
All elderly people are _____.

Do an analysis. What kind of characteristic did you write down—a positive or a negative one? Adding the modifier—*all*—accentuates the absurdity of making a claim like this. Yet this is what a stereotype communicates. We are saying that *all* people who fall into a particular category are like this. Do such generalizations help or hurt in building relationships with others? Filling in the blank of a statement like this forces us to make a judgment about each of these different types of people. While some may argue that stereotypes can be beneficial, they do not account for the individual differences within any given cultural context. We must ask ourselves, *For whom is the stereotype beneficial?*

Lead the charge in helping your congregation practice public and private, corporate and individual confession and repentance of the sins of prejudice, racism, ethnocentrism, xenophobia, hate crimes, and injustices. Spend some time parsing their specific nuances. In facing our stereotypes, we bring to our consciousness what we think of others (in our worst and even best moments). We name our sins and repent of them publicly and privately, whether these sins are in thought or in deed, sins of commission or sins of omission. We seek out and apologize to those we have hurt or offended. Educate your congregation through preaching, teaching, and workshops to develop cultural intelligence and sensitivity.[13]

Whether or not the apostle Paul is justified in using his demeaning generalization toward Cretans in Titus 1:12 is beyond our purview. Followers will mimic the behavior of their leaders. It is our

---

13. See resources from the Cultural Intelligence Center at www.culturalq.com.

responsibility as preachers and teachers of the gospel to help our people grow in discipleship and in their love for others rather than calling our sisters and brothers names or demonizing them. To love others is to not simplistically stereotype them, but rather to take the necessary time to get to know them personally and learn about their culture. Cultivating interracial and interethnic relationships will not be easy. This requires a significant time commitment, but it will be well worth it. Perhaps if we model this kindness, generosity, and hospitality in our personal lives and from the pulpit, we may help limit the collateral damage from the use of stereotypes in our own vocabulary and in that of our church members.

Principles for Reflection

1. Paul's use of stereotypes reflected the practice of ancient philosophers to make sense of people groups, ethnic groups, and cultures. The reputation of Cretans had disintegrated because of some of their attitudes and behaviors.

2. We should hesitate to make generalizations about entire groups of people. At the same time, getting to know the values and visions of cultures and how they may differ from ours gives insight into how to love them as Jesus did.

3. Do we harbor any negative feelings toward others who come from different cultural backgrounds? If so, how might the Lord work in our lives to befriend them, build a relationship with them, and introduce them to our Savior? Stereotyping is unhelpful as a general practice, but genuine cultural awareness and sensitivity can help us become better friends and disciple makers.

CONCLUSION

ERIC J. BARGERHUFF

There is inherent power in the Word of God to convert a heart and transform a life. If you believe that, then you know we are merely "earthen vessels" (KJV), or "jars of clay" (2 Corinthians 4:7), that God in his marvelous grace uses to make an impact for his kingdom. What a privilege that is, and what a responsibility! James reminds us, "Not many should become teachers, my brothers, because you know that we will receive a stricter judgment" (James 3:1 CSB).

Though this ought not to discourage us from using our gifts and finding the joy in communicating the truths of God's Word, it should bring about a healthy dose of humility and weightiness to the task at hand. We will give an account to God as those who presume to preach or teach on his behalf, and we know that people will trust us and believe that what we say is true, so we strive to get it right.

Our desire has been to present some insights into handling difficult-to-interpret texts. We don't pretend to know everything, and the task of being a student of the Bible will never be done on this side of heaven. Even in the presence of the Lord, we will spend an eternity marveling and learning. But there is much to be said for doing the hard work of study to be faithful to God's Word.

In this book we surveyed many different Bible passages. We uncovered numerous principles for interpretation and reflection. Though this is not a hermeneutics text or a comprehensive handbook on biblical interpretation, we have aimed to offer preachers/teachers ideas and creative suggestions for ways to understand these passages and make applications that are biblically accurate and culturally relevant.

With that in mind, here are several summary thoughts to help us in our preaching/teaching:

1. The main task of a teacher is to discover and communicate the original intent of the author so we can be seen as one who "correctly handles the word of truth" (2 Timothy 2:15). This involves understanding the history, culture, original audience, context (including background issues), genre, and so forth.

2. Be mindful that we are centuries away from the time these passages were written, but the timeless principles therein apply to all God's people today. It is a living and active Word. Use all the necessary tools to take yourself back to the place and time the text was written. First wrestle with the text yourself, making notes (insights and questions), highlighting relevant cross-references, and perhaps even summarizing it in your own words. Always ask, What does this text teach me about God and his character and ways? Then consult reference works and commentaries for additional insights. Remember to give the passage a chance to impact your own mind and heart before you go to study aids. Once you've done the interpretive work, proceed to the application.

3. Be mindful of the interpretive biases and experiences you bring to the reading of a text. This knowledge about yourself will help you become wise and enable you to be more objective. Further, never read into a text what you want it

to say or force your own preconceived theological framework to bend a text in a certain direction. Allow the text itself to speak on its own terms and be willing to change your view if necessary. People will respect a teacher who admits when they have changed their view after considering new evidence. But make sure any change of view is prompted by the clear study of Scripture and not by life experiences alone. Experiences can be deceiving and must be interpreted through the lens of Scripture, not the other way around. Having said that, in the right context, experiences can aid in interpretation and bring certain texts to life. Any trip to the Holy Land and ancient biblical archaeological sites will surely convince you of that.

4. If you've done your homework, don't be afraid to take a stand on an issue. You may choose to share a variety of other interpretations, but in the end, your listeners do not need a smorgasbord of options from which they can choose the one they like best. If you do share various options, be sure to share with conviction the one you believe is the best interpretation, and why. Speak and teach with authority. No one is ever truly impacted by a consistently indecisive teacher. In the end, there is only one true meaning to a text—many applications, but only one meaning.

5. You will need to work hard at getting to know your audience so you can communicate in a way they can comprehend. In time, you can feel more comfortable pushing them a bit to understand deeper and more complex subjects. Children, for example, are capable of understanding and learning far more than we give them credit for. How much more should teens and adults be challenged to think more deeply in order to grasp wonderful truths?

6. Preachers, teachers, and writers communicate in a variety of styles. Dr. Kim and I have different writing styles and emphasize different things at times. Be mindful that people will gravitate to a teaching style they learn best from, so don't be offended if your style isn't everyone's preference.

7. Use illustrations to accentuate the meaning of a text, not merely to entertain or to hold someone's attention. You want the focus to be on God and the text itself, not the brilliance of your storytelling. Illustrations can be powerful if they help connect someone to a text.

8. Use the Bible to interpret the Bible. Cross-referencing Scripture is an important tool to keep you from faulty interpretations. Being careful not to ignore context, examine what the Bible teaches on a particular topic in a different location. Keep in mind that certain biblical authors may use words and phrases differently, depending on context and purpose, but *God's moral law* never changes. The Bible is consistent and does not contradict itself. Why? Because it is inspired by the Holy Spirit, who does not lie, does not contradict himself, and is the author of truth.

9. In your preparation, spend adequate time in prayer over a passage. Before you seek to master it, make sure it has mastered you. Set apart blocks of uninterrupted time for meditation, concentration, research, and study. Include in your preparation time to connect with and worship God. Pray that God will fill you with the Holy Spirit and with deep insight into his Word.

10. Finally, avoid chronological snobbery. It is easy to rush out and buy the latest and best commentary or book on the market. But remember, God's people have a great cloud of witnesses who have gone before us and on whose shoulders our understanding of the faith rests. Insights can be gleaned from centuries of preachers and teachers, which can be immensely helpful to us.

Read the sermons and writings of Martin Luther, John Calvin, Charles Spurgeon, D. Martyn Lloyd-Jones, Jonathan Edwards, A. W. Tozer, G. Campbell Morgan, R. C. Sproul, John Stott, Watchman Nee, William Carey, J. C. Ryle, J. I. Packer, Thomas Watson, Stephen Charnock, George Whitefield, Dwight L. Moody, John Owen, and countless others. Thomas Oden edited the *Ancient Christian Commentary on Scripture,* which offers insights from the early church fathers on select passages of Scripture. God has given us great scholars today as well. Build a library, read widely, and study the original languages if you can.

Our goal is that God's people will know him better so he will be worshiped and glorified in their lives. We want to train people in the knowledge of God's Word to change their lives and equip them for ministry. The Word of God is capable of being understood with the aid of the Holy Spirit and the church. We now, more than at any other time in history, have access to information and knowledge that can assist us in interpreting this fully inerrant and inspired ancient text that still speaks God's message and his will to us today.

Some parts of Scripture are hard to understand and can be easily manipulated by false teachers and false prophets (2 Peter 3:16). But we have been given new hearts and new minds to discern the truths of God with integrity. If someone asks a question you don't know the answer to it, don't be afraid to say, "Let me get back to you on that one." Go back to your study and dig out a solid and faithful answer. God will bless the one who in humility does the hard work so that in all things, the name of Jesus Christ will be glorified and worshiped.

ACKNOWLEDGMENTS

The task of writing a book is one that involves time, energy, and occasional sacrifice. I wish to acknowledge the generous support of my colleagues at Trinity College of Florida, where I serve as the academic dean and professor of Bible and theology—with specific thanks to President Stephen P. Best for the gift of time away from the office to complete this project.

In addition, I want to thank my wife, Jennifer, for the way her love and support encouraged me daily and made writing pure joy as I worked on this project.

Eric J. Bargerhuff

I want to thank Zondervan Reflective, specifically Ryan Pazdur and Kyle Rohane, for believing in this project. Thank you for your patience as we navigated life circumstances in the process of writing this book. It was a joy to work with the entire Zondervan team! It's a blessing to teach at Baylor University's Truett Seminary, where the intersection of the academy and church is such a high value. Thanks also to Hannah Brown, my graduate assistant at Truett Seminary, for compiling a bibliography for some of the content found in this book.

Thanks to my family—Sarah, Ryan, Evan, and Aidan—for encouraging me and providing space to work on another book.

Matthew D. Kim